Culture and Everyday Life

Culture and Everyday Life

Andy Bennett

SAGE Publications

London ● Thousand Oaks ● New Delhi

SAGE Publications Ltd
1 Oliver's Yard
55 City Road
London EC1Y 1SP

SAGE Publications Inc.
2455 Teller Road
Thousand Oaks, California 91320

SAGE Publications India Pvt Ltd
B-42, Panchsheel Enclave
Post Box 4109
New Delhi 110 017

British Library Cataloguing in Publication data

A catalogue record for this book is available
from the British Library

ISBN 0 7619 6389 8
ISBN 0 7619 6390 1 (pbk)

Library of Congress control number available

Typeset by C&M Digitals (P) Ltd., Chennai, India
Printed on paper from sustainable resources
Printed and bound in Great Britain by Athenaeum Press, Gateshead

For Daniel

Contents

Acknowledgements

This book has developed from an undergraduate course on contemporary culture and media that I have taught at the University of Surrey since 2000. I would like to thank all those students who have participated in the course. I would also like to thank my academic colleagues at the University of Surrey and elsewhere for their support.

Introduction: The Problem of Everyday Life

> More than most sociological concepts 'everyday life' has proved exceedingly difficult to define. (Featherstone, 1995: 55)

Perhaps the most fundamental problem for sociologists, media and cultural theorists in addressing 'everyday life' is the sheer ambiguity of the term. As Featherstone observes, everyday life 'appears to be a residual category into which can be jettisoned all the irritating bits and pieces which do not fit into orderly thought' (ibid.). A second immediate problem facing theorists in attempting to conceptualise everyday life is its ostensibly 'ordinary' nature, that is to say, its unavoidable associations with the familiar, the taken-for-granted, the common-sensical. Thus, the study of everyday life involves 'the necessity of subjecting one's own activities to practical knowledge and routines whose heterogeneity and lack of systemicity is rarely theorized' (ibid.). However, it is precisely the inherent taken-for-grantedness of everyday life that renders it valuable as an object of social research. Amid ongoing debates concerning the interplay between 'culture' and 'structure' in the creation of the social, everyday life becomes significant as the physical site upon which this interplay takes place. As such, social theorists are increasingly utilising everyday life as an analytical model in their attempts to tease out the processes through which society is fashioned.

For early social theorists, culture was regarded as very much a 'by-product' of the structural forces underpinning society. Of major significance in shaping early approaches to the understanding of society was a need to understand the impact of the industrial revolution and concomitant urbanisation on social life during the eighteenth and nineteenth centuries. Initial interpretations of this rapid social change utilised a systems perspective which argued that taken-for-granted aspects of daily life, for example, mundane forms of social interaction and common-sense knowledges, were the product of structural forces operating beyond the consciousness of social actors. Through their raising of theoretically complex models, systems approaches sought to explain social action as the result of underlying structural processes whose influence on the individual subject, it was maintained, was comparable with that of the laws determining the behaviour of objects in the natural world.

The two principle systems approaches are associated with the respective works of founding social theorists Emile Durkheim and Karl Marx. For Durkheim, the purpose of the social system was to create order through consensus. According to Durkheim, consensual systems of norms and values were maintained through 'collective representations', that is to say, bodies of collective knowledge which existed *sui generis* (in themselves) and, thus, independently of individual actors. Marx, on the other hand, argued that the purpose of the social system was to suppress conflict between social classes given the unequal distribution of wealth and power in developing capitalist societies. The survival of industrial capitalism, Marx argued, relied upon its establishment of a 'natural order of things' which prevented the working class from perceiving and understanding the true nature of their socio-economic circumstances.

From the point of view of the systems perspective then, the sphere of everyday life is regarded as a space for the domination and exploitation of the individual subject. Thus, as Gardiner observes:

> ... social actors are effectively cultural dupes ... who internalize passively extant social roles and behavioural norms (whether consensual or a reflection of class specific interests), thus acting to reproduce, in a largely automatic and unwitting fashion, social structures and institutions. (2000: 4)

During the late nineteenth century new theoretical perspectives began to contest the systems approach, arguing that its interpretation of social action as a product of underlying structural forces took no account of the individual's capacity for agency. Indeed, it is at this point that 'everyday life', though still not commonly used in social scientific parlance, became implicitly acknowledged as a potential mediator between the individual agent and the social structure. Central to this new debate among social theorists were Max Weber and George Herbert Mead. Both Weber and Mead argued that the internalisation of social norms on the part of individuals resulted not simply in passive obedience, but rather supplied the potential for self-motivated action. Thus, for example, in examining social status, Weber argued that, while this was on the one hand ingrained in the social relations of capitalism, its actual manifestation at the level of social relations was down to the creativity of individuals in finding ways to articulate their status.

Another perspective which sought to recast the individual as an active agent in the construction of meaning in everyday life is the phenomeno-logical approach developed in the work of theorists such as Schütz and Berger and Luckman. According to this approach, the significance of everyday life is inseparable from the indexical meanings ascribed to it by individual actors (Gardiner, 2000). This interpretation of everyday life is further developed by Erving Goffman through his application of a dra-maturgical model of everyday interaction. Thus, argues Goffman (1959), through gaining a 'practical experience' of everyday life characterised by the internalisation of social roles, individuals also learn how to manage and negotiate those roles through the creation of 'front-stage' and 'back-stage' selves. In doing so, individuals creatively manipulate the everyday, making it tolerable through creating spaces for the subversion of confor-mity. As Highmore notes:

> ... Goffman recognises that the self is [a] collection of performances that take place in and across specific locations. By employing a set of tropes that are associated with theatre and gaming (play, stage, set and so on) Goffman's approach to the everyday suggests an inventory of performances spatially arranged across the geography of everyday life. (2002: 50)

According to Gardiner, however, this approach, while ascribing the indi-vidual a more active and voluntaristic role in relation to everyday life still regards the everyday itself 'as a relatively homogenous and undifferenti-ated set of attitudes, practices and cognitive structures' (2000: 5). The dia-logic process between the individual and the everyday is considered only in as much as it enables a more reflexive re-enactment of a proscribed series of roles and expectations, or, alternatively, provides spaces for minor occurrences of subversion.

During the course of the late twentieth and early twenty-first century, social and cultural theorists have begun to conceptualise the everyday as a far more dynamic and contested sphere. Thus, it is argued, the every-day can no longer be described as an homogenous whole but must rather be understood as a highly pluralistic and contested domain. At the root of this transformation of everyday life, it is argued, are a number of inter-related factors. First, the rupturing of modernity and consequent decrease in importance of modernist conceptions of identity, based around class, gender, race and occupation. Second, the increasing prevalence of media and cultural industries which, it is argued, have played a significant part in suggesting new forms of social identity based around patterns of con-sumption and leisure (Chaney, 1996, 2002a). According to Chaney (2002a), the cumulative effect of such late modern societal characteristics has been one of 'cultural fragmentation' (see also Chapter 3). As individuals in late modernity increasingly shape their own identities through reflexively appropriating images and objects from the cultural and media industries, the notion of culture as an homogenous entity, that is to say, a 'whole way of life' (Williams, 1958) underpinning a common understanding of the everyday world, becomes harder to sustain. On the contrary, culture becomes a highly pluralistic and fragmented term embracing an increasingly differentiated range of identity projects. This is not to say that local, residual elements of culture no longer play any part in the way in which identities are framed, but their influence is compromised by the effects of externally generated resources. For late modern individuals then, identity is fashioned in relation to a variety of different reference points, some of which are embedded in local cultural contexts while others derive from global media and cultural industries (Lull, 1995).

This convergence of the local with the global also has a significant impact on everyday experience itself which, in the context of late modernity, has become similarly fragmented and particularised. As with 'culture', 'everyday life' can no longer be regarded as an homogenous term that bespeaks any essential truth about the ways in which individuals experience the world around them. Rather, 'everyday life' is a culturally constructed and highly contested terrain. This fragmentation of everyday life experience has been further intensified by increasing patterns of global mobility and their impact on notions of space and place. Once clearly demarcated by relatively static and ethnically homogenous communities, the 'spaces' and 'places' of everyday life are now highly pluralistic and contested, and are constantly being defined and redefined through processes of relocation and cultural hybridisation. This is perhaps most readily noted in cities and other areas of high urban concentration. As the local population of a particular place becomes more multi-ethnic and multicultural, and its physical terrains are increasingly crossed and appropriated by more temporal groups, such as tourists (Appadurai, 1990), so the identity of that place becomes more fragmented. As Massey observes:

> If it is now recognized that people have multiple identities, then the same point can be made in relation to places. Moreover, such multiple identities can be either, or both, a source of richness or a source of conflict. (1993: 65)

In the context of late modernity then, both culture and everyday are highly complex and fragmented concepts. Rather than espousing singular and essentialist meanings, they express a range of highly differentiated and contested meanings which are underpinned by the competing knowledges and sensibilities of an increasingly heterogeneous society.

It is with this latter approach to understanding culture and everyday life and its impact on contemporary cultural practice that this book is concerned. The first part of the book presents an overview of key theoretical debates that have informed approaches to the study and interpretation of culture and everyday life in contemporary society.

Chapter 1 considers how initial readings of late capitalist media and cultural industries adopted a broadly negative view: critiques of mass culture, beginning with the Frankfurt School, suggesting that the growth and reach of such industries amounted simply to a more insidious form of capitalist control – mass deception and exploitation of the working classes masquerading under the guise of popular leisure and entertainment. The chapter also looks at the development of Cultural Studies in Britain during the 1960s and how this approach, drawing on the work of writers such as Raymond Williams and Richard Hoggart, sought to re-evaluate the social significance of mass produced popular cultural objects and images as a means through which individuals were able to resist, or at least subvert, the dominant hegemonic order.

Chapter 2 examines the influence of postmodernist theory on interpretations of culture and everyday life in contemporary society. If structuralist-influenced readings positioned individual subjects as 'trapped' within a social system over which they had no influence or control, there has been a tendency in postmodernist theory to present a broadly opposite picture. Thus, through its abandonment of modernist narratives, postmodernism decentres the social actor with the effect that, like the postmodern landscape itself, he/she becomes simply a reflection of the de-contextualised images and objects that characterise postmodernity.

Chapter 3 turns its attention to how, in their attempts to reconcile the unsatisfactory interpretations of culture and everyday life presented in both structuralist and postmodern theory, a number of writers have embarked on a new programme of cultural theory. Referred to as the 'cultural turn', this work recasts everyday life as a dynamic and interactive process centring around individuals' creative use of media and consumer products in the construction of reflexively articulated identities and lifestyle projects.

The second part of the book examines the impact of the 'cultural turn' on theoretical and empirical approaches to the understanding of culture and everyday life in contemporary society.

Chapter 4 considers the impact of media and 'new' media forms on the cultural practices that characterise contemporary everyday life. Drawing on the 'active audience' work of theorists such as Morley (1992) and Fiske (1989a, 1989b), the chapter takes as its starting point the basic premise of these theorists that media audiences are not cultural dupes but active agents who reflexively appropriate texts and images drawn from the media and inscribe new meanings in the latter. The chapter begins by looking at the significance of popular television programmes such as soap operas and game shows and how these both draw and inform the everyday life experiences of the audience. This is followed by a consideration of various forms of print media, including women's and men's magazines and fanzines. Again, it is illustrated how, in their particular ways, such print media forms act as resources for individuals in the framing of their identities and the negotiation of everyday life. The final part of the chapter looks at the cultural impact of the internet on everyday life, and in particular how ease of access to the internet has engendered new forms of trans-local, trans-temporal communication between individuals with common interests in a variety of activities from music and sport to political issues.

Chapter 5 focuses on the significance of fashion in everyday life. Beginning with a look at the pioneering work of Simmel and Veblen, the chapter considers how their understanding of fashion as a source of social status has informed successive readings of fashion consumption and its role in the construction of social identities. As the chapter illustrates, fashion plays a significant role in the identity politics of late modern individuals, both in relation to gender and ethnic identities and also in the framing of subcultural and other forms of alternative identity. The chapter also considers how the fashion industry itself has acknowledged the relationship between fashion and lifestyle to the extent that, since the advent of the designer-wear market of the mid-1980s, fashion has been vociferously marketed as an aspect of lifestyle.

Chapter 6 examines the role of music in everyday life. As the chapter illustrates, while music, in particular post-Second World War popular music, has informed a range of resistant practices and identity politics, particularly among the young, music's significance in everyday life can also been seen in relation to a series of more mundane settings and circumstances. Thus, music is frequently heard in public spaces such as pubs and bars, shopping malls, fitness centres and so on. Additionally, due to the development of the personal stereo, individuals can create their own personal soundscapes, giving rise to what Bull (2000) describes as a cinematic experience of everyday life. Similarly, music is now a central resource in advertising, providing a soundtrack for the increasingly stylish and subtle marketing of a range of products, from cars to clothes and alcoholic drinks.

Chapter 7 looks at tourism and how the varying nature of the tourist 'experience' maps onto and can be discussed in terms of lifestyle preferences and choices. Thus, it is argued, various 'types' of tourism, such as 'adventure' and 'alternative' tourism often correspond with the broader lifestyle preferences of those individuals who opt for these kinds of tourism. Similarly, it is noted how a more recent trend in 'post-tourism' feeds a desire for the exotic while simultaneously providing much desired home comforts for tourists. The chapter also considers how the tourist experience is increasingly geared towards the pre-formed expectations of tourists, whose media experience of space and place prompts what Urry (1990) refers to as a 'tourist gaze'.

Finally, Chapter 8 considers the increasing prominence of counter-cultures in contemporary everyday life. As the chapter illustrates, the increasingly technocratic nature of late modern society, and the associated reliance on rational scientific knowledge, has engendered considerable scepticism and distrust among many individuals, particularly in relation to the impact of such developments on the environment and personal health and well-being. This has manifested itself through a variety of counter-cultural sensibilities and lifestyles which attempt in their own particular ways to subvert late modernity's emphasis on technocratic progress. At one level, such subversion is achieved through a resurgence of interest in greenist issues and back-to-the-land movements. Similarly, there is a growing interest in the natural healing powers of plants and herbs, as demonstrated by the growth in popularity of alternative medicines and also in the turn to witchcraft and neo-pagan beliefs and practices. The fear and alienation experienced by many individuals in a world increasingly driven by technology has also led to an increasing interest in the occult and paranormal as areas of knowledge beyond the comprehension of rational scientific explanation.

Part I

Everyday Life and Social Theory

ONE The Mass Culture Debate

Mass Culture is imposed from above. It is fabricated by technicians hired by businessmen; its audiences are passive consumers, their participation limited to the choice between buying and not buying. The Lords of *kitsch*, in short, exploit the cultural needs of the masses in order to make a profit and/or to maintain their class rule. (Macdonald, 1953: 60)

The arguments and debates around which this book is written are rooted in the growth of leisure and consumerism in the developing capitalist societies of the early twentieth century. As workers gained more rights, wages increased and the working day became shorter, the demand for leisure and entertainment grew. At the same time, breakthroughs in media and technology gave rise to new forms of mass communication and the mass production of leisure goods. By the middle of the twentieth century, the importance of leisure had grown to the extent that it had become a dominant aspect of everyday activity in late capitalist society. Work, which had once been a means to survival, now became a means to an altogether different end. Wages were no longer used simply to acquire the necessities of life, such as food and clothing, but also became a means through which to acquire goods and services associated with the new leisure markets (Bocock, 1993). Consumer and media products were now considered as important to the quality of life as those goods directly necessary for the sustenance of life. In other words, everyday life in late capitalism no longer turned around the value of 'utility' items alone, but also around more aesthetically valued objects and accessories – music, fashion, films and television programmes, sport, tourism and so on.

The shift from work to leisure-centred capitalist societies gave rise to a new phase in the sociological debate concerning the nature of social order under capitalism. Central to this debate were arguments concerning the relationship between new forms of leisure and consumption and the capitalist industries that facilitated these. While certain theorists, notably

Weber (1978 [1919]), Benjamin (Buck-Morss, 1989), Simmel (Frisby and Featherstone, 1997) and Veblen (1994 [1924]), argued that leisure and consumption opened up spaces for new forms of collective expression and creativity (see Chapter 3), this was countered by a rather more pessimistic interpretation which suggested that the apparently more 'civilised' spaces of late capitalist society merely served to veil an advanced, and in many ways more brutal, form of capitalist oppression which exploited new forms of mass leisure and consumption to its own ends. This chapter considers a number of critical responses by twentieth century social theorists to the increasing centrality of mass culture in capitalist society, its relationship to capitalist ideology and power, and its ultimate role in the reproduction of culture.

Feeding a fickle culture?

Critical theories of mass culture were greatly inspired by the work of Marx, and in particular Marx's explication of the systematic and highly complex processes of ideological and social control necessary for the maintenance of the capitalist system. According to Marx, the significant social upheavals brought about by industrial revolution of the mid-eighteenth century – the rapid shift from rural to urban living and a new form of cash nexus relationship in which workers were forced to sell their labour to capitalist entrepreneurs – altered the nature of social relations significantly. The survival of industrial capitalism, Marx argued, relied upon the establishment of a 'natural order' of things, the latter being achieved through the imposition of a social hierarchy which prevented the working classes from perceiving and understanding the true nature of their socio-economic exploitation by the bourgeoisie. Thus, as Löwith observes:

> Because the producers of commodities (i.e. the producers of objects of every kind with the form or structure of commodities) enter into human-social relationships only through the exchange of commodities as commodities – hence as 'things' – the social relations which underlie commodities do not appear to the producers themselves as social relations of the human social labour process. On the contrary, these real underlying social relations seem to be purely 'objective' relations among themselves as producers, while conversely, the 'objective' relations between commodities assume a character of quasi-personal relations which act independently in a commodity market which has its own laws. (1993: 101)

By dent of their socio-economic subordination, argued Marx, the working class were also subject to a form of ideological domination which turned upon the bourgeoisie's ability to construct a particular form of social reality in which workers were deemed, and deemed themselves, subservient to the needs of capitalism. As Morrison observes, 'individuals bec[a]me outcomes of capitalist social functions and appear[ed] to enter into economic activity as if it were their nature' (1995: 77). The everyday cultural experience of the working class was, therefore, held to be little more than a by-product of their economic exploitation, the economic core or 'base' of society, according to Marx, being mirrored in the cultural institutions or 'superstructure'. From a Marxist perspective:

> A culture is organized in relation to sets of interests within society and dominant interests are the articulation of power. Power, in turn, is ... mediated through the existing systems of stratification in society (in relation to class, gender, race, ability, age and so on) which are, in general, taken for granted by most of the people, most of the time. (Jenks, 1993: 72)

For Marx then, the 'everyday culture' of capitalist society is little more than an elaborate trick of illusion, a vehicle for the ruling class's economic and ideological exploitation of the working class. Such is the force of the illusion held in place by the combined economic and ideological power of the ruling class, according to Marx, that the working class are effectively prevented from collectively comprehending the true conditions of their socio-economic existence, such comprehension being a necessary element in the process of social change.

The increasing technological sophistication of capitalist societies during the twentieth century was argued by many theorists to add weight to Marx's arguments concerning the nature and ownership of power and control under capitalism. In particular, it was suggested that the increasing prevalence of mass communications technologies in advanced capitalist societies was resulting in the exercise of ever more pervasive forms of social control from above due to the more ready manipulation of the ideas and beliefs of the working classes facilitated by such technologies. Key theorists in this debate were German neo-Marxist thinkers Adorno, Horkheimer and Marcuse, leading writers within a group collectively known as the Frankfurt School. According to the Frankfurt School, 'the possibilities of manipulation of mass opinion through the media [were] particularly threatening' (Holton and Turner, 1989: 22). The mass cultural critique formulated by the Frankfurt School theorists was influenced considerably by events in Germany during the 1930s when Hitler's Nazi Party made extensive and highly effective use of the mass media in its national propaganda campaign (see Bottomore, 1984).

During a period of exile in the US between 1933 and 1950, Adorno and Horkheimer developed their ideas into a more sophisticated critique of mass culture through a series of observations on the centrality of the media and other forms of mass entertainment in American life (see Bottomore, 1984; Stevenson, 1995). Mass culture, it was claimed, represented a new, technologically enhanced form of social control, surpassing Marx's notion of the ruling ideology as the instrument of social control through its ability to manipulate leisure as a form of mass distraction. Ironically, argued Adorno and Horkheimer, despite their apparent everyday significance as spaces of freedom from work and avenues for relaxation, leisure and entertainment actually served the capitalist process in a very effective way by preserving the routinised pattern of working life outside of the workplace:

> Amusement under late capitalism is the prolongation of work. It is sought after as an escape from the mechanized work process, and to recruit strength in order to be able to cope with it again. But at the same time mechanization has such power over a man's leisure and happiness, and so profoundly determines the manufacture of amusement goods, that his experiences are inevitably afterimages of the work process itself. (1969: 137)

A particularly good example of this, according to Horkheimer and Adorno, was the Hollywood film industry, the formatted nature of Hollywood films underpinning the regulated nature of the work experience.[1] The predictability of films, whatever their genre – romance, thriller, horror or comedy – mirrors the mundane predictability of working life with the result that the individual cannot escape this routine even when supposedly engaged in the leisure pursuit of going to the cinema. This rationalisation of the cinematic experience, it was argued, also extended to children's cartoon films, the animated characters of such films portraying acceptable social roles or, alternatively, acting as examples of what young viewers could expect when the line between acceptable and unacceptable behaviour was crossed:

> In so far as cartoons do any more than accustom the senses to the new tempo, they hammer into the brain the old lesson that continuous friction, the breaking down of all individual resistance, is the condition of life in this society. Donald Duck in the cartoons and the unfortunate in real life get their thrashing so that the audience can learn to take their own punishment. (ibid.: 138)

Adorno was also highly critical of mass produced popular music which, he argued, constituted one of the worst examples of capitalism's intrusion into the world of art (Jay, 1973). A musician himself, Adorno was repulsed by what he regarded as the standardisation of music when reduced to a commodity form. In an essay entitled 'On Popular Music', Adorno makes a distinction between serious, or 'art', music and 'popular' music, the key difference in these musical forms, according to Adorno, being the contrasting demands they make of the listener. In the case of art music, suggests Adorno, its key purpose is to convey a specific meaning, as intended by the composer, to the listener in much the same way that a painting is supposed to convey the intended meaning of the artist to the viewer. Moreover, according to Adorno, the intended meaning becomes apparent only after a considerable degree of listening skill has been learned and applied. Listening to art music is, therefore, an educational experience; 'correct' listening becomes an exercise in grasping the 'concrete totality' of a musical piece (Adorno, 1990 [1941]: 303). Once this totality has been understood, a door is opened on a new inner world of heightened experience which allows the listener to transcend the mundane world of everyday experience (Paddison, 1996).

In the case of mass produced popular music, argues Adorno, no such individual meaning is conveyed by the music, and thus no listening skill is necessary. For Adorno, the essence of popular music is its standardised format. This in turn ensures that the social reception of popular music is pre-programmed, that musical composition and production follow exacting guidelines which are calculated to produce a specific and uniformed response among listeners:

> The composition hears for the listener ... Not only does it not require effort to follow its concrete stream; it actually gives him models under which anything concrete still remaining may be subsumed. The schematic build up dictates the way in which he must listen while, at the same time, it makes any effort in listening unnecessary. Popular music is 'pre-digested' in a way strongly resembling the fad of 'digests' of printed material. (Adorno, 1990 [1941]: 306)

As with the Frankfurt School's critique of Hollywood films and other mass cultural forms, Adorno suggests that the formulaic nature of popular music, and its dumbing down effect on the listener, contributes to the patterning and regulation of leisure time in capitalist society. According to Adorno, the 'patterned and pre-digested' nature of popular music offers relief 'from both boredom and effort simultaneously' with the result that periods of leisure can be tailored to provide maximum relaxation and refreshment (ibid.).

For Adorno and Horkeimer then, such was the level of technocratisation and rationalisation inherent in the production and dissemination of mass culture that it effectively constituted a 'culture industry', infiltrating in ever more seductive ways the spaces of everyday life in late capitalist society (Kellner, 1995). The seductive power of the culture industry, they argued, was illustrated perfectly in the context of American society. Thus, by means of the newly developed mass media communication technologies a nation the size of the United States could be force-fed a uniform diet of images, information and consumer products on a daily basis with the result that the pursuit of leisure and entertainment became standardised, with individuals choosing from a proscribed range of leisure and entertainment activities tightly controlled by the media and cultural industries. As the media and producers of consumer goods worked increasingly together, it was argued, the result was a ruthless and systematic flooding of everyday life with a never ending flow of advertisements for products, thus ensuring a complete fetishisation of leisure and entertainment. In this way, argued Adorno and Horkheimer, the culture industry acquired control over the desires and, ultimately, the destinies, of its increasingly 'captive audience'. As Inglis and Hughson observe with reference to Adorno and Horkheimer's reading of mass culture:

> Large media corporations' monopoly on cultural life was made possible through bureaucratically organised means of distribution, which ensured that the products on sale reached everyone in a given population ... Just as in Hitler's Germany all means of communication had been under the control of certain powerful interest groups, so too were the airwaves and film-houses of democratic America under the rule of the powerful. (2003: 49)

As a result the logic of capitalism became an all pervasive form of control, central not only to the workplace but also to the domestic sphere of family life and leisure. Just as Marx had argued that the power of the bourgeoisie during the period of industrial capitalism turned on their ability to impose a particular version of reality upon the everyday lives of the working class, so the Frankfurt School suggested that late capitalism refined this system of control using the seductive pleasures of mass cultural products to dupe the masses into blithe acceptance of the capitalist consumer system. As Stevenson notes:

> The effectiveness of the culture industry was not secured through a deceptive ideology, but by the removal from the consciousness of the masses of any alternative to capitalism. The dominant culture of late capitalism served to promote the repression of all forms of conflict, heterogeneity and particularity from the cultural sphere. This form of 'affirmative culture' both fetishises exchange over the use value (where the value of a concert is secured through the cost of the ticket rather then the quality of the performance) and produces in the audience the desire for the ever same over and over again. (1995: 53)

Of the original Frankfurt School theorists, only Marcuse, displays any degree of optimism regarding the centrality of mass culture to everyday life in late capitalist society. Having originally subscribed to the same critical views as Adorno and Horkheimer (see Marcuse, 1964), Marcuse subsequently witnessed the rise of the hippie counter-culture during the late 1960s and reviewed his interpretation of mass culture (see Bottomore, 1984). In particular, Marcuse was struck by the way the counter-culture appeared to use the very products of the late capitalist leisure and consumer industries, notably mass produced music and fashion, in a direct revolt against dominant capitalist institutions, such as work, education, the family and mainstream politics. Marcuse's views were echoed in the work of Theodore Roszak who additionally suggested that the fact that the counter-cultural 'revolution' appeared to be driven by *middle-class* youth suggested that a radical deconstruction was taking place within the very ideological power base that neo-Marxist theorists had identified as key to the continuing domination of capitalism in technologically advanced consumer-based societies. Thus, observed Roszak:

> ... by way of a dialectic Marx could never have imagined, technocratic America produces a potentially revolutionary element among its own youth. The bourgeoisie, instead of discovering the class enemy in its factories, finds it across the breakfast table in the person of its own pampered children. (1969: 34)

Nevertheless, the relatively short-lived era of the counter-culture, and also subsequent music and style-driven youth cultural movements such as punk rock (see Hebdige, 1979), served to confirm for many the fundamental accuracy of the Frankfurt School's mass cultural critique. Thus, according to Bottomore, 'the limited scope and the rapid disappearance, or assimilation, of the counter-culture [could] in fact [be taken to] reveal the strength of the culture industry' (1984: 46).

For the Frankfurt School, the rise of the mass media and 'culture industry' and their steady infiltration of everyday life during the twentieth century signalled a shift from the 'self-regulating liberal capitalism of the nineteenth century [to a] planned and totally administered "organised capitalism"' (Swingewood, 1977: 77). According to fellow Frankfurt School theorist Habermas, this shift in the nature and function of capitalism would forever seal the fate of the masses. Thus, the everyday lives of the masses, or the 'lifeworld' as Habermas terms this, becomes fundamentally shaped by the mediatisation processes that act upon it to the extent that mediated information becomes the very basis of everyday knowledge. Due to ubiquitous and all-embracing nature of the media, no avenue exists for the forming and articulation of critical thought or action on the part of individuals themselves. All forms of everyday knowledge, understanding and communication are effectively controlled by the over-arching system of bureaucratic and administrative control through which organised capitalism is managed and maintained. The wishes and desires of individuals are so tightly controlled that the lifeworld becomes 'ratio-nalised' by the capitalist system that controls it. At the same time, how-ever, the masses remain entirely oblivious to the overarching system that controls their consciousness and determines their needs. As Habermas observes, the lifeworld:

> ... takes on the character of deception, of objectively false consciousness. The effects of the system on the lifeworld, which change the structure of contexts of action in socially integrated groups, have to remain hidden. The reproductive constraints that instrumentalize a lifeworld without weakening the illusion of its self-sufficiency have to hide, so's to speak, in the pores of communicative action. This gives rise to a structural violence that, without becoming manifest as such, takes hold of the forms of intersubjectivity of possible understanding. (1987: 187)

The ultimate effect of this colonisation of the lifeworld, according to Habermas, is a withering away of individuals' capacity for critical thought and collective action, with the consequence that the lifeworld becomes incapable of acting back on the system that shapes it. This results in what Habermas refers to as a 'de-coupling' of the system from the lifeworld. Having being robbed of their power to critically engage with and synthe-sise knowledge and information received from above, individuals con-tinue to exist in the lifeworld in a disengaged state, unthinkingly accepting their daily routines and regarding them as simply second nature.

The legacy of the Frankfurt School

The Frankfurt School's highly critical interpretation of the effects of mass culture on society have continued to exert a powerful influence. Key to this influence is the Frankfurt School's identification of an apparently unshiftable dualism inherent in the social effects of mass culture, mak-ing it a both highly efficient means of ensuring the economic survival of capitalism and a vehicle for the exertion of a powerful form of ideologi-cal control. As a principal arm of organised capitalism, mass culture con-stitutes, according to the Frankfurt School, a simultaneous economic and ideological exploitation of the masses. This interpretation of mass culture and its effects upon everyday life has been taken up and developed by various theorists for whom there is a general consensus that mass culture's fetishisation of consumer objects and its powerfully imposed false consciousness pose considerable barriers to the transformation of everyday life into a more liberal and reflexively enacted sphere through which individuals may regale against the stifling conditions of late capitalism.

A particularly pessimistic reading of the effects of mass culture in this respect is offered by Heller. Heller argues that the mediatisation of late capitalist society results in 'a trivialization of human personality' (1984: 223). The fetishisation of objects and images, according to Heller, has created a desire in individuals to be continually bombarded with information. Indeed, according to Heller, even such taken-for-granted everyday expressions as 'being well-informed' bespeak at a deeper level the fate of the individual as a mere 'recipient' of information generated from above and circulated down to the masses. In contemporary societies, argues Heller, the emphasis is upon receiving rather than acting upon information, the capacity for critical discussion and assessment of stories and events having being replaced by a straightforward acceptance of information received via the mass media as 'given'. This in turn illustrates, according to Heller, how individuals in late capitalist, media-driven societies are deprived of any capacity to act on their lives and implement change: 'If the desire to be well-informed completely ousts the urge to act on the basis of information received, human knowledge tends to be passive rather than active, and ceases to play a significant role in the structuring of life (which is what everyday knowledge is supposed to do)' (ibid.). In Heller's view, robbed of their ability for dialogic interaction, individuals turn increasingly inwards, focusing only upon themselves and their own immediate everyday lives. It is this feature of late modern society, argues Heller, that most effectively prohibits radical collective action. Lacking a capacity for critical thought, individuals revel in a state of pseudo-individualism, created by the combined forces of the media and cultural industries, the former serving to further fragment forms of collective consciousness based around class, community and tradition. Such social fragmentation has an acutely pathological effect, eroding the collective moral fibre on which social cohesion and a potential for radical collective action ultimately depends. Thus, as Gardiner observes:

> For Heller, everyday life under modernity ... is an alienated form of existence, because instrumental thinking and acting dominate our lives, and the concrete 'other' disappears as a genuine dialogical partner. Revelling in a kind of solipsistic particularism gives us the illusion of autonomous freedom, but a genuine moral attitude must be attuned to the demands of more

universalistic notions of human responsibility and freedom, based on such overarching considerations as mutual recognition, interpersonal dialogue and what [Heller] calls 'radical tolerance'. (2000: 21)

Lefebvre is similarly critical of what he perceives as mass culture's systematic manipulation of individual consciousness and action. For Lefebvre, the mass produced everyday experience of late capitalism 'separates what men are from what they think they are, what they live from what they think they live' (1991: 146). According to Lefebvre this feature of capitalism is made all the more pervasive through the consumer goods and services associated with everyday life in late capitalism: 'you are being looked after, cared for, told how to live better, how to dress fashionably, how to decorate your house, in short, how to exist' (1971: 107). The parallels with the Frankfurt School's pessimistic reading of mass consumer culture are very clear in Lefebvre's observation. Unlike the Frankfurt School, however, Lefebvre does not perceive individuals as doomed to exist in a lifeworld disengaged from the capitalist system that presides over it. Rather, he believes that individuals retain a capacity for agency that could ultimately be used to effect social change through the rejection of the false representation of the everyday offered up by late capitalist cultural industries. For Lefebvre, such radical action depends upon the renurturing of the individual's capacity for critical judgement, something which has been stripped away by the alienating forces of capitalism. According to Lefebvre, the cracks in this visage are already beginning to show and will become more evident as individuals increasingly gain power over themselves, that is to say, as reason, morality and self-realisation triumph over the rational-scientific core of late capitalist order:

... progress in the way life is organized cannot be limited to the technical progress in external equipment, cannot be confined to an increase in the quantity of tools.

It will also be a qualitative progress: the individual will stop being a fiction, a myth of bourgeois democracies – an empty, negative form – a pleasant illusion for each human grain of sand. He will cease being 'private' by becoming at the same time more social, more human – and more individual. (1991: 248)

For Lefebvre, a crucial element in the renurturing of the individual's capacity for critical thought is a rejection of the fetishised products of mass culture and a reinvestment in objects of real 'cultural worth', that is to say, the high cultural forms which Adorno and Habermas claimed were key to the intellectual and critical capacity of the individual subject. However, if Lefebvre remains optimistic regarding the possibility of a return to 'high culture' and the subsequent reversal of organised capitalism's economic and ideological domination of the masses, other theorists take a far more negative view, arguing that the seductive and all embracing nature of mass culture may ultimately lead to a widespread cultural malaise including the objects of high culture championed by elite theorists.

Such pessimism is exemplified in the work of US mass cultural theorist Dwight Macdonald whose writing during the 1950s issued a severe warning concerning the danger of allowing the production and distribution of mass cultural goods and services to keep on growing unchecked. Following Adorno, Horkheimer and other Frankfurt School theorists, Macdonald makes a distinction between high culture and mass or 'low' culture, identifying in these respective forms the same liberatory and exploitative qualities that the Frankfurt School attached to them. However, while the Frankfurt School regarded high and low/mass culture as occupying two relatively distinct cultural spheres, Macdonald warned of a steady encroachment of mass culture upon the high cultural domain. This he argued stemmed both from the relative ease with which the mass cultural sphere was expanding on a daily basis and the highly seductive characteristics of mass cultural products. Thus, observes Macdonald:

> Good art competes with *kitsch*, serious ideas compete with commercialized formulae – and the advantage lies all on one side ... bad stuff drives out the good since it is more easily understood and enjoyed ... [Kitsch] threatens High Culture by its sheer pervasiveness, its brutal overwhelming *quantity*. (1953: 61)

The irony of this, according to Macdonald, is that those who seek to economically exploit mass audiences through the production and dissemination of mass cultural products ultimately engineer the demise of the high culture through which they had hitherto differentiated themselves from the masses:

> The upper classes, who begin by using [kitsch] to make money from the crude tastes of the masses and to dominate them politically, end by finding their own culture attacked and even threatened with destruction by the instrument they have thoughtlessly employed. (ibid.: 61–2)

A similarly pessimistic view of mass culture and its ultimate transformation into *the* culture of modernity is offered by Swingewood. According Swingewood, however, it is not the case that mass culture simply replaces high culture as the dominant cultural form; rather, he suggests, vast elements of what was previously regarded as high culture are subsumed by mass culture and become aspects of the 'popular' everyday culture consumed by everyone. The result of this, according to Swingewood, is that the aura of 'true' art is lost as great works of art, novels, poetry, music and so on are clinically reproduced on a mass scale and consequently reduced to a commodity form: 'Thus the inexorable levelling of standards: capitalist culture and its artifacts become commodities, their function to entertain, divert and reduce consciousness to a state of total passivity' (Swingewood, 1977: 2).

Everyday life and Cultural Studies

Against the tide of pessimism regarding the growing power and domination of mass cultural forms during the mid-twentieth century, a new academic project began to take shape. Referred to as Cultural Studies, this provided the basis for an alternative way of interpreting the impact of mass culture upon society, and in particular the working classes for whom, for reasons already discussed, the consequences of mass culture had been deemed to be particularly dire. Cultural Studies drew much of its early inspiration from the work of British literary critics such as F.R. Leavis and T.S. Eliot. Eliot was highly critical of what he regarded as the 'unrestrained egoism and individualism' of modern capitalism and its 'weaken[ing effect on] the moral bonds of a traditional common culture' (Swingewood, 1977: 7). Leavis shared Eliot's concern regarding 'loss of community', but regarded this as a potential rather than actual effect of the mass culturalisation of society (ibid.: 10). Moreover, Leavis accepted that historical change is an inevitable part of the civilisation process. Thus, for Leavis the key task of the critic was to emphasise how 'human values, community and the common culture' could be maintained and strengthened even as the fabric of society underwent substantial changes as a consequence of capitalism's ongoing development and deeper colonisation of everyday life (ibid.: 10). Indeed, Leavis argues that even mass culture could have potentially subversive qualities through its appropriation and use by ordinary people in everyday contexts. Thus, as Swingewood observes:

> ... at the heart of [Leavis's] analysis is the idea of culture as simultaneously popular and discriminating. Leavis's emphasis [is] on the essential link between 'life' as the common culture, the everyday experience of common people within a morally binding community, and creative intelligence. (ibid.: 10)

Leavis's notion of culture as a contested and creative domain was to become a core element of the Cultural Studies project, which gathered momentum during the 1950s through the work of Raymond Williams and Richard Hoggart. In particular, Williams's contention that culture is 'ordinary', and thus the basis upon which a *whole way of life* is established, furthered the attempts initiated by Leavis to wrest culture away from its exclusively 'highbrow' associations with, for example, works of art, literature, classical music. According to Williams, such high art forms are but single elements in the sphere of cultural activities which also includes a range of more mundane, 'everyday' practices:

> The analysis of culture ... is the clarification of the meanings and values implicit and explicit in a particular way of life, a particular culture. Such analysis will include ... historical criticism ... in which intellectual and imaginative works are analysed in relation to particular traditions and societies, but will also include elements in the way of life that to followers of the other definitions are not 'culture' at all: the organization of production, the structure of the family, the structure of institutions which express or govern social relationships, the characteristic forms through which members of the society communicate ... It seems to me that there is value in each of these kinds of definition. For it certainly seems necessary to look for meanings and values, the record of creative human activity, not only in art and intellectual work, but also in institutions and forms of behaviour. (1961: 57–8)

Hoggart, although similarly concerned with broadening the definition of culture to encompass mundane everyday practices, is often associated with a far more pessimistic reading of cultural relations in class-based societies. In particular Hoggart's work is said to present a damming picture of post-war popular culture and its impact on the British working class. In a now famous observation, Hoggart (1957) claimed that the seductive qualities of popular culture imported into Britain from the US induced an urge for self-gratification, effectively 'unbending the springs of action' and reducing the working class to a passive audience duped by effete and feckless forms of popular entertainment. More recent readings of Hoggart's work, however, suggest that its alleged pessimism may have been overstated. For example, with reference to Hoggart's work on popular music, Laing notes that this 'demonstrates a detailed knowledge of the variety of popular song in the mid-1950s and considers the complexity of the response of working-class listeners to even the most inconsequential lyrics' (1994: 185).

In 1964 Hoggart established the Centre for Contemporary Cultural Studies (CCCS) at the University of Birmingham. During the next twenty years the CCCS produced a series of studies focusing on the everyday cultural practices of the British working class. Key to CCCS's analysis of culture was its adoption of aspects of the cultural-Marxist approach developed by Italian neo-Marxist Antonio Gramsci. Although subscribing to the view that social change on the scale predicted by Marx was increasingly unlikely in the context of late capitalism, Gramsci also argued that social control in any absolute sense by the bourgeoisie was unachievable due to the constant struggle between class interests. Contrary to the negative outlook of the Frankfurt School and mass cultural theorists such as Macdonald (1953) regarding the fate of the individual in late capitalist society, Gramsci argued that the reduction of working hours combined with increasing outlets for leisure and recreation had functioned to create a more critical and articulate society. The consequence of this, contended Gramsci, was a shift in the basis of power in capitalist society. Thus, he argued, the bourgeoisie are no longer able to maintain power purely on the basis of their economic dominance but must strive exercise it 'in moral and intellectual terms' as well (Bennett et al., 1981: 198).

Gramsci refers to this process as 'hegemonic rule', hegemony expressing the dominant system of ideas and beliefs through which the bourgeoisie are able to consolidate their power over society. Some observers have suggested that hegemonic control is simply a more concentrated form of the original economic power exercised by the bourgeoisie. May, for example, argues that hegemony simply allows the bourgeoisie to '[exercise] its social control through both coercion *and* consensus within institutions. What presents itself as common sense is actually symptomatic of ideological distortion' (1996: 42). Such an interpretation suggests that, through its utility in the presentation of the social order as a given and normal set of circumstances, hegemony simply enhances the elaborate smokescreen set in motion and perpetuated by the bourgeoisie as a means of tricking the working class into subordination. For Gramsci, however, hegemony has an altogether different effect on the nature and function of social order. Thus, he argues, the ruling hegemony is susceptible to challenges from below. Although such challenges are in themselves incapable of usurping the bourgeoisie from their dominant position they can, nevertheless produce a 'crisis of authority' (Bennett et al., 1981: 199). This, in turn has significant implications for the bourgeoisie's ability to exert its social power through consensus. Thus, states Gramsci: 'If the ruling class has lost its consensus, i.e. is no longer "leading" but only "dominant", exercising coercive force alone; this means precisely that the great masses have become detached from their traditional ideologies, and no longer believe what they used to believe previously, etc.' (1971: 275).

Faced with this situation, the only means available to the ruling class to reassert and maintain its hegemonic power is through the 'accommodation [of] opposing class values' (Bennett, 1986a: xv). This, in turn, necessitates a new understanding of cultural forms and the everyday life processes in which they are embedded as sites of hegemonic struggle and contestation. Culture becomes the ideological terrain on which issues of power are continuously negotiated and redefined. Moreover, as a result of such struggle and contestation, the ideological divisions existing between social classes are weakened. As Bennett notes:

> As a consequence of its accommodating elements of opposing class cultures, 'bourgeois culture' ceases to be purely or entirely bourgeois. It becomes, instead, a mobile combination of cultural and ideological elements derived from different class locations which are, but only provisionally and for the duration of a specific historical conjuncture, affiliated to bourgeois values, interests and objectives. By the same token, of course, the members of the subordinate classes never encounter or are oppressed by a dominant ideology in some pure or class essentialist form; bourgeois ideology is encountered only in the compromised forms it must take in order to provide some accommodation for opposing class values. (ibid.)

The concept of hegemony has considerable implications for more pessimistic interpretations of mass cultural theory in that it effectively explodes arguments concerning the allegedly conspiratorial nature of mass culture and offers scope for the redefinition of mass cultural products, texts and images as offering spaces of resistance. Power in society is no longer considered to be a purely top down process; rather, through the prism of mass culture, power is recast as process of compromise and constant readjustment, the maintenance of power being entirely dependent upon the bourgeoisie's ability to absorb and rearticulate values and ideas projected upwards from the lower levels of the social strata.

The Birmingham CCCS's analysis of contemporary culture as a process of hegemonic struggle was most famously examined in Hall and Jefferson's (1976) *Resistance Through Rituals*, a study of style-based working-class youth cultures in post-Second World War Britain (see also Chapter 5). During the 1950s, many observers suggested that Britain was becoming a classless society. Thus, it was argued, post-war affluence was resulting in an erosion of class differences as the working class effectively became middle class in their leisure and lifestyle habits (see, for example, Zweig, 1961). Post-war youth cultures were considered to be a primary illustration of this process in that they demonstrated working-class youth's assimilation into a unified teenage consumer culture (Abrams, 1959). The CCCS argued against this interpretation of post-war youth. Thus, they contended, if the emergent style-based youth cultures of the 1950s were indeed indicative of working-class youth's newly acquired spending habits, at a deeper level they symbolised the fact that class divisions were still very much a feature of post-war British society. The increased spending power of working-class youth, it was argued, may have risen their profile as consumers but did nothing to alter their life chances in real terms. Thus, it was argued:

> There is no 'subcultural solution' to working-class youth unemployment, educational disadvantage, compulsory miseducation, dead-end jobs, the routinisation and specialisation of labour, low pay and the loss of skills. Subcultural strategies cannot match, meet or answer the structuring dimensions emerging in this period for the class as a whole ... They 'solve', but in an imaginary way, problems which at the concrete material level remain unresolved. (Clarke et al., 1976: 47–8)

The CCCS went on to argue that fashion styles appropriated by young working-class people from the emergent youth market became resources in strategies of resistance staged by working-class youth against the material conditions of their existence. Drawing on Gramsci's concept of hegemony, the CCCS maintained that working class youth's use of style in this way represented a new chapter in the '"Theatre of Struggle" [which Gramsci had argued characterises the social relations of late capitalism], a repertoire of strategies and responses – ways of coping as well as of resisting' (ibid.: 44). According to the CCCS, working-class youth's creation of 'subcultural' solutions to material problems was to be seen most readily in their act of winning 'cultural space in the neighbourhood and institutions, real time for leisure and recreation, actual room on the street corner' (ibid.: 45).

This Gramscian interpretation of class struggle, and the latter's enhanced articulation through the prism of mass popular culture, was further developed during the 1980s in research by cultural theorists such as Stuart Hall and Tony Bennett at the Open University. For Bennett, a key effect of popular culture in late modernity has been its facilitation of 'cultural and discursive spaces ... in which positive forms of self-recognition and estimation [can] be produced' (1986b: 12). According to Bennett, the mass production and dissemination of popular culture made possible through technological advances in late modernity has facilitated its ready augmentation into mundane everyday practices. This, in turn, has empowered individuals with new levels of expression and creativity, thus transforming everyday life into a reflexively articulated cultural process. Bennett argues that popular culture facilitates a greater level of pluralism in everyday life, the hegemonic struggle between the classes becoming more pronounced rather than diminishing:

[Popular culture] consists of those cultural forms and practices ... which constitute the terrain on which dominant, subordinate and oppositional cultural values and ideologies meet and intermingle, in different mixes and permutations, vying with one another in their attempts to secure the spaces within which they can become influential in framing and organising popular experience and consciousness. It consists not of two separated compartments – a pure and spontaneously oppositional culture 'of the people' – but is located in the points of confluence between these opposing tendencies whose contradictory orientations shape the very organisation of the cultural forms in which they meet and interpenetrate one another. (ibid.: 18–19)

While Cultural Studies has done much to enrich the theoretical and empirical understanding of mass culture through arguing its significance as a site of hegemonic struggle in late modern everyday life, its approach has been criticised on a number of accounts. A key criticism points to the problems inherent in the concept of hegemony itself. Thus, it is argued, by fixating on the nexus of the structural relations of capitalism, hegemonic interpretations of conflict and struggle in everyday life conspire to rob the individual of reflexivity and self-will, suggesting an essentially automatic and subconscious form of action. Thus, as Harris notes in relation to CCCS readings of youth cultures as pockets of resistance to the structural circumstances of their everyday existence, the actors themselves 'are not subjectively aware of these structural meanings' (1992: 90).

A further criticism points to the emphasis of Cultural Studies theorists upon textual analysis rather than actual engagement with those individuals using the products of mass culture in the course of their everyday lives. That theorists have drawn so extensively on textual analysis stems directly from the theoretical tools underpinning the Cultural Studies project. Thus, it is argued, the cultural significance of everyday working-class practices can only be grasped through the use of theoretical abstraction as a means of rolling back the overlying mundaneness of everyday life and revealing the underlying struggles for power that inform such practices and their connection to the ongoing class struggles that characterise late capitalist society. As Hall observes:

... to think about or to analyse the complexity of the real, the act of practice of thinking is required; and this necessitates the use of the power of abstraction and analysis, the formation of concepts with which to cut into the complexity of the real, in order precisely to reveal and bring to light relationships and structures which cannot be visible to the naked eye, and which can neither present nor authenticate themselves. (1980: 31)

Ultimately, however, this refusal on the part of cultural studies theorists to empirically engage with the social subjects at the heart of their work creates an irresolvable paradox in Cultural Studies work, in that cultural meanings are being imposed upon the actions of individuals for them by theorists who claim such individuals remain oblivious to such meanings. This approach is borne out by Dick Hebdige, who at the end of his celebrated study of the semiotic meaning of punk, *Subculture: The Meaning of Style*, concludes: 'It is highly unlikely ... that members of any of the subcultures described in this book would recognise themselves reflected here' (1979: 139). Such a bold statement prompted critics to ask very pointed questions concerning the verifiability of a body of work that claimed to address highly subjective issues such as stylistic meaning when the bearers of the style themselves remained unconsulted. Thus, as Cohen argued in response to Hebdige's claims:

> Displaying a swastika shows how symbols are stripped from their natural context, exploited for empty effect, displayed through mockery, distancing, irony, parody, inversion ... But how are we to know this? We are never told much about the 'thing': when, how, where, by whom or in what context it is worn. We do not know what, if any, difference exists between indigenous and sociological explanations. (1987: xvii)

Harris is similarly critical of the absence of empirical data to support theoretical claims made in Open University Cultural Studies research on television audiences. As with critics of the CCCS work on youth culture, Harris argues that the absence of empirical research results in highly tenuous links being made between media content and its effects upon the audience. Again, for Harris, recourse to empirical work is a crucial element of such work, especially because of its claims to speak for real people living in real world contexts where issues of cause and effect may be due to a range of specific local circumstances that are not easily comprehended using a detached theoretical perspective. According to Harris: 'Asking the actual audience what they think of programmes [becomes necessary in order] to fix the floating signifiers and ground analysis, to check the dangers of endless but fanciful speculation about the significance of texts' (1992: 134).

Another criticism directed at the Cultural Studies project relates to its essentially inflexible definition of class in late modernity. Thus, not only is conflict and struggle in everyday life wholly circumscribed by the fact of class, class is also presented as an inescapable constraint on the individual. The fact of class is simply assumed to permeate all aspects of the individual's lifeworld. The shortcomings of such a position are effectively captured by Chaney who argues that:

> The problem with theories of hegemony ... is that they try to close off the processes of the production of meaning. Such theories cannot allow the

free play of irony and reflexivity in cultural discourse ... the fundamental
mistake is to assume that there are differences in kind between social and
cultural concepts. Putting it at its simplest, such theories assume that social
entities such as class exist, one might say in the real world, and then they
are talked about, represented and experienced as cultural matters. It follows
that the dynamic relations of the former can be used to explain the character
of the latter. (1994: 48–9)

According to Chaney then, the problem with the Cultural Studies perspective is that, while it acknowledges the presence and significance of
mass culture as a 'resource' in everyday life, this is done only insofar as
mass culture is seen to facilitate articulations of ingrained and subconscious class-based social sensibilities. The possibility that mass culture
may offer individuals the possibility to transcend such class-based sensibilities, or to draw on them in a more reflexive fashion in strategies of
resistance and negotiation, is never considered.

In defence of the Cultural Studies project, however, it should be noted
that its particular form of engagement with cultural processes in late capitalist society provided the impetus for more progressive understandings
of everyday life. Most significantly, Cultural Studies sought to recast individuals as agents who are at some level active in the production of their
cultural reality, rather than passive recipients of a ready made culture
imposed from above. This approach has been continued and developed in
the work of more recent Cultural Studies theorists such as John Fiske
(1989a, 1989b) and Mike Featherstone (1991) and in media studies research.
Key examples of this work are considered in detail in Chapter 3.

Conclusion

This chapter has considered a range of critical responses to the increasing centrality of mass culture in late capitalist society and its impact on
the everyday lives of individuals. Beginning with an overview of the
work of the Frankfurt School, it was illustrated how theorists such as
Adorno and Horkheimer were deeply pessimistic regarding what they
saw as the highly seductive qualities of mass popular cultural entertainment, notably in relation to film and popular music. According to the
Frankfurt School, the veneer of harmless fun and relaxation surrounding
these new leisure pursuits was merely an illusion, the underlying rational of mass produced leisure being a furthering of the economic and
ideological exploitation of the masses upon which capitalist society was
dependent for its survival.

The ideas of the Frankfurt School were to have a lasting influence on social and cultural theory. As considered in subsequent sections of this chapter, many theorists addressing the social impacts of mass culture during the latter half of the twentieth century shared the Frankfurt School's pessimism concerning the fate of the individual in mass society. Indeed, a common aspect of mass cultural critiques was the view that mass culture resulted in a withering away of the individual's capacity for critical thought. Thus, it was argued, while the appreciation and enjoyment of high cultural forms required an intellectual capacity – through which came a constant strengthening of the critical mind – the fickle pleasures associated with mass culture resulted in a desire for instant and unthinking gratification.

Against this canon of mass cultural criticism, the Cultural Studies project offered a more progressive solution to the 'problem' of mass culture. For theorists working out of the Cultural Studies paradigm, the terrain of the everyday was one of constant struggle, the resources of mass and popular culture being used by the working class in ways that constituted collective 'cultural' responses to their socio-economic circumstances, thus challenging the hegemonic order that the bourgeoisie attempted to impose on them. As critics of the Cultural Studies approach have observed, however, while at one level allowing for challenge and negotiation in the context of mass cultural society, the interpretation of culture put forward by Cultural Studies theorists is grounded in a belief that the structural experiences of individuals are rigidly fixed and essentially monolithic.

If structuralist and Cultural Studies approaches can be said to bind the individual too tightly into a world of predetermined structural responses, during the 1980s, the rise of a new school of social and cultural theory, influenced by postmodernism, was to redefine the fate of the individual. Postmodernism, it was argued, signalled an end to the modernist social structures around which industrial capitalism had been erected and the dominant ideological discourses of capitalist society maintained. According to postmodernists, the effect of postmodernism was to rupture the ideological project of modernity and transform individuals into de-centred subjects, at liberty to choose between an endless flow of images, texts and commodities, each of whose meaning was as malleable and shifting as the next. The postmodern era, it was argued, was one in which dominant discourses had given way to a continuous play of multiple and conflicting discourses. The following chapter considers the contribution of postmodern theory to our understanding of everyday life and the cultural forms through which the latter is constructed.

Note

1. Indeed, as Strinati (1995) notes, the Hollywood studio system was based upon and highly consistent with other forms of mass production perfected during the twentieth century, including strict separation between different stages of film production and a very specialised division of labour within production teams.

TWO Postmodernism

As noted in Chapter 1, a central aspect of mass cultural criticism is a belief in the ongoing nature of the economic and ideological exploitation of the masses by the ruling class. According to this approach, social *reality* is regarded as merely the sum of its representation by the ruling class, that is to say, an elaborate smokescreen put in place to ensure the 'taken-for-grantedness' by the masses of the structural relations on which the capitalist mode of production crucially depends. The individual, it is argued, is thus governed by subconsciously internalised norms and values whose primary function is to maintain the social hierarchy. During the latter part of the twentieth century, such social perspectives were challenged by a new school of thought which suggested that significant changes taking place in the social fabric signalled an overarching change in the nature of society. Such changes were argued to be characterised by a transition from a 'modern' to a 'postmodern' social condition (Lyotard, 1984). A key element in this 'postmodern turn' (Best and Kellner, 1997), it was argued, was the erosion of the dominant discourse which had previously sustained and legitimated the project of modernity and its replacement by a plurality of competing discourses co-existing alongside each other. This transition is summed up by Connor who argues that postmodernity involved 'a shift from the muffled majesty of grand narratives to the splintering autonomy of micronarratives' (1989: 32).

The onset of postmodernity has been attributed to a range of factors, including the loss of faith in rational 'scientific' explanations (Bell, 1976), the declining centrality of work in daily life and the rise of a post-industrial society based on consumerism and leisure (Featherstone, 1991), and the increasing power of the media to circulate a plurality of images and texts to a global audience (Kellner, 1995; Ang, 1996). At its most extreme, postmodern theory suggests that the fixity of meaning associated with modernity has been subsumed by a series of unstable and ever-changing representations, or free-floating signifiers (Baudrillard, 1983); in this sense, it is argued, the 'real' has, in effect, been transformed into the hyper-real (Eco, 1987). The postmodern turn is also argued to have had a considerable impact on the notion of individual identity, the erosion of those ideological forces that once proscribed identity giving rise to an endless array of possible identities from which individuals are able to choose, thus assuming multiple and shifting personas (Shields, 1992a, 1992b). Additionally, it is suggested, the weakening of the ideological constraints associated with modernity has also led to more pluralistic and fragmented cultural, political and religious identities (Chambers, 1990; Bhatt, 1997). This chapter examines the basic tenets of postmodern theory and their relevance for our understanding of culture and everyday life in contemporary social settings.

Defining postmodernism

Postmodernism is, as Smart points out, an extremely 'controversial term, a term that elicits highly charged reactions across intellectual disciplines and associated theoretical and political constituencies' (1993a: 11). This view is supported by Hebdige who describes postmodernism as 'neither a homogenous entity nor a consciously directed "movement" [but rather] a space, a "condition", a "predicament" an *aporia* ... where competing intentions, definitions, and effects, diverse social and intellectual tendencies and lines of force converge and clash' (1988: 200). As these observations imply, it is not only the social sciences where postmodernism is in current and widespread use. On the contrary, the influence of postmodernism can be seen across a range of academic disciplines, including geography, theological studies, literary criticism and art. Among each of these different disciplines, and the differing interpretations that they apply to postmodernism, however, there is one particular area of consensus. Thus, all parties agree that postmodernism relates to significant social transformations that have been taking place at the global level since at least the end of the Second World War. At the root of these transformations, it is argued, is a declining belief in the defining ideas and principles of the Enlightenment project. It was the latter's emphasis on rational, scientific explanations, and upon the human capacity for reason and judgement, that fundamentally shaped the physical and ideological properties of modernity. As Jenks notes:

> The Enlightenment established a set of typical characters, with typical motives and a shared goal, that is to say, it provided the 'grand' narrative form for the history of modernity. Reason was to triumph over faith, humankind was

to become the measure of all things, nature was to be quelled and put to the service of humankind, and time was to be measured in terms of a transition from darkness into the light, a transition and an implicit theory of moral evaluation that came to be known as *progress*. (1993: 138)

During the latter half of the twentieth century, the modernist ideologies that had held such values in place began to crumble. Growing cynicism about technology and rationalisation, engendered by the memory of world war and persecution, together with an increasing concern about industrial waste and pollution of natural resources, led to a declining faith in modernity's emphasis on science and progress (Smart, 1993a). Indeed, as Kumar notes, this 'crisis of confidence has [also] extended to the scientists themselves. Not only do they now question the wholesale application of science to the world; they also raise disturbing questions about the very status of science as a privileged method of understanding' (1995: 134). An additional factor in the decline of modernist ideology was a growing unrest and dis-satisfaction in many parts of the world with western domination and colonial rule. This began to highlight at a public level longstanding philosophical and moral debates concerning the way in which the West's emphasis on scientific and technological development had translated into a powerfully enacted cultural imperialism that imposed a western template of development and progress on third world nations (Tomlinson, 1991).

Key to the rise of postmodernism, then, was a waning of modernity's claim to be an authoritative voice in relation to the world order. As Lyotard observes, postmodernity involves a delegitmation of modernity's claims to such ideological and moral authority: 'In contemporary society and culture – postindustrial society, postmodern culture – the question of the legitimation of knowledge is formulated in different terms. The grand narrative has lost its credibility' (1984: 37). According to Lyotard, this decline in the power and influence of modernity's grand narrative corresponds directly with 'the blossoming of techniques and technologies since the Second World War' which have imbued everyday life with a plurality of discourses and knowleges (ibid.). Crucially significant in this respect, suggests Lyotard, were new forms of electronic media which, from the 1950s onwards, played an increasingly central role in everyday life. Indeed, as Stevenson (1995) observes, such is our reliance today on the media for everyday needs – news, education, leisure and entertainment, and so on – that contemporary cultures are, in effect, 'media cultures'. A similar view is expressed by Gergen who suggests that the products of media cultures constitute 'the major sources of daily motivation' (1996: 123; see also Kellner, 1995). The flow of images and texts facilitated by the media have played a significant part in subverting the discourse of modernity, not only in relation to knowledge and ideas but also in relation to the meanings attached to images and objects. According to Connor, the power to define meaning and authenticity in images and objects has effectively been wrenched from the hands of the individual artist or creator and propelled into the infinitely pluralist and subjective domain of the audience:

> ... mass-cultural media ... seem structurally to embody a surpassing of the modernist narrative of the individual artist struggling to transform a partic- ular physical medium. Uniqueness, permanence and transcendence ... seem in the reproducible arts of film and video to have given way irrevocably to multiplicity, transience and anonymity. (1989: 158)

As the above observation suggests, it is not simply the flow of images and information from artist/creator to audience which results in such a 'loss' of meaning. Rather, the media itself functions in an increasingly arbitrary fashion, continually decontextualising and recontextualising images and information in ways that cut across modernist distinctions – spatial, tem- poral, political or discursive. Discussing this in relation to television and video, Connor argues that, from a postmodernist perspective, these forms of media 'represent in their very forms challenges ... [to] the hegemony of modernist aesthetic models' (ibid.: 163). A similar point is evident in Kellner's observation: 'If for most of the history of television, narrative story-telling has been the name of the game, on a postmodern account of television *image* often decenters the importance of narrative' (1995: 235). This aspect of 'postmodern' visual media is further explored by Kaplan in a study of MTV. According to Kaplan, 'MTV blurs distinctions between past, present, and future, along with its blurring of separations such as those between popular and avant-garde, between different aesthetic gen- res and artistic modes' (1987: 144). In this respect, argues Kaplan, MTV conforms to a pattern which is also to be seen in other forms of contem- porary media whose theme and content reflect a postmodern turn, notably advertising, film and new media such as IT and the internet. Each exhibits what Hebdige has referred to as a playful '"fascination" with mirrors, icons and surfaces' (1988: 192) as texts and images are taken from their original contexts and subject to arbitrary re-orderings in which original meanings are lost and new ones derived.

The 'sign' and the 'signified'

The direct result of such visual and textual re-orderings in postmodern society is a rupturing of the once fixed relationship between the sign and the signified; in effect texts and images become free-floating signifiers (Baudrillard, 1983). According to Baudrillard, postmodernity has so effectively removed the fixity between the sign and the signified that all textual and visual meanings are now essentially fluid and arbitrary. Baudrillard's argument is supported by Best and Kellner through their observation that:

> No longer constrained by an objective reality or by pre-existing needs or use value, the signifier is free to float and establish its own meanings through its manipulation in coded differences and associative chains ... Freed from any stable relationship with a signified, where the sign points to a distinct referent in the world, the signifier becomes its own referent. (1997: 99)

The consequence of this is a blurring of the boundary between 'simulation and truth, image and reality' (Bauman, 1992: 150). The individual is thus plunged into a world of simulation, a world in which a rapid sequence of images and representations becomes the primary form of reference. Meaning, as much as this has a currency in postmodern society, is inherently fragile and contested. Thus, as Porter observes:

> Thanks to the twentieth century revolutionization of consciousness – through mass communications, hi-tech media, the advertising and publicity industries, the empire of images throughout the global village – modern human beings now inhabit an artificial, hermetically sealed pleasure dome. Nothing is constant, everything reflects everything else in a theatre of dazzling simulations dominated by the proliferation of the sign ... Meaning is produced by endless, symbolic exchanges within a dominant code, whose rhetoric is entirely self-referential. (1993: 1–2)

According to Baudrillard, the result of this is a *death of the real*, that is to say, 'a radical transformation of experience, a neutralisation if not a destruction of meaning and signification' (1983: 53). Baudrillard's most famous, and controversial, example of this process is to be found in his interpretation of the 1991 Gulf War. In an account of the war written for the British newspaper The *Guardian* before the commencement of the allied bombing campaign (see Stevenson, 1995), Baudrillard (1991) suggested that the reality of the Gulf War was the sum of its representation in the media, with the effect that it was 'a "virtual war" ... a war of words and images, of simulated murder and destruction, not actual death' (Stevenson, 1995: 194). This led Baudrillard to claim that the Gulf War could 'not happen', that images and texts had been manipulated by the media to produce a 'simulated' conflict. While Baudrillard's account was subsequently overtaken by the harsher reality of the Gulf War, it has been argued that the essence of Baudrillard's argument, that is its broader analysis of the effects of media representation and simulation on individuals' perceptions of 'reality', contains an irrefutable truism. Thus, according the Best and Kellner:

> ... the 1991 Gulf War demonstrated the incredible power mass media has in constructing 'reality'. Although the devastating effects of the war on the Iraqi people and the environment were all too real, its true enormity was buried in the barrage of media messages that coded it as the struggle of Good against Evil. (1997: 108)

The alleged effect of the media on everyday lived experience in post-modern society is further considered by Lash who extends the discussion to the more familiar and mundane sphere of everyday leisure and con-sumption practices. According to Lash:

> In postmodernism the change is not so much the way we perceive time and space as in terms of *what* we are perceiving. What we are perceiving, in TV, in video, in the spread of information technology, on the Walkman, on the audio cassettes we listen to in cars, in advertisements, in the huge increase in popular magazines we look at, are representations, are mostly images. We are living in a society in which our *perception* is directed almost as often to representations as it is to 'reality'. These representations come to consti-tute a very great proportion of our perceived reality. And/or our perception of reality comes to be increasingly by means of these representations. (1990: 23–4)

In postmodern society then, the force of representation is such that it becomes a primary form of everyday experience. In effect, the everyday becomes little more than 'a gigantic simulacrum ... never again exchanging for what is real, but exchanging in itself, in an uninterrupted circuit without reference or circumference' (Baudrillard, 1992: 152). As Baudrillard suggests here, in postmodern society, individuals experience the everyday as a series of decontextualised images and referents, that relate only to each other rather than to a fixed, objective notion of reality. Baudrillard (1988) famously expounds this argument in his book *America*. In what has become a cele-brated travelogue of the postmodern *flâneur*, *America* documents Baudrillard's car journey through the rural and urban landscapes of the US, the images that pass by the windscreen being likened by Baudrillard to the images on a television screen. As Turner notes in reflecting on Baudrillard's theorisation of this journey: 'Reading the car screen as tourist and *flâneur* is parallel to the channel hopping viewer as voyeur ... Reading the car screen is a voyeuristic consumption of a series of signs, the detached and therefore cynical cruise through hyperreality' (1993: 154).

Baudrillard's America, then, is essentially the sum of its media-representation, a version of the 'truth' which, according to Baudrillard, is the only version readily available to individuals living in contemporary societies whose everyday experience is one of media-saturation. For Baudrillard, engagement with the everyday amounts to a precarious sifting through decontextualised visual and textual fragments, the resources from which individual experiences of everyday life are constructed in the postmodern condition.

The hyper-real

The effect of postmodernity in transforming 'reality' through a continuous play of texts and images has also been explained in terms of a shift from the 'real' to the 'hyper-real' (Eco, 1987; Baudrillard, 1992). According to Eco, the hyper-real describes the seductive array of simulated experiences, notably theme parks and related leisure facilities, that increasingly prevail in urban and rural locations around the world. In his book *Travels in Hyperreality*, Eco (1987) considers the impact of the hyper-real on contemporary everyday life in the US. According to Eco, the centrality of the hyper-real to the postmodern condition is reflected in the American obsession with realism. Thus, argues Eco, the ubiquitous presence in the American landscape of 'perfect' replicas and 'authentic' reproductions of everything from medieval European castles to wild west towns, has effectively dissolved the boundaries between 'true' and 'false', reality and reproduction, creating 'a spatio-temporal haze where virtually everything appears present' (Smart, 1993b: 53). As Perry observes, such an arbitrary recontextualisation of once fixed cultural referents in new everyday contexts says much about the 'changing relations between cultures and the status and cognitive efficacy of those categories that are purportedly internal to them' (1998: 97). Relating Perry's observation back to Eco's description of postmodernity's hyper-real landscape, the full effect of the postmodern turn on cultural symbols and artefacts becomes clear. What once stood as markers of distinction between specific national cultures and cultural groups now flow into the melting pot of postmodernity. Like the objects of late modern consumerism, aspects of traditional cultural heritage have been dramatically loosened from their original cultural contexts and repositioned as ephemeral objects of spectacle and gaze, to be consumed and disposed of in much the same way as any other consumer object.

Baudrillard goes a step further in mapping the trajectory of the hyper-real onto everyday lived experience. Thus, according to Baudrillard, such is the force of simulation in postmodernity that it has effectively over-taken the 'real'; the omni-presence of the hyper-real is now such that any distinction between the real and the hyper-real is purely illusionary. Baudrillard expounds this argument using the example of Disneyland which, he argues, has assumed a metaphorical presence in a national landscape in which all has, in effect, been subsumed by simulation and hyper-reality. Thus, argues Baudrillard: 'Disneyland is presented as imaginary in order to make us believe that the rest is real, when in fact all of Los Angeles and the America surrounding it are no longer real, but of the order of the hyper-real and of simulation' (1992: 154).

Postmodern identities

If postmodernity is perceived as a process which brings about fundamental changes in the social fabric, this in turn is argued to carry significant implications for the individual, particularly in relation to the concept of identity. The increasing force with which the postmodern condition is argued to saturate everyday life in contemporary social settings has become a key issue in the debate concerning the nature and fashioning of individual identities. Opinions as to the precise implications for the individual are broadly divided into three main points of view. One group of commentators argue that postmodernism has served to decentre the individual subject to such an extent that identities have become shallow and superficial, corresponding with the continuous play of texts and images that form the basis of everyday 'reality' in postmodern societies. According to Kumar: 'The "de-centred" subject of [postmodernity] no longer thinks of his/her identity in historical or temporal terms ... Instead the postmodern self considers itself a discontinuous entity, as an identity (or identities) remade in neutral time' (1995: 147). The erosion of modernity is argued to have had a withering effect on the grounding, structural features of everyday life – class, gender, race, occupation, education, and so on – through which individuals formally understood themselves and their relationship to others. The onset of postmodernity is thus deemed to be accompanied by a disintegration of the individual subject 'into a flux of euphoric intensities, fragmented and disconnected ... [that] no longer possesses the depth, substantiality, and coherence that was the ideal of the modern self' (Kellner, 1992: 144). A similar view is offered by Jameson who suggests that the postmodern subject has 'succeeded in transcending the capacities of the individual human body to locate itself, to organise its immediate surroundings perceptually, and cognitively map its position in a mappable external world' (1992: 175).

Schacht advances this pessimistic reading of postmodernism's effect on the individual subject, arguing that the cultural fragmentation associated with the postmodern condition has resulted in a deepening sense of alienation. According to Schacht, human beings possess a basic 'need for some sort of identity they can affirm' (1996: 1). In the context of modernity, this affirmation of identity is achieved through a formulation of community based upon family, kinship and occupation ties. It is through such forms of grounded daily existence that individuals gain a sense of who they are and the value and significance of their relationships with others. As Schacht observes, 'all human identity or selfhood that is not merely physiological is grounded in (if not simply a function of) relations of involvement in one's environing world' (ibid.: 6). The postmodern turn, argues Schacht, has produced a sudden shift from such grounded forms of social identity to a new state of fluidity in which individuals, having being alienated from the original bonds that once shaped their everyday cultural existence, become increasingly self-orientated and self-interested. According to Schacht, individuals 'involve themselves in identity-shaping games ... [on] the open seas of postmodernity' (ibid.: 13), this in turn having a profound, and potentially pathological, impact on the nature of everyday life: 'In place of the likes of dominant cultures, peoples, social substances, and their latter-day remnants, there will be only a profusion of social and cultural formations, participation in any of which is optional and normatively neutral' (ibid.: 10).

According to a second school of thought, however, postmodernity has had a very different effect on the individual. Thus, it is argued, postmodernism does not result in a loss or weakening of the 'self', but rather has a liberating effect on the individual. The 'postmodern' self is one which operates free of the structurally grounded restrictions that held sway in modern society, the latter imposing limits and constraints on individual expressions of identity. As MacCannell and MacCannell note, a key effect of postmodernism is its 'demonstrat[ion of] the arbitrariness of all "values"', not least of all those which held categories of status and distinction in place in modern society (1993: 126). From this perspective, a central feature of postmodernity is its empowering of the individual subject by allowing them to construct identities which are freed from the confines and restraints of class and tradition. In postmodern society, the freedom to consume is the freedom to choose one's identity, to adopt an image and attendant sensibilities according to personal preference. This view is supported by Featherstone who suggests that postmodern individuals 'display their individuality and sense of style in the particularity of the assemblage of goods, clothes, practices, experiences, appearances and bodily dispositions which they design together into a lifestyle' (1991: 86). It follows, therefore, that if postmodern identities are effectively fashioned from consumerist objects and resources, then identity can no longer be described as fixed but must be seen as a more fluid construct which can be refined and changed. Indeed, according to Shields, the contemporary individual exhibits a 'postmodern "persona" [whose] multiple identifications form a *dramatis personae* – a self which can no longer be simplistically theorized as unified' (1992a: 16). A similar view is expressed by Bauman who suggests that in a postmodern world fashioned through ephemeral and disposable consumerist images and items, 'identities can be adopted and discarded like a change of costume' (1997: 88).

Other observers, argue that a key effect of postmodernism has been to create 'a "third" space' for the articulation of identities which are neither rigidly bound by pre-determined structural features nor entirely free-floating and arbitrary (Langman and Scatamburlo, 1996: 128). As Langman and Scatamburlo observe, such a 'dialectical approach' to the understanding of postmodern identities allows for the negotiation and adjustment of identity while at the same time 'locating selves and various identity formations within broader political, economic, and cultural contexts' (ibid.). This notion of a postmodern 'third space' has resulted in a number of attempts to rethink the process of identity formation in relation to structurally defined categories such as class, gender and race. Rather than claiming that such categories completely disappear or become irrelevant in postmodern society, this work suggests that they are transformed into more fluid and reflexively articulated expressions of social identity. As Chambers observes:

> The realities of race, gender, class, sexuality and ethnicity are not only increasingly represented (both in the æsthetic and political sense), but socially conditioned and constituted, through the 'artificial' languages, the hieroglyphs, of commodities and their accompanying symbology. (1990: 71)

According to Chambers then, in postmodern society individuals display a more active and reflexive investment in their identity. Inherent in this is a process of modification that seeks to reject or, at best, negotiate the restrictive ideologies which governed the ascription of identity in modernity. A notable effect of this, argue Langman and Scatamburlo, has been the deconstruction of modernity's privileging of the white male identity accompanied by a 'celebration of difference, diversity and indeterminability' (1996: 128).

This view is supported by McRobbie's assertion that postmodernity has facilitated 'the coming into being of those voices that were historically drowned out by the (modernist) narratives of mastery' (1994: 15). As an example of this process, McRobbie cites postmodernism's apparent undermining of the dominant patriarchal discourses associated with modernity and the appearance of what she terms *new femininities*. According to McRobbie, new femininities reflect a series of new female sensibilities that challenge 'the old domestic settlement which tied women (and young women's futures) primarily to the family and to low-paid or part-time work' (ibid.: 157). Such essentialist notions concerning the social role of women and the nature of femininity have, argues McRobbie, been subverted by a new discourse of femininity which is concerned less with defining the female gender role and more with exploring the multiple possibilities which exist for the creation and articulation of femininity. The result of this, observes McRobbie, is 'a greater degree of uncertainty in society as a whole about what it is to be a woman' (ibid.).

A parallel range of arguments has been put forward in relation to the influence of postmodernism on religion and concomitant notions of identity. Bhatt, for example, observes that religious identities are now very much the product of a complex interplay of media representations and traditional discourses. As a consequence of this, doctrines that were once fixed by religious institutions and the state are now routinely challenged and contested. One salient feature of this, notes Bhatt, are new 'transnational strands (such as pan-Islamic revival) that disrupt the idea of ... identit[ies] based on ethnic nationalism' (1997: 91). Postmodernity is also argued to have had a considerable impact on the collective identities of diaspora populations, that is, displaced peoples from Africa, the Indian subcontinent and other areas of the world from which individuals have either been forcibly removed or have voluntarily elected to remove themselves due to a variety of factors including slavery, political or religious unrest or poor socio-economic conditions (Gilroy, 1993; Lipsitz, 1994). The attempts of such diasporic populations to adjust to new everyday circumstances, often in cities and locales very different from their own, has given rise to the formation of new expressions of ethnic identity that draw selectively on aspects of tradition, religion and political ideology, combining these with cultural elements taken from their new surroundings. Over a period of several generations, such creative experimentation with cultural sensibilities and imagery has resulted in the creation of what Back (1996) refers to as 'new ethnicities'. This has been effectively illustrated in work on hip hop, a form of music, dance and street art which emerged from the South Bronx district of New York during the early 1970s (Lipsitz, 1994; Potter, 1995; see also Chapter 6). Potter describes hip hop as an 'ongoing, and highly sophisticated postmodernism' (1995: 13). Crucially, argues Potter, hip hop has allowed African-Americans to prize open the dominant historical and cultural discourses in the US relating to race and power and revaluate these according to alternative, critical criteria. Thus, according to Potter:

> If postmodernist art can be said to be haunted by a sense of belatedness, a sense of living in the ruins of the abandoned structures of modernism, then it should come as no surprise that African-American art in general – and hip hop in particular – has come into its own at this juncture of history ... For many African-Americans in the United States, the disappointment of the political and economic dreams of the civil rights movement of the 1960s, along with the worsening economic situation of the inner cities have combined to bring about a similar sense of life on the edge ... [hip hop] 'turn[s] the tables' on previous black traditions, making a future out of fragments from the archives of the past, turning consumption into production. (ibid.: 18)

For Potter then, hip hop's critical levering of modernist ideologies constitutes an important form of empowerment for African-Americans as an historically disempowered group. Moreover, as Lipsitz observes, when placed in a global context hip hop can be seen as a cultural form that symbolically links members of dispersed African-diasporic communities throughout the world, 'opening up cultural, social and political space for struggles over identity, autonomy and power' (1994: 27–8).

Postmodernity and the 'social'

As the contradictory readings of postmodern identities might suggest, there has also been considerable discussion concerning the fate of the 'social' in the postmodern condition. Baudrillard (1983) argues the implosion of meaning associated with media saturation in postmodernity creates a state of mass indifference which ultimately results in the 'death of the social'. As Smart notes, according to Baudrillard: 'The masses oppose and resist the "ultimatum of meaning", countering it with a refusal of meaning and a "will to spectacle"' (1993: 54). This postmodern 'death of the social' is also central to Beck's (1992) concept of 'risk society', albeit for somewhat different reasons to those outlined by Baudrillard. According to Beck, at the heart of risk society is an anxiety and distrust of society's increasing reliance on science and technology and the emphasis on specialist jargon and scientific terminology that 'makes the world more complex and unknowable' (Beck, 1998: 13). As Beck observes: 'As knowledge and technology race ahead, we are left behind panting in ignorance, increasingly unable to understand the machines we depend on and so less able to calculate the consequences of their going wrong' (ibid.).

Beck goes on to consider how such anxiety has, in turn, engendered concern over a range of issues, from the threat of global environmental disasters to the spread of life-endangering viruses and diseases, such as Aids and CJD. The direct consequence of risk and uncertainty, Beck argues, is a new individualist sensibility, that is, a prioritising of individual needs over the collective well-being of social networks (see also Douglas, 1992). This aspect of Beck's work is developed by Furedi who argues that the threats and uncertainty engendered by risk have resulted in a 'culture of fear', based upon a collective feeling that the world has suddenly become a very unsafe place in which to live. According to Furedi, the reaction of individuals to such perceived circumstances has been a mass 'blocking out' of the social world, with individuals striving to attain the maximum amount of personal comfort and safety for themselves and their immediate dependents. Thus, observes Furedi:

> The spread of risk consciousness has influenced the way in which people make sense of their circumstances … Heroes are definitely out of fashion … Not taking risks is positively advocated. Since people's powerlessness relative to risks is widely affirmed, limited ambition has become increasingly acceptable … Knowing your limits, accepting yourself, is held to be more important than actual outcomes. (1997: 64–5)

Beck's concept of risk society has also been influential on the work of a number of other social theorists. According to Giddens, such has been the impact of risk and uncertainty on individual consciousness that it now infuses decisions and orientations towards 'relationships and involvements' at all levels (1998: 28). This observation is supported by Dürrschmidt who suggests that risk society has engendered an individual perspective that is more inward looking, rather than the individual perceiving him/ herself as part of a social/community network of peers, relatives and friends. Thus, according to Dürrschmidt, living in the shadow of risk, individuals come to regard 'biography as the primary frame of reference for generating and structuring lived space' (2000: 17).

Countering such pessimistic readings of postmodernism's effects on the social, other theorists have sought to understand how the changes in the social fabric brought about by the postmodern turn may function to '[generate] new sources and sites of solidarity' (Crook, 1998: 533). This, in turn, has given rise to an alternative series of debates concerning the nature and function of social action in postmodern societies. For example, Hetherington, drawing on the work of Schmalenbach (1977), argues that the social has not disappeared in postmodern society, but rather manifests itself through temporal gatherings or *Bünde* (bondings) created through affective forms association. Hetherington is referring here to collective forms of contemporary cultural practice, such as fandom and spectatorship, shopping, participation in clubs and sporting activities and so on. In each of these instances, collectivity is maintained not through commonly held traditional, community-based norms and values but through shared emotional and material investment in a particular activity and the sensibilities of belonging and commitment that this activity engenders. As Hetherington observes: 'A *Bund* is an intense form of affectual solidarity, that is inherently unstable and liable to break down very rapidly unless it is consciously maintained through the symbolically mediated interactions of its members' (1992: 93).

According to Hetherington, the relevance of *Bünde* for our understanding of collectivity in postmodernity relates directly to their temporal and fluid quality. Unlike traditional community ties, which are essentially fixed, *Bünde* are ties between individuals that are collectively achieved and reflexively understood through the display and exchange of particular forms of knowledge and belief and/or the involvement in a shared form of activity or practice. Moreover, as Hetherington notes, *Bünde* do not manage individuals but are managed by them, the survival of a particular *Bund* being down to the continual and conscious investment of individuals in their preservation.

A similar interpretation of the social in postmodern society is put forward by Maffesoli in his concept of neo-tribes. Significantly, if Hetherington regards *Bünde* as inherently fragile and unstable entities which are in danger of collapsing if not maintained, for Maffesoli the very essence of the neo-tribe is its inevitable fragility, this being the key to the value of neo-tribe as means of understanding the altered nature of postmodern social gatherings and their aura of sociality. Thus, according to Maffesoli, the neo-tribe is 'without the rigidity of the forms of organization with which we are familiar, it refers more to a certain ambience, a state of mind, and is preferably to be expressed through lifestyles that favour appearance and form' (1996: 98). Using the concept of neo-tribes, Maffesoli maps the character of everyday life in postmodern social settings in terms of a series of temporal associations based around patterns of leisure and lifestyle. Thus, he observes: '[Neo-tribes] are perceptible in the various sporting gatherings which, through the influence of the media, take on a familiar significance. We can see them at work in the consumer ... frenzy of department stores, supermarkets and shopping centres' (ibid.).

As noted by Crook, Maffesoli has been criticised for his seeming lack of attention to the political dimensions of everyday life, neo-tribal theory appearing to limit itself to a celebration of the carnivalesque – a romanticised escapism from the more restrictive aspects of everyday life. According to Crook, however, Maffesoli is less concerned than other social and cultural theorists with 'resistance to established power. Resistance, in the sense of the affirmation of sociality and puissance, is an end in itself' (1998: 537). A similar interpretation of neo-tribal affiliation is offered by Bauman who suggests that:

> Neo-tribes 'exist' solely by individual decisions to support symbolic tags of tribal allegiance. They vanish once the decisions are revoked or the zeal and determination of members fades out … They are much too loose as formations to survive the moment from hope to practice. (1992: 137)

According to theorists such as Hetherington, Maffesoli and Bauman then, the onset of postmodernity does not signal the death of the social, but rather gives rise to new forms of sociality, based around more temporal forms of collective practice. Moreover, given the infinite range of information and resources available in postmodern society, individuals are held to be far more at liberty to pick and choose between particular affective groupings, thus giving rise to an inherent instability of collective gatherings.

Criticisms of postmodernist theory

Postmodernist theory provides a number of valuable insights into the nature of everyday life, social identity and the formation of collective cultural practice in contemporary social settings. At the most fundamental level, postmodernist interpretations of social development have led to a more sophisticated understanding of the ways in which identities and their attendant cultural practices are 'constructed' in the course of everyday life, reinforcing the post-structuralist argument that contemporary expressions of identity and culture must be understood as reflexively drawn rather than simply 'given' or 'ascribed' from the top down. This said, however, postmodernist theory has not been without its critics, many of whom argue that if traditional models of sociological theory lay too much emphasis on the role of structural forces in shaping and controlling the cultural fabric of the everyday, postmodernist theory lurches towards the other extreme, assuming a world where all such constraints have been subsumed by a new social (dis)order in which social meanings and the actions they engender are governed by spontaneous impulses, driven by a never-ending flow of decontextualised images and texts whose significance has been reduced to that of free-floating signifiers.

Callinicos advances this argument by suggesting that to accept this basic tenet of postmodernism is to consent to a loss of critical agency on the part of social and cultural theorists. Thus, he contends, postmodernism:

> ... license[s] a kind of intellectual dandyism. In a world that has taken on the properties of a Modernist artwork, the radical intellectual must abandon the traditional task of theoretical enquiry, of uncovering the underlying structure responsible for the way things seem. (1989: 147)

Callinicos goes on to argue that in equating theoretical enquiry with the project of modernity, Baudrillard and other exponents of postmodernism strip academic enquiry of its analytical voice. The result is a blasé outlook which fails to acknowledge how, even if one is to acknowledge that everyday life in contemporary societies has taken on 'postmodern' characteristics to a greater or lesser degree, in many parts of the world the more negative features of modernity, notably inequality and capitalist exploitation, remain firmly entrenched. Callinicos makes this critique of postmodernism most pointedly in relation to Lytoard's famous observation that in postmodern society: 'Eclecticism is the degree zero ... one listens to reggae, watches a western, eats McDonald's food for lunch and local cuisine for dinner, wears Paris perfume in Tokyo and "retro" clothes in Hong Kong' (Lyotard, 1986–7: 76). In response to this, Callinicos argues that much:

> ... depends, of course, on who 'one' is. This is more than an ad hominem remark, though it is a bit rich that Lyotard should ignore the majority of the population even in the advanced economies to whom such delights as French scent and Far Eastern travel are denied. (1989: 162)

A broadly similar point is made by Best and Kellner in a criticism of Baudrillard's work that describes it as 'the ideological perspective of a French, urban middle-class intellectual enmeshed in a very specific mode of experience and divorced from the complex realities of diverse groups of peoples and their daily struggles' (1997: 117). Indeed it could be further argued that, even if we can accept that consumerism is now a far more accessible and ubiquitous activity in many contemporary social settings than was previously the case, postmodernist theorists tend to overlook the fact that the achievement of a broader consumer base is inherently linked to capitalism, and key to its survival of in a postindustrial age. According to Callinicos what some theorists perceive as postmodernism can also be interpreted as a transition to late capitalism characterised by the 'promotion of a mass market geared to the instant fulfilment of desires' (1989: 144; see also Jameson, 1984). Moreover, observes Callinicos, inevitably the same processes of mass production and exploitation which drove industrial capitalism remain an inherent aspect of late capitalism, the only difference being that they have now shifted from first world to third world locations.

According to some theorists, this repositioning of production outside the sphere of consumption further fuels the 'myth' of the postmodern turn in contemporary society. Thus, as MacCannell and MacCannell observe: 'It is the genius and enormous good fortune of late capitalism to be able to externalize most of the costs of code creation on which the production of simulacra depends and to detach itself from responsibility' (1993: 138). According to MacCannell and MacCannell then, the processes of production and concomitant exploitation on which capitalism depends have not disappeared but simply go on 'behind the scenes', allowing the more affluent individuals in westernised, consumer-based societies to engage in their accepted and taken-for-granted everyday practices of consumption without sight of or consideration for those in the third world factories and sweat shops who produce the products central to the continuity and enjoyment of western consumerism and leisure. A corresponding view is offered by Best and Kellner who argue that the 'play of signs', identified by Baudrillard and others as symptomatic of the postmodern condition, can also be read alternatively as the seductive strategy of a high-tech, late capitalism harnessing the full power of global capitalist enterprise in an effort to extend its reach across a wider spectrum of lands and peoples:

> [Baudrillard's] analyses erase the institutional forms of advanced capitalism, which seem to have determined his discourse to such an extent as to (mis)lead him into concluding that capitalism no longer exists. Baudrillard's insistence on the hermetic nature of postmodern simulacra is better seen as the introjection and projection of the capitalist imaginary – the dream of seamless closure, complete mystification and perfected hegemony – than as an accurate description of contemporary social reality. (1997: 117)

Similar criticisms have been directed at postmodern theorists' claims regarding a shift from the 'real' to the 'hyper-real' (Eco, 1987; Baudrillard, 1992), the argument again being that such readings refer only to those westernised citizens with the available leisure time and economic capital (Bourdieu, 1984) to enjoy the seductive simulations of the media and consumer industries. Moreover, it is suggested, because western social theorists are themselves effectively trapped in and thus a product of this media and consumer-driven world, their postmodern interpretations of the everyday are often tainted by the limits of their own (mis)perceptions (Callinicos, 1989; Best and Kellner, 1997). This drawback in postmodernist writing is effectively captured in Smart's (1993b) critique of Baudrillard's (1988) study *America*. According to Smart, Baudrillard's vision of America, despite the novel and compelling nature of its media-informed gaze, is very much a product of the writer's own romanticised narrative: 'the America Baudrillard presents is one seen (scene) through (on) the screen of his car (cinema). One journey, one route, one form of travel, and one vision' (1993b: 54–5). Smart goes on to argue that Baudrillard's reading of America is merely an indication of how pervasively Hollywood has intoxicated the minds of its audiences. Thus, suggests Smart: 'Baudrillard arrived already in possession of his America, possessed by it, a colonized subject of its empire of cinematic signs' (ibid.: 55). A similar criticism of Baudrillard's work is offered by Denzin:

> [Baudrillard] could easily have taken a slow train from Minneapolis and followed the Mississippi river to New Orleans. Another version of the country would have revealed itself: the erotic rhythm of the rails, faded Amtrak coaches filled with boozy blacks, microwave dinners, Japanese tourists with Walkmans, conductors calling out Memphis in the early morning and pointing to Graceland, urban and rural landscapes painted in Edward Hooper colours, all-night diners, country-western music, New Orleans jazz, the bayou country with cajuns, bridges which extend forever over waterways that run to the Gulf of Mexico ... But American trains aren't for European travellers and Baudrillard wasn't in search of this version of America. (1991: 125)

According to Denzin then, Baudrillard's reading of America is acutely one dimensional; a reading that overlooks the country's deeply ingrained social divisions and rich cultural diversity. As Denzin observes, such images of the American landscape are wholly absent from Baudrillard's 'cinematised' version of America.

Postmodernity or reflexive modernity?

As the various criticisms of postmodernist work begin to illustrate, considerable debate continues as to the extent to which postmodernity has in fact overtaken and replaced modernity as the dominant social condition. Thus, while one school of thought maintains that the onset of postmodernity denotes 'an epochal shift or break from modernity involving the emergence of a new social totality with its own distinct organizing principles' (Featherstone, 1988: 198), other theorists suggest a more subtle transition from the modern to the postmodern. Such a view is typified by Lyotard who suggests that postmodernism 'simply indicates a mood, or ... state of mind' (1986–7: 209). This position is strongly supported by Kellner who argues that 'claim[s] concerning a new postmodern rupture in society and history' have been exaggerated and that, rather than having witnessed an abrupt end of modernity and the rapid rise of postmodernism 'we are now living in a transitional era between the modern and the postmodern' (1995: 9). A similar argument is put forward by Rojek who suggests that:

> Some aspects of modernity are evident in postmodernity. Perhaps this is only to be expected for postmodernity is explicitly theorized as emerging from modernity. Indeed some accounts present this process as still in gestation. Instead of referring to the postmodern 'condition' they allude to 'intimations' or 'glimpses' of postmodernity. (1995: 6)

Bauman, on the other hand, suggests that: 'Postmodernity may be conceived of as modernity conscious of its true nature – *modernity for itself*' (1992: 187). Such a view echoes Berman's concern that postmodernists' tendency to strip modernity of its relevance is to overlook the extent to which so-called postmodern features in everyday life, for example, recent breakthroughs in cybernetics and computer animation, adhere to a characteristically modernist concern with knowledge and progress. Moreover, argues Berman, such aspects of modernity are an inevitable part of the human condition: 'a process of incessant enquiry, discovery and innovation, and a shared determination to transform theory into practice, to use all we know to change the world' (1992: 35). Inevitably, this countering of the postmodern turn has led to a questioning of the actual level and nature of material and cultural changes that have occurred in contemporary society, with a number of theorists arguing that what is now routinely termed 'postmodernity' might be better understood as a more sophisticated and seductive form of modernity. This corresponds with Jameson's (1984) view that some of the features typically associated with the perceived transition from modernity to postmodernity are, in fact, closely tied to the shift from industrial capitalism to late capitalism. According to Jameson, if the rise of industrial capitalism involved society becoming centred around an increasingly rationalised industrial production base, the shift to late capitalism has resulted in another transformation, the dominance of work being replaced by leisure and consumption. This in turn, Jameson suggests, has given rise to 'a prodigious expansion of culture throughout the social realm, to the point at which everything in our social life – from economic value and state power to practices and to the very structure of the psyche itself – can be said to have become "cultural" in some original and as yet untheorised sense' (1984: 87).

A number of theorists, notably Chaney (1994, 1996, 2002a), have suggested that this shift from the 'social' to the 'cultural', holds the key to understanding the actual essence of what many have regarded as a wholesale postmodern turn. Thus, it is argued, the rise of the cultural domain, facilitated through the quickening circulation of images, texts and consumer goods, has resulted in a deepening level of reflexivity in everyday life as individuals appropriate such resources, inscribe them with personal meanings and build them into strategies for engaging in the practice of everyday life. This, in turn, has led to the suggestion that what we are witnessing in contemporary society is not a postmodern turn, but a turn towards a state of 'reflexive modernity'. The concept of reflexive modernity is extensively discussed by Giddens (1991) who argues that factors contributing to the weakening of hold on modernity, notably the greater plurality of ideas facilitated through the rise of media cultures, has empowered contemporary individuals by making them more critical both of themselves and the world around them. All levels of social prac-tice, from the formation of identity to the acquisition and enactment of cultural beliefs and social sensibilities, no longer present themselves as 'given' but rather result from processes of negotiation between agency and structure, between the individual and the everyday. In this new 'post-traditional order', social identities become 'reflexive project[s] con-tinuously worked on and reflected' (1991: 53) Thus, observes Giddens:

> What to do? How to act? Who to be? These are all focal questions for every-one living in the circumstances of late modernity, and ones which, on some level or another, all of us answer, either discursively or through day to day social behaviour ... Everyday choices about what to eat, what to wear, who to socialise with, are all decisions which position ourselves as one kind of person or another. (ibid.: 70, 81)

From the perspective of reflexive modernity, the rupturing of dominant dis-courses and consequent instability of meanings associated by Baudrillard, Lyotard and others with a state of postmodern fragmentation, is regarded as having driven individuals to seek actively their own meanings, and to ground these in the fabric of their everyday lives through the symbolic appropriation of images, texts and objects. As McGuigan notes, in a state of reflexive modernity, 'individuals expect to control their fates, to spend their money and time as they wish, to be in command of their bodies and their living spaces' (1999: 129). Key to this is the transformation of every-day life into a manageable, bearable and, above all, 'liveable' space, such a transformation being brought about through what Chaney (1994) has referred to as a 'cultural turn'. Culture, in this sense, is being used to describe the *aestheticization* of everyday life (Featherstone, 1991) through creative and symbolic practices designed to block out, or symbolically negotiate the more oppressive and restrictive features of everyday life. In this sense the 'cultural' has increasingly become the reflexively enacted domain of individuals, power and authority over and engagement with everyday life being an essentially 'cultural' process.

Some observers have suggested that reflexive modernity can be seen as an integral feature of the risk society (Beck, 1992), a fragmenting of the social as contemporary societies become more individualised. Thus, it is argued, if reflexive modernity leads to greater subjective awareness, and the autonomy to realise this through the commanding of a particular look, style sensibility, series of beliefs and so on, then this leads to a decline in the significance of the social (see McGuigan, 1999). According to Chaney, however, reflexivity results not in the demise of the social, but rather its refinement. Even as previous forms of social order, grounded in modernist practice and belief, are seen to decline in importance, and new self-fashioned knowledges and sensibilities take their place, individuals still seek out and adhere to forms of authority, notably the fashion and media industries, which act as cultural markers. Thus, argues Chaney,

> ... if we have been forced into more personal choices about what to believe, there is likely to be a greater demand for new sorts of expertise and guidance. And thus a paradoxical intensification of the social process of reflexivity is a proliferation of expertise and authority in fragmented culture. The reason why a more intense reflexivity is associated with greater uniformity becomes clearer if it is appreciated that the processes of heightened reflexive consciousness are articulated through textually mediated discourses more generally. (2002a: 24)

According to Chaney then, the shift from modernity to a state of reflexive modernity does not result in the erosion or 'death of the social' (Baudrillard, 1983). Rather the desire for sociality (Maffesoli, 1996) becomes re-entrenched as a basic human need but is redrawn according to the criteria of a more reflexively articulated everyday sphere, in which individuals construct their identities according to cultural signposts provided by the cultural and media industries of reflexive 'late' modernity.

Conclusion

This chapter has examined the contribution of postmodernist theory to our understanding of everyday life in contemporary society. This began with a review of various attempts to define postmodernism and to map its rise against a backdrop of the failing project of modernity. As was subsequently noted, while most theorists attribute the rise of postmodernity to a range of factors, for many a key element underpinning the postmodern turn is the increasing centrality of audio-visual mass media in contemporary societies. For theorists such as Baudrillard and Lyotard, the arrival of the 'media culture' has played a significant part in undermining the dominant discourse of social reality upon which modernity relied as a means of exerting power and influence over the masses. According to postmodernist theorists, the never ending flow of images and texts that characterise media cultures disrupt the once accepted relationship between the sign and the signified, allowing for a plurality of arbitrary interpretations. Within this postmodern haze, it is argued, forms of individual identity and social collectivity are significantly redefined, the individual becoming a more reflexively defined subject whose associations with others take on a more fluid and temporal nature.

Critics of postmodern social and cultural theory argue that what may on the surface seem to be large-scale changes in the social fabric, are in fact local phenomena brought about by the increasing sophistication of leisure and consumerism in late capitalist societies. In other words, what appears to be 'postmodern' is simply an elevated form of media saturation and consumerism reserved for those first world individuals who can afford such a lifestyle. This in turn has led a number of theorists to question whether the social changes observed during the latter part of the twentieth century really do constitute a postmodern turn, or if they could rather be described as transition towards a state of 'reflexive' modernity? According to exponents of this argument, while capitalism continues to be a motor force in the everyday lives of individuals, their experiences of leisure and consumption are radically altered as they become active participants in the production of those cultural meanings attached to the products of the media and consumer industries. Such reflexive engagement with media and consumer resources provides individuals with a basis for active negotiation of their day-to-day experiences. The following chapter examines how theorists have attempted to map what they perceive as the reflexively articulated cultural terrain of everyday life in late modernity.

THREE The Cultural Turn

... although modernity is marked by a logic of control and domination, the Orwellian nightmare of a thoroughly bureaucratized social existence is always deferred, partly because controllable systems are simply not possible ... but also because we subvert the total commodification and homogenization of experience through myriad (if sometimes fleeting) expressions of passion, non-logicality and the imaginary. The emancipatory moments are endemic in the everyday, and remain opposed to the utilitarian greyness of official society. (Gardiner, 2000: 15)

In the course of the previous chapter it was noted that a number of theorists engaged in debates concerning the nature and consequences of postmodernism have argued that many key features associated with post-modernity can, in fact, be re-interpreted as signalling an altered form of modernity or, more specifically, a shift towards 'reflexive modernity'. The centrality of media and consumerism in late capitalist society, it is suggested, has opened up a greater space for individuals to become more 'reflexively' aware of themselves as social subjects. The cultural resources made available through media and consumer channels allow individuals scope to creatively modify and negotiate the structurally experienced nature of class, gender and race, thus giving rise to new, reflexively derived articulations of identity. The concept of reflexive modernity also has significant implications for our understanding of everyday life. Thus, it is argued, rather than existing as a site of exploitation and oppression, everyday life is a site of contestation and struggles; a site on which a plurality of cultural values give rise to competing sensibilities through which individuals reflexively define themselves, their relationship to others and their place in the physical and symbolic order of things. This interpretation adds an important new dimension to the use of everyday life as a conceptual framework in contemporary social and cultural theory, its 'sensitivity to everyday experience as both problematic and problem solving offer[ing] an important challenge to accounts in which the only dynamic in everyday life is that of routine and repetition' (Crook, 1998: 529).

Since the early 1990s this position has been extensively examined by sociologists, cultural and media theorists who have sought to locate the individual at the centre of cultural meaning and action as this manifests itself in contemporary everyday life. Terms such as 'active audience' (Fiske, 1989a, 1989b; Morley, 1992; Ang, 1996) and 'lifestyle' (Featherstone, 1991; Chaney, 1996) seek to invest the individual with the power to inscribe cultural meanings in the images, texts and objects that characterise everyday life in late modernity. Such power, it is argued, crucially manifests itself at the level of the local, that is to say, in the context of everyday lived experience. The local, it is maintained, acts as a framing device for individuals in inscribing cultural resources with meaning. The inscription of meaning in cultural resources forms part of a strategy through which individuals make sense of everyday life. As such, it is argued, these strategies directly correspond with and are imbued by forms of local knowledge. This chapter presents an overview of the key ways in which everyday life has been reconceptualised as a space for the enactment of collective patterns of reflexive cultural practice.

Everyday life and cultural production

The recasting of everyday life as a reflexively constructed cultural space owes much to the work of Michel de Certeau. Unlike his contemporaries Heller (1984) and Lefebvre (1971, 1991) (see Chapter 1) de Certeau takes a far more optimistic view regarding the centrality of mass culture in late capitalist society. Thus, rather than viewing the production of mass culture as a one-way flow, and coterminous with subordination and a surrendering of will, de Certeau considers issues of meaning in the products of the media and cultural industries to be a two-way process. For de Certeau, both producers *and* consumers play their part in determining the aesthetic meanings of images, texts and objects provided by the media and cultural industries. Thus argues de Certeau:

> ... once the images broadcast by television and the time spent in front of the television has been analyzed, it remains to be asked what the consumer *makes* of these images during these hours. The thousands of people who buy a health magazine, the customers in a supermarket, the practitioners of urban space, the consumers of newspaper stories and legends – what do they make of what they 'absorb', receive and pay for? What do they do with it? (1984: 31)

For de Certeau then, the transformation of capitalist societies from centres of industrial production to centres of leisure and consumption has created space for an accompanying transformation of individual consciousness. In effect, individuals have become *more* and not *less* aware of themselves as critical agents through the process and practices of late modern consumption. Thus, according to de Certeau, the act of consumption is, in effect, the act of self-realisation, the point at which individuals assume a more reflexive awareness of themselves as subjects, with a will, an identity and a desire to move in a particular direction; in other words, individuals come to perceive of themselves as 'projects' to be worked on and perfected through self-realisation and development. In doing so, individuals transform the everyday from a pre-determined script into a series of personal quests – voyages of individual discovery through which they attempt to control or at least actively fashion their own destinies. As de Certeau argues:

> Unrecognized producers, poets of their own affairs, trailblazers in the jungles of functionalist rationality, consumers ... trace 'indeterminate trajectories' that are apparently meaningless, since they do not cohere with the constructed, written and prefabricated space through which they move. They are sentences that remain unpredictable within the space ordered by the organizing techniques of systems. Although they use as their *material* the *vocabularies* of established languages (those of television, newspapers, the supermarket or city planning), although they remain within the framework of prescribed syntaxes (the temporal modes of schedules, paradigmatic organizations of places, etc.), these 'traverses' remain heterogeneous to the systems they infiltrate and in which they sketch out the guileful ruses of different interests and desires. (1984: 34)

For de Certeau then, everyday life is the combined product of individual efforts to bring their particular life projects to fruition, a terrain on which vibrant struggles take place. The cultural fabric of the everyday, once unproblematically assumed to be a sphere of forced ideology and resultant false consciousness, is recast as a series of conflicting discourses and practices through which the world is continually defined and redefined.

The ideas of de Certeau are further developed by Fiske (1989a, 1989b). In what has become a celebrated reappraisal of the relationship between the individual and late modern consumer culture, Fiske argues that the act of cultural production is largely down to the creative potential of individuals whose consumption of cultural products and images results in the creation of new meanings. According to Fiske, at the level of their industrial mass production, objects and images are simply 'products', created for economic gain. It is only when such products enter the public sphere and are appropriated by individuals for use in everyday life that they become culturally meaningful:

> What is distributed is not completed, finished goods, but the resources of everyday life, the raw material from which popular culture constitutes itself. Every act of consumption is an act of meaning. At the point of sale the commodity exhausts its role in the distribution economy, but begins its work in the cultural. Detached from the strategies of capitalism ... it becomes a resource for the culture of everyday life. (Fiske, 1989a: 35)

According to Fiske, cultural meanings are derived as much through the creative negotiations of individuals as through the images, texts and objects they consume. As such, Fiske ascribes the individual a more reflexive role in the production of cultural meanings than earlier mass cultural theorists, or indeed postmodernists for whom, as illustrated in Chapter 2, the individual is merely an empty vessel consuming an endless flow of free-floating signifiers (Baudrillard, 1983). Despite its more progressive interpretation of late capitalist media and consumer driven society and its effect upon the individual, Fiske's work has not escaped criticism. For example, Chaney suggests that in his interpretation of consumerism as the expression of 'struggle and resistance against the corporate hegemony', Fiske paints an overly romantic impression of the subversive potential associated with the act of consumption (1994: 215). Similarly, Stevenson argues that Fiske's optimism concerning the audience's ability to empower itself through the inscription of meaning in mass cultural products is achieved only at the expense of a more critical appreciation of the 'forms of manipulation [that continue to be] evident in our culture' (1995: 58). Taken together, these identified problems in Fiske's work have led some theorists to label his approach 'cultural populism' (McGuigan, 1992; Kellner, 1995). Thus, according to Kellner, Fiske 'collapses the distinction between culture produced by the people, or "popular classes", contrasted to mass-produced media culture, thus revelling in a "cultural populism" ... that often uncritically celebrates media and consumer culture' (1995: 33). Voicing a broadly similar concern, Rojek argues that, in adopting an essentially uncritical position in relation to consumerism, Fiske's approach runs the risk of simply rehearsing 'the stereotypical argument of capitalist entrepreneurs that the market delivers genuine freedom, choice and self-determination for consumers in their leisure and consumption activities' (1995: 106).

Despite the criticisms directed against it, however, it could be argued that Fiske's work has at least provided the basis for a new understanding of how the politics of everyday life involve instances of cultural production and transformation in which objects of consumerism and global media play a central role. Similarly, Fiske's portrayal of the audience not as cultural dupes but as active producers of the cultural meanings inscribed in texts, images and objects has been of paramount importance in the development of the study of everyday life. Thus, as Lull observes, whatever view one takes of Fiske's interpretation of the audience as participants in 'ongoing semantic and cultural guerrilla warfare ... He has certainly helped to dispel the idea that media audiences are passive consumers or victims' (1995: 142).

The active audience

Fiske's acknowledgement of the audience as active participants in the construction of cultural meaning in their everyday lives has had a considerable impact upon the field of media studies, inspiring a wholesale rethinking of the pessimistic interpretation of the Frankfurt School and mass cultural theorists such as Dwight Macdonald (see Chapter 1). The notion of the 'active' audience was first alluded to in the work of Benjamin (see Buck-Morss, 1989). A contemporary of Frankfurt School theorists Adorno and Horkheimer, Benjamin was highly critical of the latters' interpretation of mass culture and its effects on audiences. According to Benjamin, rather than turning audiences into cultural dupes, the 'technological *re*production [associated with mass culture] gives back to humanity that capacity for experience which technological *production* threatens to take away' (Buck-Morss, 1989: 268). During the mid-1980s significant attention began to be paid to the role of the audience in the construction of textual and visual meanings. Following innovative audience research, notably Morley's (1986) *Nationwide* study (see Chapter 4), theorists began to take more seriously the notion of the audience as active agents in the production of media texts. The result was a new body of work which recast the audience as an authenticating power in its own right, that is, as agents capable of critical reflection and evaluation rather than an empty vessel passively receiving information and images from the media. Inherent in this redefinition of the audience, it was argued, was a weakening of the interpretive authority of the intellectual to define the meanings of mediated texts and images for audiences. As Ang observes:

> 'The audience' no longer represents simply an 'object of study', a reality 'out there' constitutive of and reserved for the discipline which claims ownership of it, but has to be defined first and foremost as a discursive trope signifying the constantly shifting and radically heterogeneous ways in which meaning is constructed and contested in multiple everyday contexts of media use and consumption. (1996: 4)

The basis of Ang's argument here is that the academic pursuit of meaning and cultural significance in media texts and images can no longer restrict itself to top-down narrative accounts. On the contrary, media meanings, as these manifest themselves in everyday life, can only be properly understood through the use of empirical research as a means of engaging with the views and perceptions of audiences themselves. Similarly, Morley argues that a key effect of ethnographic audience research has been a greater understanding of how 'media consumption practices ... are embedded in the context of everyday life' (1996: 321–2). Moreover, according to Moores, it is not simply media images and information which assume their concrete meaning at the level of the everyday. Rather, he argues: 'Like the sounds and images which constitute the "software" of mass communication, its "hardware" might equally be seen as a collection of signs that have multi-accentual social meanings – capable of being decoded and appropriated in a plurality of ways' (1993: 9).

If the sphere of the everyday is deemed crucial to an understanding of the ways in which media products acquire their cultural meaning, this, in turn, has led to an increasing emphasis on the significance of the local circumstances which inform everyday experience. Thus as Thompson notes:

> The appropriation of media products is always a localized phenomenon, in the sense that it always involves specific individuals who are situated in particular socio-historical contexts, and who draw on the resources available to them in order to make sense of media messages and incorporate them into their lives. And messages are often transformed in the process of appropriation as individuals adapt them to the contexts of everyday life. (1995: 174)

Implicit in Thompson's observation is the need for an understanding of the local as the bedrock of everyday life experience, and thus as a significant factor in the ways that individuals respond to and make sense of media products. This view is supported by Lull who is concerned to illustrate how globally mediated resources are appropriated and reworked in specific local contexts. According to Lull, individuals, whose perceptions of the world are grounded in particular forms of local knowledge and experience, culturally 'reterritorialise' images, texts and objects from the flow of global culture through acts of symbolic appropriation:

> Reterritorialization ... is a process of active cultural selection and synthesis drawing from the familiar and the new. But creative construction of new cultural territories also involves new ways of interpreting cultural icons in processes of resignification. The entire cultural milieu ... become symbolic resources to be used in ways that differ radically from their original meanings and functions. (1995: 161)

In many respects Lull's concept of cultural reterritorialization shares Fiske's (1989a) concern with recasting individuals as active agents in the creation of cultural meanings. At the same time, however, Lull is careful to point out that the local circumstances in which individuals consume media resources also serve to limit their potential to engage in the creation of meaning. In effect, argues Lull, while the resources that individuals access through the media do indeed engender creative projects through which individuals strive to inscribe new meanings in images and texts, thus effecting forms of resistance to and symbolic negotiation of the everyday, this achieved only in so far as such things are possible within pre-existing local constraints:

> Despite all the ambiguity and richness of texts, and for all the interpretative creativity people routinely exhibit in everyday life, no semantic negotiation takes place without constraints ... Any interpretation made of the symbolic environment will, to some extent, reflect hierarchies represented in message structure and social structure. (1995: 170)

A similar point is made by Morley who suggests that 'the meanings of both [media] texts and technologies have to be understood as emergent properties of contextualized audience practices' (1992: 195). The observations of Lull and Morley are substantiated by Liebes and Katz's work on the popular 1970s' US soap opera *Dallas* and its different reception in various parts of the world. Liebes and Katz suggest that local audiences form part of distinctive 'interpretative communities' whose 'active "negotiation" of the text' is informed by knowledges and sensibilities shaped by local circumstances (1989: 204; see also Chapter 3).

Consumerism and lifestyle

If work on the active audience has endeavoured to provide new frameworks for our understanding of the relationship between media and audiences in everyday life, a parallel series of studies have looked at the everyday significance of consumerism. Such is the centrality of consumerism to everyday life in westernised (and 'westernising') societies, that it has become a deeply ingrained, and largely taken-for-granted, feature of everyday life (Miles, 1998). As Abercrombie notes: 'Not only are the denizens of modern society consumers, they are also consumer*ist* ... Th[is] involves[s] a stress on pleasure rather than the duties of work, on the rights of the individual to decide on courses of action, and on the centrality of consumer desires to the conduct of life' (1994: 44–5). Abercrombie goes on to note how the spread and importance of consumerism in contemporary social life has led to it becoming a new form of 'authority' which undermines more traditional forms of authority, notably class background and family, opening up a space for new forms of individual expression and identity.

Central to this interpretation of consumerism is 'lifestyle', a term originally introduced by Weber (1978 [1919]) as a key conceptual element in a multi-dimensional model of the social strata which challenges the economically determined model put forward by Marx (see Chapter 1). As Reimer observes according to Weber: 'Society is not only stratified economically; it is also stratified according to status [and] the way that status is most clearly expressed is via different groups' lifestyles' (1995a: 121). For Weber then, the cultural sphere of society needs to be understood as *both* the product of economic factors *and* the processes engaged in by social actors as a means of marking themselves out as belonging to a particular status group. Such processes, argues Weber, involve the creative appropriation of particular goods and services made available through the burgeoning consumer industries of the late nineteenth and early twentieth centuries. Thus, in opposition to Marx, Weber suggests that notions of status and of belonging go beyond straightforward issues of class, encompassing issues of 'good taste' and the latter's visual articulation through, for example, fashion and leisure preferences. Thus, as Inglis and Hughson observe, Weber:

> ... denied what he took to be Marx's contention that membership of a class is the primary way an individual in a class-based society will think about themselves. There are other culturally mediated identities people may have, such as the pride in being a member of a particular group such as a sports club. Sports club membership and the feelings it provokes will be related to class issues (e.g. most of the members will be middle class), but this is an indirect relationship, and it is this possibility of other identities being more crucial than class membership that Marx does not allow for. (2003: 29)

The significance of lifestyle as a means understanding the articulation of wealth, status and power in consumer-based society is effectively illustrated in Veblen's (1994 [1924]) study of the emergent American leisure class of the late nineteenth century. This leisure class comprised individuals who had generated wealth and status through hard work and capital accumulation. Veblen notes how these individuals attempted to articulate their newly acquired status by mimicking the lifestyles of the European upper classes through adopting the latter's tastes in fashion, eating and leisure activities, an activity for which Veblen coined the term 'conspicuous consumption' (see also Chapter 5).

Similarly influential on contemporary lifestyle theory is the work of Simmel. Simmel was primarily concerned with 'the fragmentation and diversity of modern life' as this manifested itself in the urban spaces of the late nineteenth- and early twentieth-century city (Urry, 1995: 9).

According to Simmel, the relative anonymity experienced by individuals in the city created a need for personal distinction, a means of marking oneself out from the crowd. As Hamilton notes:

> At the same time as Simmel insists on the social construction of the modern way of life of the metropolis, he also makes clear that the city itself, as a large social organism, does have major consequences for individuals within it. Their reactions to the metropolitan way of life, to the 'modernity' of the city, require that individuals have to 'resist being levelled down or worn out' by this 'social-technological mechanism'. One characteristic form of this resistance is to be found in the search for ways of emphasizing social difference (what we might now term *identity*). (2002: 104)

According to Simmel, it was the act of consumption which provided one of the key elements in the construction of such urban identities (see also Chapter 5). This aspect of Simmel's work is examined by Chaney who suggests that:

> ... [for Simmel] the metropolis is mediated through symbolism – it is a lifeworld in which symbols mutually refer in ever more complex layers of association and in which the play of meanings can only be understood reflexively and as a constant process of innovation. The increasingly differentiated world of goods of modernity is not a simple process of enrichment, but neither is it straightforward alienation. *The cultural terrain of the metropolis simultaneously offers new potentials for individuals to enhance their subjectivity.* (1996: 51; my emphasis)

Following its initial application in the work of, respectively, Weber, Simmel and Veblen, the concept of lifestyle became unfashionable in sociology for a number of years during which time it was more readily associated with market research (Reimer, 1995a). During the early 1990s, however, lifestyle was reintroduced through the work of contemporary social and cultural theorists such as Bourdieu (1984), Featherstone (1991), Shields (1992a, 1992b), Reimer (1995a) and Chaney (1996). Bourdieu's (1984) celebrated study *Distinction* develops the ideas of Weber, Simmel and Veblen through its conceptualisation of lifestyle as a reflection of social status. Bourdieu argues that the lifestyle practices engaged in by individuals send out messages about their level of wealth, achievement and status in society. According to Bourdieu, even though lifestyles appear to be autonomously constructed and reflexively articulated forms of cultural practice, they remain inextricably bound up with the experience of class, a social process which Bourdieu refers to as 'habitus'. For Bourdieu, 'habitus' is indelibly stamped on the identity of the individual to the extent that there is a direct link between a person's habitus and their accumulation of particular forms of 'cultural capital', a primary resource through which lifestyles are constructed:

> ... class constitutes a relatively autonomous space whose structure is defined by the distribution of economic and cultural capital among its members, each class fraction being characterized by a certain configuration of this distribution to which there corresponds a certain life-style. (1984: 260)

According to Bourdieu, in the context of late capitalist consumer-based society, the fact of class itself becomes a mediation, something that is learned and understood through particular forms of consumption practice in relation to a particular array of goods and services. It follows then, according to Bourdieu's interpretation, that such experiences of class remain with the individual, continuing to shape their identity even as they become more socially mobile.

Subsequent work has challenged Bourdieu's interpretation of lifestyle as the subconscious practice and articulation of rigidly established class-based sensibilities. According to Chaney, Bourdieu's insistence on the structuring role of class amounts to a crude negation of the reflexive and oppositional qualities that late modern consumerist practices have introduced into the cultural sphere of the everyday. Thus, argues Chaney:

> To assume that objectifications [of cultural capital] are only displays of a lesser or greater mastery of cultural codes is to presume that there is a pre-existing and unchanging hierarchy of codes – or perhaps more accurately, it is to presume that culture is an inescapable environment which envelops social action in the way that social structures envelop individual experience. (1996: 66–7)

In Chaney's view, the significance of *lifestyle* lies precisely in its illustration of the weakening hold of class and attendant forms of structured experience on the individual within the context of late capitalist consumer-based society. Chaney regards lifestyles as demonstrative of the increasing reflexivity exhibited by individuals in both the practice and negotiation of everyday life. Of central importance here are the possibilities offered by late modern consumerism for individuals to negotiate the constraints of class and associated forms of structured inequality, notably gender and race. Key to Chaney's interpretation of lifestyle is his distinction between *lifestyles* and *ways of life*. Thus argues Chaney, lifestyles are 'creative projects' which rely on 'displays of consumer competence', while *ways of life* are 'typically associated with a more or less stable community [and] displayed in features such as shared norms, rituals, patterns of social order and probably a distinctive dialect' (1996: 97, 92).

There are certain similarities between Chaney's reading of lifestyle and Shields's (1992a) concept of the *postmodern persona* examined in Chapter 2. In both cases, identity is seen as something that is reflexively constructed rather than 'given', that is to say determined by structural factors. It is fair to say, however, that while the *postmodern persona* is suggestive of an entirely 'free-floating' and decentred subject, lifestyle, as applied in Chaney's work, remains sensitive to the continuing importance of local factors and to the on-going engagement between individuals and their everyday surroundings. Thus, according to Chaney, the way in which lifestyles are constructed and enacted corresponds with a series of 'sites and strategies' that correspond in turn with attempts to negotiate, local, everyday experience. Thus, observes Chaney, 'lifestyles are creative projects, they are forms of enactment in which actors make judgments in delineating an environment' (1996: 92). As such, argues Chaney, lifestyles constitute an important form of individual empowerment in the context of late modernity, such empowerment being linked to 'the creative organisation of experienced space' (ibid.: 74).

Although remaining a central element in the way in which late modern lifestyles are enacted, local circumstances do not determine lifestyle in any totalistic sense. Rather, the local becomes a point of reference for the individual, a stock of knowledges and sensibilities which individuals draw upon selectively in constructing lifestyles. To speak of a late modern 'lifestyle' then, is to speak of a way of being in which aspects of locality – local traits, knowledges, mannerisms and so on – are both reflexively managed and creatively combined with a range of appropriated cultural resources in the construction of identity. There is then, a clear sense in which, through their lifestyles, late modern individuals exhibit a continued tiedness to the local spaces in which they live out their everyday lives. However, such tiedness encompasses a dynamic interplay between the individual and the circumstances of everyday life, rather than a determined relationship in which individuals are unwitting victims of structural constraints.

An alternative approach to understanding the potential of consumerist practices to empower the individual, but that displays some similarities with Chaney's approach, is Willis's concept of *grounded aesthetics*. Like Chaney, Willis is concerned with how late modern individuals appropriate objects and images and inscribe them with their own meanings and significance. According to Willis, individuals achieve this through the process of grounded aesthetics, which, he explains 'refer to the specifically creative and dynamic moments of the whole process of cultural life' (1990: 22). Again then, Willis regards mass cultural products as having a liberatory effect on the individual through their facilitation of a broadened range of identities and modes of personal expression:

If it ever existed at all, the old 'mass' has been culturally emancipated into popularly differentiated cultural citizens through exposure to a widened circle of commodity relations. These things have supplied a much widened range of symbolic resources for the development and emancipation of everyday culture. (ibid.: 18)

As with more recent work on media audiences, studies of late modern consumer culture position individuals as 'active' agents, creatively adopting and adapting consumer resources in the construction of reflexive, individually fashioned identities. Again then, such work seeks to recast the cultural terrain of contemporary everyday life as a contested domain within which individuals struggle to win space for the articulation of distinctive forms of identity practice.

The local and the global in everyday life

It has been noted above how sociological, cultural and media theorists have drawn respectively on 'active audience' and 'lifestyle' as conceptual frameworks for understanding everyday life in late modernity as reflexively experienced and enacted. It has further been noted how, in utilising these conceptual frameworks, theorists emphasise the importance of local knowledge as a resource through which the raw materials appropriated from the media and cultural industries are inscribed with meaning. Clearly, in the context of late modernity, the concept of the 'local' is complicated by the process of globalisation. Indeed, it has been suggested by some theorists that key to the globalisation process is a 'flattening out' of local cultures, the latter becoming subsumed by a uniform global culture. This argument is typified in Ritzer's (1993) concept of McDonaldization. Drawing on Weber's (1968 [1921]) theory of rationalisation, Ritzer uses the same analogy of the 'iron cage' to describe a progressively developing global culture in which local variations are gradually, but systematically, eroded away and replaced by a uniform, technologically and bureaucratically 'McDonaldized' version of the world. According to Ritzer:

... McDonaldization not only affects the restaurant business, but also education, work, travel, leisure-time activities, dieting, politics, the family, and virtually every other sector of society. McDonaldization has shown every sign of being an inexorable process as it sweeps through seemingly impervious institutions and parts of the world. (1993: 1)

As Tomlinson notes, such fears concerning the fate of local cultures are not restricted to academic work but are also to be seen in documents produced by international bodies such as UNESCO. The argument commonly expressed is that globalisation is a thinly veiled form of cultural imperialism, the latter acting as 'an *homogenising* cultural force' (Tomlinson, 1991: 26). Thus, observes Tomlinson:

> The perception here is that everywhere in the world is beginning to look and feel the same. Cities in any part of the world display uniform features determined, for example, by the demands of automobiles; architectural styles become similar; shops display a uniform range of goods; airports, the potential gateway to cultural diversity – have an almost identical 'international' style. Western popular music issues from radios and cassette players from New York to Delhi. (ibid.)

Such pessimistic interpretations of the globalisation process have been countered by an alternative series of arguments which maintain that the observed effects of globalisation have been far less predictable, more gradual, and often have the opposite effect to that suggested by Rizter and others. For example, Featherstone argues that 'one paradoxical consequence of the process of globalization, the awareness of the finitude of the boundedness of the planet and humanity, is not to produce homogeneity but to familiarize us with greater diversity, the extensive range of local cultures' (1993: 169). This view is developed and refined in a series of studies that have sought to rethink the local/global relationship in ways that allow for localised patterns of appropriation and creativity 'within a stream of globally available media products and information' (Bennett, 2000: 196). A key theorist in this debate is Robertson who argues that the interface between the global and local gives rise to what he terms a process of *glocalization*. According to Robertson:

> It is not a question of *either* homogenization or heterogenization, but rather the ways in which both of these tendencies have become features of life across much of the late-twentieth century world. In this perspective the problem becomes that of spelling out the ways in which homogenizing and heterogenizing tendencies are mutually implicative. (1995: 27)

Glocal cultures, suggests Robertson, are neither local or global but have undergone a process of cultural hybridity in which aspects of residual local culture (Williams, 1961) become seamlessly interwoven with new global cultural forms. This view is supported by Kraidy who contends that: 'A recognition that all contemporary cultures are to some extent hybrid is required to understand the micro-politics of local/global interactions' (1999: 460). A similar argument is put forward by Nederveen Pieterse who defines 'globalization as a process of hybridization which gives rise to a global mélange' (1995: 45). What Nederveen Pieterse means here is that globalisation is not only experienced differently in different parts of the world but that the physical and aesthetic manifestations that the globalisation process assumes at a local level are also qualitatively different. Thus, he observes, 'globalization [is] a multidimensional process which, like all significant social processes, unfolds in multiple realms of existence simultaneously' (ibid.).

Indeed, one need look no further than the McDonald's restaurant concept itself for confirmation of the way in which local cultural sensibilities shape the reception of global products and services. As Miller and McHoul observe:

> In France, where fast food is still new (about 5 per cent of the restaurant business, but growing rapidly since the late 1980s), McDonald's has gone through a series of transformations. In the 1970s, it was chic: the intelligentsia frequented the few outlets, and fashion shows associated themselves with hamburger stands. But by 1989 this otherness had become ordinary fare. (1998: 51)

Miller and McHoul further note how the growth of fast food restaurants in France with 'American' sounding names has also met with an element of local resistance, culminating in the French government's creation of a 'National Council of Culinary Art within the Ministry of Culture', the former being charged with the protection of local cuisine 'from fast food and other stresses' (ibid.). The presence of such local forms of reception and resistance clearly problematise the notion of McDonaldization as a straightforward and relentless process of eroding cultural difference. Similarly, it is important to note the local variations in the menu of McDonalds and other fast-food chain restaurants in different parts of the world, such adjustments being necessary in order to cater for local dietary preferences. For example, in Japan and other parts of the Far East McDonald's offers noodle dishes, while in Scandinavia more fish dishes are served. Thus, as this brief example illustrates, if McDonald's is now a global icon, this has been achieved only through the acknowledgement and incorporation of local culinary taste and tradition.

Globalisation relates not only to the global flow of capital, goods and information but is also characterised by the increasing global mobility of people. This aspect of the globalisation process is vividly captured in Appadurai's concept of *ethnoscapes*, that is 'landscape[s] of persons who constitute the shifting world in which we live: tourists, immigrants, refugees, exiles, guestworkers and other moving groups and persons' (1990: 297). Again, this scenario has raised questions about the value of the 'local'; the argument here being that as increasing amounts of people become globally mobile local cultures are diluted, urban centres becoming melting pots for an array of fragmented and diffuse cultural sensibilities. This view is typified in the work of Dürrschmidt who argues that cities in the contemporary world 'are certainly not just nodal points of flows of capital, finance and information, but also central to the flows of people, their social practices and beliefs' (2000: 13).

Other theorists, however, argue that although global mobility has now become a fact of life for many people, aspects of the local remain ingrained in the way that everyday life is constructed and symbolically negotiated. In effect, it is suggested, such sensibilities of 'localism' (Calabrese, 2001) become a crucial form of situating practice for those who must find ways of adapting to or negotiating the everyday culture, customs and general goings-on of a new social environment. Such situating practice takes a variety of forms. Thus, for example, Hannerz notes how, despite the increasing opportunity, or indeed necessity, for global mobility, many global travellers remain essentially 'anti-cosmopolitan'. As Hannerz explains, anti-cosmopolitans are

> ... people (mainly business travellers) who would rather not have left home; people who are locals at heart ... who would want to know what restaurants in Tokyo offer Sweet'n'Low, which hotel in Madrid has king-size Beauty-rest mattresses, and whether there is a Taco Bell in Mexico City. (1990: 241)

As Hannerz's example illustrates, even as 'categories of people are emerging who lead more mobile lives' (Featherstone, 1995: 154), individuals retain a strong sense of their local identity based around a series of shared sensibilities embedded in taken for granted everyday objects and practices. Moreover, it is not just itinerant business travellers who crave such 'home comforts' in this way. For many expatriates, exported aspects of their national culture perform an important role in enabling them to frame their identity, to 'know who they are'. This point has been illustrated effectively in relation to music. For example, as Frith notes: 'In London's Irish pubs ... "traditional" Irish folk songs are still the most powerful way to make people feel Irish and consider what their "Irishness" means' (1987: 141). Similarly, Baumann (1990) considers how bhangra, originally a Punjabi folk music which has became globally popular due to its fusion with western pop styles by British-Asian musicians, is performed at festivals, weddings and other celebrations held by Asian diaspora populations in Britain and elsewhere in the world. For such populations, bhangra provides an important means of maintaining a link with their cultural roots (see also Bennett, 2000).

In many ways then, a key effect of globalisation in late modernity has been the transformation of the 'local' into an even more potent symbol for the construction of identity. The key here is to think of the local not as a bounded physical space but as a metaphorical and discursive construct. This re-emphasises Chaney's (1996) point concerning the significance of late modern lifestyles as reflexively chosen, yet socially embedded forms of cultural practice; a crucial part of the embedding process being the subjective use of those discourses and metaphors that circumscribe the 'local', and thus inform local knowledges and sensibilities. Thus, rather than withering in terms of importance, the local has become an increasingly important situating strategy, that is to say, a means through which individuals negotiate their place in contemporary everyday life using 'a range of locally embedded images, discourses and social sensibilities centred around the *familiar*, the *accessible* and the *easily recognisable*' (Bennett, 2000: 197; emphasis in original).

If late modernity has seen the transformation of the 'local' from a fixed entity into a series of discourses and metaphors of space and place, it follows that there need be no ready consensus as to the nature of the local and local identity. This view is supported by Carter et al. who suggest that physical spaces are both plurally understood and culturally malleable; 'populated neither by atomistic individuals nor cohesive communities, this public sphere will be the site of contestation between groups of distinct, located (physically and culturally) identities' (1993: xiv). Such contestation involves the collective construction of space in particular ways, something which is primarily achieved through the use of narratives. Within a given space there will exist, at any given time, not one but a multiplicity of local narratives:

> ... in referring to the 'local', we are in effect speaking about a space which is crossed by a variety of different collective sensibilities each of which imposes a different set of expectations and cultural needs upon that space. In doing so, such sensibilities also construct the local in particular ways, a process which ensures that terms such as *locality* and *local identity* are always, in part at least, subjective elements which begin by utilising the same basic knowledges about the local, its social and spatial organisation, but supplement such knowledges with their own collectively held values to create particular narratives of locality. (Bennett, 2000: 66)

The fleshing out of such local narratives is achieved through the selective appropriation of resources, typically those produced by the global media and cultural industries. Through these acts of appropriation, groups create strategies for the negotiation and 'management' of their everyday lives, cultural resources being inscribed with particularised meanings and significance drawn from stocks of local knowledge. Such resources thus become woven into the local cultural fabric, assuming their own particular role in the normal everyday surroundings of individuals. In this way, late modern individuals are empowered through taking a hand in the production and realisation of their cultural milieu.

The aestheticisation of everyday life

So far this chapter has examined a range of theories and concepts that endeavour to present contemporary everyday life as the product of a continuous interplay between the symbolic creativity of individual agents and the local circumstances in which they find themselves. Images, information and products provided by the media and cultural industries become resources for use by individuals in the negotiation of the everyday, a process that involves the construction and articulation of reflexive identities and the carving out of habitable spaces. As such, it becomes possible to perceive of the everyday as an aestheticised space (Featherstone, 1991), that is to say, a site upon which individually derived lifestyle projects are articulated, cohere and become collective strategies. Thus, as Chaney observes, lifestyles may be regarded as 'aesthetic projects – in their practice particular ways of understanding actors, their possibilities and their inter-relationships are recommended' (1996: 147). Lifestyle projects, then, are one of the key ways that boundary work (Nippert-Eng, 1996; Lury, 2002) is achieved between groups in contemporary everyday life. As Lury observes:

> ... while [such] boundaries may be purely conceptual, they often also result in physical forms, in objects and everyday practices and rituals that reinforce and make visible the categories they create. In other words, by shaping the very way we think about and act toward each other and things, classificatory boundaries are an essential element of social life. This is because placing lines here or there has definite implications for how we treat each other and the world around us. In drawing boundaries, we perpetuate a particular way of thinking, and enact our membership of distinctive social groups. (ibid.: 140)

Lury, therefore, supports the contention of lifestyle theorists such as Chaney (1996) and Featherstone (1991) that, in contemporary society, social boundaries can no longer be regarded as rigidly ascribed – along lines of class, gender or race; rather social boundaries are reflexively drawn by groups whose collective identities are derived through common patterns in taste, habit and interest, each of which are centrally defining components of lifestyle projects (Chaney, 1996). In the context of late modernity, the significance of lifestyles as aesthetic projects designed to articulate a distinct play of identity politics has become increasingly more apparent. Thus, to take one example, stylistically-based youth cultures, once deemed to be the direct product of class (Hall and Jefferson, 1976; see also Chapters 1 and 5), are now more commonly viewed as the product of reflexively chosen identities (see, for example, Bennett, 2000; Muggleton, 2000). As this book will presently consider, such reflexivity can also be seen in relation to use of media entertainment, choice of fashion and even preference for particular tourist resorts and activities.

While the academic study of lifestyle has, so far, been largely confined to a relatively narrow range of activities, typically consumerism (see, for example, Featherstone, 1991), a number of other associated collective practices can also be studied and mapped in terms of their significance as lifestyle strategies (Chaney, 1996). The various forms of fandom, for example in relation to sport (Redhead, 1997; Brown, 1998), film (Gledhill, 1991; Lewis, Lisa A., 1992) and music (Bennett, 2000) can each be seen as components of wider aesthetic practices through which collective lifestyle strategies are produced and articulated. Aesthetically informed lifestyle strategies are similarly evident in the growing number of counter-cultural sensibilities, each of which embody an openly directed critique of late modern society (see Chapter 8). Beck (1992) suggests that one of the key features of late modernity has been a loss of faith in the authority of science and technology. First evident as a form of lifestyle 'politics' during the late 1960s with the hippie counter-culture's rejection of the 'technocracy' and concomitant turn to spiritualism and Eastern beliefs (Roszak, 1969; Reich, 1971), counter-cultural activity has become more widespread and increasingly pluralistic in terms of the ideologies and practices that it encompasses. Examples here include 'new social' and DIY political movements, such as Reclaim the Streets and the Anti-Road Protest (see McKay, 1998). Similarly relevant are the various revivals in pre-industrial customs and beliefs, for example paganism (Magliocco, 2001) and witchcraft (Greenwood, 2000).

A further dimension for critical engagement with everyday life has been created through recent advances in domestic technologies, such as the internet, collectively referred as 'new media' (see Chapter 4). Such devices have made communication, at both local and global levels, far more instantaneous while at the same time opening up new avenues for individual and collective creativity. This is particularly noticeable among the young. Thus, as Reimer (1995b) observes, in every decade of post-war society it is youth who have most readily embraced newly developed forms of media technology. Due to their more interactive qualities, new technologies such as the internet open up creative possibilities for young people which are not associated with previous forms of media. Hall and Newbury suggest that the creative potential of the internet takes two forms. First, they argue, it offers new 'opportunities for cultural participation'. Second, they maintain, the internet provides a highly accessible medium through 'which young people are able to explore and promote their own identities and concerns' (1999: 100–1).

As the above examples illustrate, due to the increasing range and diversity of lifestyle projects in late modern society the possibilities for reflexivity and critical practice become ever greater, thus enriching the vibrancy of everyday life in contemporary social settings. Indeed, according to Chaney, a key effect of mass consumer culture on everyday life has been its facilitation of a state of 'cultural fragmentation'. What Chaney means here is that, through the proliferation of images and resources that mass culture offers individuals, it suggests to them a plurality of cultural sensibilities; a range of ways in which to be themselves and to negotiate everyday life. The upshot of this, argues Chaney, is that dominant cultural ideologies, which have in the past been used as a key form social control, become increasingly difficult to uphold in late modern society. Culture, Chaney suggests, 'is becoming harder to mark off as a distinct "space"' (2002a: 170). To put this another way, culture can no longer be regarded as a distinct ideological construct bespeaking a series of essentialist representations, pertaining, for example, to national identity, custom and habit, that function to maintain social order. Although individuals remain subject to forms of power and control in the course of their everyday lives, they nevertheless 'seek forms of resistance or escape; everyday life has [therefore] become a field or a site of struggle in which meanings are contested or reclaimed from ungraspable others' (ibid.: 175).

The second part of this book examines some of the key forms of leisure and consumerism in contemporary society, and considers how individuals utilise them in the framing of collective lifestyle projects through which to engage with and effectively manage their everyday lives.

Part II

The Cultural Terrains of Everyday Life

FOUR Media and New Media

... media culture has become a dominant force of socialization, with media images and celebrities replacing families, schools, and churches as arbitors of taste, value and thought, producing new models of identification and resonant images of style, fashion and behaviour. (Kellner, 1995: 17)

As the above observation by Kellner illustrates, popular media, that is mediums of communication such as television, newspapers and magazines, are a central aspect of everyday life in late modernity. For over half a century, popular media have not only been a primary source of information but have also played a significant part in shaping individuals' perceptions of the world around them. Since the late twentieth century advances in digital technology have meant that 'traditional' forms of visual and print media have been joined by a range of 'new media', notably email and the internet. Not only have the latter resulted in more rapid and instantaneous forms of communication, but they are also diminishing the boundaries between 'public' and 'private' space (Regan Shade, 1996).

Contemporary culture is then a media saturated culture. Nevertheless, as studies reveal, the everyday uses of both traditional and new media forms challenge the pessimistic predictions of mass cultural theorists who argued that the expansion of media would lead merely to more effective forms of ideological control of mass audiences (see Chapter 1). To begin with, such is the range and complexity of media in contemporary society that it is now possible to question the very concept of the mass audience (Ang, 1996). Rather, it appears that contemporary media audiences are increasingly heterogeneous, comprising a complex array of highly differentiated taste cultures. Similarly, if audiences have arguably always been more 'active' than mass cultural theory suggested, new media forms such as email and the internet allow for enhanced levels of audience interaction with media images and texts. This chapter examines the interplay between media and audience in the context of contemporary everyday life.

Media cultures

According to Stevenson, to speak of late modern cultures is to speak of media cultures. Such is the embeddedness of media in late modern everyday life, he argues, that it has become an integral part of the latter's cultural fabric. Issues of knowledge, identity, taste and lifestyle, some of the centrally defining features of culture in late modernity, are invariably conceptualised and operationalised by individuals through their consumption of media texts and images. Thus, as Stevenson observes:

> ... much of modern culture is transmitted by the media of mass communication. The various media disseminate classical opera and music, tabloid stories about the lives of politicians, the latest Hollywood gossip and news from the four corners of the globe. This has profoundly altered the phenomenological experience of living in modernity. (1995: 3)

As Stevenson implies, the very basis of lived 'reality' in late modernity absorbs and is thus articulated through visual and textual representations received via the media. This point is supported by Chaney who suggests that 'all aspects of our lived experience are formulated, made manifest, through the constitutive activity of representational resources' (1994: 67). The representational power of the media can be observed at a number of levels. Thus, for example, dominant notions of national and/or cultural identity in contemporary society are strongly informed by the ways in which they are 'represented' in key everyday media such as television and cinema (see, for example, Morley and Robins, 1989; Van den Bulck, 2001). Similarly, in times of war and other forms of socio-political conflict when national issues are at stake, the media plays a central role in enforcing dominant ideological positions. According to Kellner, 'Media culture produces representations that attempt to induce consent to certain political positions, getting members of the society to see specific ideologies as "the way things are"' (1995: 59).

As Bausinger notes, however, it is important not to overstate the power of the media in this respect. Indeed, to do so is to simply repeat the failings of the original mass cultural critique which saw audiences as little more than cultural dupes. Although the media may supply audiences with representational resources and 'ways of seeing', there is no straightforward relationship between dissemination, reception and everyday use of such resources. On the contrary, in making sense of media information and applying it to their own everyday life experience, audiences draw on a range of local knowledges and sensibilities, through which mediated information is framed and contextualised. As Bausinger observes:

> ... television and other media do not impart a slice of reality ... reality consists of that which has been mediated both by the media and by other things, and is consistently constructed anew. [Media content] radiates out into the rest of reality, which therefore cannot be separated from it. (1984: 350)

It is this view of the media, as a resource that both shapes and is shaped by the everyday knowledges and sensibilities of audiences, which informs much of the current thinking about the cultural significance of media in contemporary societies. The rest of this chapter examines a range of popular media from the point of view of their significance as cultural resources in everyday life.

Television

Until relatively recently, a large amount of the academic research on media and media audiences centred around television. This focus on television can be attributed to two main factors. First, it is a highly accessible medium, being found in the majority of family homes in many different countries around the world (Lull, 1988). Second, television provides a key source of information about both local and world events and developments (Hall, 1971). Early television research focused on news and current affairs programmes, a key example being the series of seminal studies conducted during the 1970s and early 1980s by the Glasgow Media Group on news coverage of events such as the Falklands War and the 1984–85 Miner's Strike (see Eldridge, 1995). During the 1980s, however, the remit of television research gradually broadened to consider audience responses to a more diverse range of television programmes including soap operas, game shows and 'Reality TV'.

Three distinct phases can be identified in television audience research (see Alasuutari, 1999). The first phase centred around the encoding/decoding model developed by Hall (1973) which argued that 'certain messages are sent and then received with certain effects' (Alasuutari, 1999: 3). Unlike earlier mass cultural approaches, however, the encoding/decoding model allowed for the fact that audience meanings of television texts may vary from those intended by producers of those texts. As Alasuutari notes: 'A message was no longer understood as some kind of package or ball that the sender throws to the receiver' (ibid.). A classic example of this approach is Morley's (1980) *The 'Nationwide' Audience*, an in-depth ethnographic study of audience responses to the former early evening BBC news programme *Nationwide*. Morley's study revealed considerable differences in audience reactions to and interpretations of news stories featured on the programme. As Moores observes:

> ... Morley was able to confirm Hall's proposition that consumers are not passive recipients of encoded meanings and identities. Even those viewers who made sense of the *Nationwide* message within the dominant code performed active, if partly unconscious, semiotic labour. Their general acceptance of the programme's preferred reading was the outcome of an interdiscursive encounter – rather than a result of them being 'blank sheets' for the text to write on. (1993: 22)

Morley's findings, in particular their challenging of earlier mass cultural assumptions concerning the homogeneity and passivity of media audiences, provided the basis for a new paradigm in television research which lay emphasis on obtaining ethnographic accounts from audience members themselves regarding the meanings they derived from the visual and textual messages of television programmes. This new approach became known as the 'constructionist' approach which, as Alasuutari explains,

> ... entail[ed] questions about the meaning and use of particular pro-grammes to particular groups of people [and] also include[d] questions about the frames within which [they] conceive of the media and their con-tents as reality and as representations – or distortions of reality. (1999: 7)

Ethnographic studies of television audiences also revealed the presence of strongly gendered patterns of television viewing, and in particular the preference among female viewers for romantic serials and other forms of television drama in which gender roles and relationships were a key sub-ject matter. According to Alasuutari, research on this issue argued that 'woman viewers interpret and make use of the offered readings [of gender relationships] against the background of their everyday life and experiences' (ibid.: 5). This was particularly evident in relation to female audiences' reception of soap operas. Researchers suggested that part of the endearing quality of soap operas for women viewers is the way in which they are able to relate storylines, characters and weekly scenarios to their everyday lives. Thus as Geraghty observes: 'Soaps have traditionally dealt with the fabric of social relationships ... pos[ing] the question of how one's personal life [is] to be lived and [giving] endless opportunities to examine issues of fidelity, consistency, disappointment and personal choice' (1992: 133). As Geraghty's observation suggests, for soap operas to work in this way a high degree of audience engagement with the text is necessary. Thus, rather than simply viewing soap operas as 'finished narratives', audiences actively work on soap texts, taking their narratives apart and reworking them in ways that make sense in the contexts of their own everyday lives.

According to Geraghty, such creative work on the part of soap audiences also extends to the continuity of the soap text. Soap operas are shown on average around three times a week, often with afternoon and evening showings for each episode (see Rosen, 1986). In between times soap characters lead what Geraghty (1981) refers to as an 'unrecorded existence' which somehow needs to be brought to life. Such textual gaps are filled by audiences through their individual thinking about and collective discussion of particular soap characters, incidents involving them and probable outcomes. As Creeber notes, through eliciting such audience responses, soaps have the capacity to 'capture an audience's involvement in a way equalled by few contemporary media' (2001: 441). Indeed, as such observations suggest, the appeal of soap operas extends far beyond the viewing context, with audiences collectively discussing plots, storylines and soap characters in a range of daily settings. According to Hobson:

> A large part of the enjoyment which is derived from watching soap operas is talking about them with other people ... at school, at work or at leisure ... Talking about soap operas forms part of the everyday work culture of both men and women. It is fitted around their working time or in lunch breaks. The process takes the form of storytelling, commenting on the stories, relating them and assessing them for realism, and moving from the drama to discussing events which are happening in the 'real world', as reported in the media. (1989: 150)

Hobson's comments provide an effective illustration of how, by discussing the thematic content of soaps among themselves in non-viewing contexts, audiences effectively fill in the 'off-air' gaps in soap texts by applying their everyday life knowledges and experiences as a means of keeping the storylines alive and preserving their continuity. Hobson's work also demonstrates that the viewing of soap operas can no longer be regarded as a specifically gendered activity; rather, she suggests, the everyday appeal of soaps has generated both male and female viewers of all ages. This observation is supported by Geraghty who argues that the diversification of the soap audience has 'stretched the boundaries of the soap genre and shifted it away from the traditional concerns of women's fiction' (1991: 167). The broadening audiences for soap operas has prompted questions about how different sections of this audience perceive and respond to soap operas. Thus, according to Allen, soap audiences can be seen as comprising different 'interpretive communities' who engage in 'discursive relationships' framed around 'a variety of perceived textual features' of soaps (1988: 45).

Allen's observations are supported by Barker and Andre's empirical study of the significance of soap operas for teenage audiences. The study argues that one of the key values of soap opera for teenagers is its function as 'a forum for discussion of topics that are difficult or embarrassing to talk about' (1996: 27). This is illustrated through reference to a discussion that took place among a group of young people about the sexuality of particular characters in certain soaps. As Barker and Andre explain, through these discussions the young people were able to formulate and articulate their personal views on the topic of sexuality: 'Some speakers try to secure themselves a fixed heterosexual identity while others, adopting a more flexible position, are open to the plasticity of sexuality' (ibid.).

The broadening appeal of soap operas has also given rise to questions regarding the way soaps are interpreted in different national settings. For example, in a study of the reception of the popular US soap opera *Dallas* among different national audiences, Liebes and Katz noted a range of localised responses to the show. Thus, for example, among Arabs in Israel, *Dallas* was commonly viewed as symbolic of their perception that western capitalism has led to moral degeneration through its promotion of economic altruism and financial greed. In Japan, by contrast, viewers complained about the fast moving pace of the storylines and did not approve of the cliffhanger style endings of weekly episodes, a standard device in serialised western drama designed to maintain the interest of the audience. As Liebes and Katz note: 'This incompatibility between the formula and viewers' expectations gives a clue to the reason why American family dramas have failed in Japan' (1989: 213). On the basis of their findings, Liebes and Katz suggest that local audiences form part of distinctive 'interpretative communities' whose 'active "negotiation" of the text' is informed by everyday knowledges and sensibilities shaped by local circumstances (ibid.: 204).

Significantly, a rather different audience reception aesthetic has been noted in relation to local appropriations of serialised television programmes featuring ethnic minorities. An example of this is provided in Havens's study of the popular US sitcom, *The Cosby Show*, whose central characters are an African-American middle-class family. According to Havens, while localised reception patterns were evident, for example in South Africa where '*The Cosby Show* was so incendiary that a Member of Parliament publicly criticized the show for its "ANC messages", the appeal of the programme also appeared to stem largely from its ability to communicate a series of commonly understood messages to "variously situated audiences"' (2000: 373). In effect, suggests Havens, *The Cosby Show* reinforces a sense of trans-national identity which provides an affective link for globally dispersed African and other non-white diasporic communities:

> ... many black and non-white postcolonial viewers express an affinity with *The Cosby Show* because of a shared history of racial-colonial exploitation and contemporary class oppressions that derive from that history ... These affinities extend beyond mere economic conditions to include similar histories of imperial exploitation and terror, including Western efforts at cultural genocide. These diverse audiences express admiration for *The Cosby Show* because it avoids conventional black stereotypes while retaining distinctly black cultural references like jazz. (ibid.: 374–5)

The relationship between television and audience constructions of ethnic identity is also central to Gillespie's (1995) work on the South Asian diaspora in London. As noted elsewhere (see, for example, Sharma et al., 1996) generational tensions continue to exist in South Asian communities around Britain as younger members of these communities struggle to reconcile the pre-emigration sensibilities of older members of their families with their own need to carve out a cultural space for themselves in contemporary British society (Baumann, 1997). As Gillespie observes, a pertinent frame of reference for such everyday struggles are the Hindi films viewed by South Asian families in the context of the family home. The representations of 'Asian-ness' portayed in such films are the source of much debate at an inter-generational level. According to Gillespie:

> ... the viewing of Hindi films is often accompanied by an airing of views and intense debates on tradition and modernity; indeed there is evidence that the content of Hindi films is discussed far more, by viewers in India and Britain alike, then is the content of western films. (1995: 80)

A strong element of audience-text interaction has also been demonstrated in research on audience responses to television game shows. Such is popularity of the game show, that it has become an essentially integral part of television programming in many different countries throughout the world. Writing in the late 1980s, Fiske noted how, in the US alone, 'more than 300 different quiz and game shows [were broadcast], most of them in the daytime, and most of them aimed at the woman as consumer' (1989b: 133). Over the last decade the popularity of quiz and game shows, and the scope of their target audience, has broadened considerably.

According to Fiske, a large part of the appeal of the game show is its 'valorization of an everyday knowledge and set of life skills that ... can be transformed directly into material goods or the pleasures of a holiday' (ibid.: 136). Clearly, the appeal of the game show in this respect is not merely confined to contestants themselves. Rather, through applying their knowledge and answering questions correctly, audiences watching television quiz shows at home put themselves in the role of the contestant. Moreover, such involvement in game shows by home audiences often transcends individual viewing, becoming occasions for collective participation. This view is supported by Morley (1992) who suggests that television viewing is often a family-centred activity, with family members invariably discussing programmes among themselves, shouting out comments at the television screen, and so on. Quiz shows, allowing for displays of individual knowledge and expertise, are a key example of this interactive dynamic between national and global television entertainment and the domestic space of the living room.

A further aspect of the link between on- and off-screen participation in game shows is addressed in Syversten's study of game show participants. According to Syversten, taking part in a television game show 'involves not only participants themselves but also their wider social networks' (2001: 320). Syversten notes how when asked about the circumstances leading to their game show appearance, many respondents said they had been encouraged to do so by family, friends or work colleagues. As such, participation in a game show becomes a collective event involving not only the individual but also his/her wider social network.

This blurring of the distinction between everyday life and television, between the *private* and the *public* sphere (Reimer, 1995b) is also central to van Zoonen's study of the reality television show *Big Brother*. Originally a Dutch concept, local variations of *Big Brother* have now been produced in a number of different countries, including the UK and the US. The show revolves around a communal 'Big Brother House' inhabited by a number of 'contestants'. Every evening television viewers can watch the activities of those resident in the house live on air, while those with access to the internet can also engage in 'off-air' viewing. At the end of each week viewers are invited to vote on whom they think should be evicted from the 'Big Brother House'. According to van Zoonen, *Big Brother* 'turn[s] the private lives of ordinary people, with all their normal, everyday, seemingly unimportant experiences, into a daily spectacle' (2001: 670). As with the soap opera, part of the appeal of *Big Brother* undoubtedly relates to the fact it deals with issues that people are confronted with on a daily basis, the difference here being that the fictional devices used to sensationalise such portrayals in soaps are replaced by 'real life' scenarios. Indeed, van Zoonen argues that the success of the *Big Brother* concept, and resulting attempts by national television companies to diversify the formula 'toward particular target groups' (ibid.: 673), bespeaks a desire on the part of an atomised public for a return to a collective experience of the everyday. Thus, suggests van Zoonen:

> The combination of television and internet platforms in *Big Brother* has created a collective experience characterized by a desire for everyday communality and by a rebellion against the norms of 'civilized' public culture. That desire, not provoked by exceptional events like a skating marathon, a royal wedding, a disaster of national proportions or a soccer championship, but rooted in ordinary daily hum drum experience, forms the basis of *Big Brother's* success. It springs from the contemporary bourgeois division between a private realm and a public realm that has isolated private life, marginalized it and made it invisible. (ibid.)

A further point of significance concerning the inter-textual relationship between television and its audience is the way that this relationship changes over the lifecourse. This is illustrated in a study by Gauntlett and Hill which considers the personal meanings derived from television programmes using a demographic perspective stretching from childhood to old age. In relation to retired and elderly audiences Gauntlett and Hill discovered that, while the latter 'are a diverse group who watch all kinds of material', there are still identifiable viewing traits that correspond with sensibilities acquired in later life (1999: 175). Thus, just as younger audiences found much of their everyday discourse and experience mirrored in soaps and fast action drama, older audiences demonstrated a preference for programmes that conformed more closely with their pace of life and everday experience. According to Gauntlett and Hill, older people's choice of television programmes:

> ... do not tend to feature large amounts of on-screen violence, sex or bad language, they often have light, 'pleasant', nostalgic and middle-class themes (as opposed to reflecting the 'gritty realities' of modern urban life), and they often feature leading characters who are themselves no spring chickens. (ibid.)

If television is perhaps the dominant form of media in everyday life, it is supported by a range of other media, notably print media publications. Like television programmes, the range and content of print media publications have also diversified in response to different target markets.

Print media

The last twenty years have seen dramatic developments in print media. In particular, there has been a substantial increase in the number and range of 'niche' media, that is, specialist publications, such as 'lifestyle' magazines, designed to appeal to a specific section of the market (see also Chapter 5). According to Thornton, this increase in niche media was the product of three inter-related factors: more detailed market research, tighter target marketing, and the availability of new technologies such as desktop publishing (1995: 151). Early examples of niche media were aimed at the youth market and focused on topics such as music and fashion. Such magazines also carried advertisements from the record, fashion, beverage and tobacco industries. Thornton suggests that by targeting particular sections of the youth market and catering for specific tastes in music, style and other leisure pursuits, niche media have played a fundamental role in the formation of youth cultural groups. Thus, argues Thornton, youth-orientated niche media 'categorize social groups, arrange sounds, itemize attire and label everything. They baptize scenes and generate the self-consciousness required to maintain cultural distinctions' (ibid.).

The growth of the niche media market has also seen a significant increase in the number and range of women's magazines. As Winship notes, traditionally women's magazines have been concerned to uphold conservative notions of femininity, focusing on accepted female activities and leisure pursuits, notably 'motherhood, family life, beauty and fashion, love and romance, cooking and knitting' (1987: 6). Ballaster et al. argue that this 'representation of the woman reader as "housewife" has been closely linked with the representation of the magazine as work manual' (1991: 123). This *gendering* quality in magazines aimed at female readers has also been noted in relation to publications aimed at teenage female audiences. For example, in her study of the popular 1970s teen magazine *Jackie*, McRobbie argued that its articles and stories were dominated by images and role models designed to condition teenage girls in relation to the roles they were expected to assume in adult life. According to McRobbie:

> *Jackie* sets up, defines and focuses exclusively on the 'personal', locating it as the sphere of prime importance to the teenage girl. This world of the personal and of the emotions is an all-embracing totality, and by implication all else is of secondary interest. Romance, problems, fashion, beauty and pop all mark out the limits of the girl's feminine sphere. (1991: 205)

During the 1980s, girls' women's magazines began to move away from such forms of representation. New publications such as *Elle, Marie Claire, Just*

Seventeen and *Mizz* 'aimed to break with the traditions of the domestic magazine' and expressed a new 'self-confidence and openness to the world' (Ballaster et al., 1991: 123; McRobbie, 1997: 191). As McRobbie points out, this new range of women's magazines responded to changing modes of femininity in the wider society. Even the representation of male pop idols in such magazines embodied a new element of irony 'which allows girls to be fans without being simply "stupid girls"' (ibid.: 199).

According to Stevenson, women's magazines no longer seek to reproduce the existing order of gender relations in society but focus increasingly on feminist concerns, ranging 'from more emancipated definitions of sexuality to health and women in employment' (1995: 172). As Stevenson observes: 'While such texts barely seek to politicize relations of sexual dominance, the feminine subject has become a more unstable construction and spaces for more autonomous forms of development have thereby been opened up' (ibid.). The dynamic between shifting patters of socio-cultural convention and the reader's reception of textual messages in women's magazines is further illustrated by Hermes (1995). Drawing on the work of Morley (1986), Hermes argues that magazine readers, like television audiences, can be seen as active participants in the creation of textual meanings. Thus, according to Hermes: 'Texts may be said to have "preferred meanings" that invite a reader to read them in line with dominant meaning systems ... However, this invitation need not be taken up. Readers may negotiate with texts or even read them against the grain' (1995: 25).

Hermes subsequently develops this analysis through a consideration of the critical selectivity exercised by women in their reading of women's magazines. As Hermes points, this 'continuing dialogue between readers and magazine' problematises the gender coded content of women's magazines (ibid.: 51). Thus, rather than aspiring to 'be' the female characters and role models portrayed in women's magazines, readers were often highly sarcastic about them or viewed them as unrealistic. On other occasions such magazines were read because of the support they offered to readers, particularly if they identified with personal situations and scenarios described in magazines. A key point to emerge from Hermes's study is that as female identities have become more unstable and subjectively positioned, this has had an influence on both the way in which media representations of femininity are interpreted by female audiences and also upon forms of representation themselves. According to Hermes, the success and appeal of women's magazines today depends on their effectiveness 'in addressing any of a wide range of "selves", for example, your "practical self", or your "worried partner or parent self", or your "cultured person self", which are given form through the different repertoire a reader uses' (ibid.: 65).

In more recent years, there has also been an increasing number of magazines aimed at a male readership. As Winship observes: 'The influence of feminist ideas, the rise of the gay movement in transforming masculinity, together with unemployment and capitalism's relentless penetration of new consumer markets, all account for this development' (1987: 150). Significantly, however, among the most successful of the new crop of men's magazines have been those that subvert the 'new man' ideology of the 1980s and revert back, albeit, with a more reflexive and ironic stance, to a more 'traditional' male sensibility. Particularly successful in this respect are publications such as such as *GQ* and *Loaded* which cater for the so-called 'new lads', young, single males, typically between the ages of 18 and 30. The emphasis in such magazines is squarely upon unrestrained male pleasure. According to Jackson et al., if the 'new man was what women wanted men to be' the new lad signifies 'men throwing off this synthetic media image for something more in tune with reality' (2001: 86). In effect, the 'new lad' image represents an attempt to achieve a renewed distance between men and women through the adoption of 'unacceptable, anti-politically correct behaviour' (ibid.: 85). As Jackson et al. observe:

> ... the cultural construction of the new lad acts as a means of enforcing boundaries between men and women ... The accompanying fear seems to be that unless men and women are rigidly rendered apart, this would then introduce a small grain of uncertainty within the representation of masculine identity, thereby threatening to undermine it altogether. (ibid.: 86)

GQ, Loaded and comparable magazines act as a resource for the articulation of this new lad identity. Through their portayal of particular 'new lad' images and personality traits, such magazines provide templates for readers to draw upon and act out in the course of their everyday lives. These magazines provide both tips on essential commodities for the 'new lad image, 'including hair gel, deodorant, fashion and other lifestyle accessories', as well as articles and stories written by 'experts' on issues such as how to manage personal relationships (ibid.: 86). The new lad image is a clear example of reciprocity between media, identity and everyday life in late modern society. New laddism illustrates the media's success in accurately predicting social trends and punctuating the latter with new images designed to resonate with the cultural sensibilities that inform such trends.

Another area in which men's magazines engage with contemporary notions of masculinity is in relation to danger and risk. A notable example here is the increasing number of men's magazines devoted to 'extreme sports', such as snowboarding, skyboarding, paragliding, climbing and white-water rafting. According to Jackson et al. the danger and risk associated with extreme sports corresponds accurately with the presentation of the male self in contemporary everyday life, maleness being more readily associated by many men with feats of personal courage, strength and bodily endurance than with tests and challenges associated with emotional involvement. Thus, note Jackson et al. the aspects of danger and risk associated with extreme sports:

> ... are representative of the externalization of risk away from the more dia-logic emotional encounters that are involved in interpersonal relations. Contemporary masculinity is more attuned to imagining and projecting itself through visual and discursive figurations of bodily risk than emotional engagement. In this respect, what [exteme sports] magazines offer can be interpreted as short-term resolutions of more systematic anxieties and contradictions. (ibid.: 90)

Men's magazines also engage with the desire among contemporary males for greater control over and management of their bodies. Increasingly, men have made the realisation that control and management of body image and physical shape depends on a series of lifestyle choices regarding health issues such as diet and exercise. Such lifestyle choices are now regarded as being equally integral to the construction and articulation of the male identity as fashion and other forms of 'conspicuous consumption'. Jackson et al. note that, in the context of late modern society, the body 'is seen as a project that can only become completed once we have made certain lifestyle choices. How we choose to regulate our bodies becomes increasingly open to question in a culture where it is read as an expression of individual identity' (ibid.: 91). Magazines for men devoted to health and fitness issues play a central role in helping readers understand how to manage their bodies through making particular lifestyle choices designed to achieve and maintain a good health and physical fitness for as long as possible. In a society where people live longer and cultural values focus on the desirability of 'pleasure, youth, health and fitness [the body] is increasingly viewed as a passport to the good life' (ibid.). Thus, as Jackson et al. observe: 'The culture of health magazines can be seen as a form of magical thinking that involves a narcissistic fight for life against a time-related future' (ibid.).

The alternative media and zine culture

In addition to niche media, advances in computer technology and desk-top publishing have also led to increases in the number and quality of alternative and 'subcultural media' publications (Thornton, 1995). The roots of the alternative media can be traced back to the 1960s and the rise of the alternative underground press. Examples of underground publications produced at this time include *Time Out*, *Oz* and *Realist* (see Fountain, 1988). Although alternative media vary both in terms of theme and format, they are generally characterised by two common features. First, such publications are generally low budget, do-it-yourself productions put together by an individual or small, unpaid production staff. Second, alternative media are often established to provide 'alternative' points of view/interpretations of local, national or global issues, thus working in a counter-hegemonic fashion to the mainstream media. A prevalent form of subcultural media in contemporary society are 'zines', 'zine' being derived from 'magazine' and deliberately shortened to bespeak an alternative DiY ethic both in terms of production and content. As Duncombe notes, 'The form of the zine lies somewhere between a personal letter and a magazine. Printed on a standard copy machine, fastened together on the side or corner, or folded widthwise to form a folio and stapled in the crease, zines typically run from ten to forty pages' (1997: 10).

Zines cover a broad spectrum, including politics, music, unexplained phenomena, religion, occupation and career, health, sex, travel, comic fiction, literature and art (see Duncombe, 1997: 11–13). According to Duncombe, zines frequently provide a voice for groups and individuals who do not have access to mainstream media channels but nevertheless wish to express their opinion in relation to a given issue. Moreover, through acting as a vehicle for those with alternative, anti-mainstream opinions, zines perform a social function through bringing such individuals together. Indeed, Duncombe suggests that, although zines have a subcultural or 'underground' character, the concerns shared by zine writers have much in common with those of other social groups. As, Duncombe argues: 'Although the world of zines operates on the margins of society, its concerns are common to us all: how to count as an individual, how to build a supportive community, how to live a meaningful life, how to create something that is yours' (ibid.: 15).

The hands-on and often anti-hegemonic character of zines is perhaps observed most readily in relation to youth culture. In her study of the moral panic instigated by the mainstream British media against rave culture and acid house music during the late 1980s and early 1990s, Thornton (1994) notes how zines produced by members of the rave scene took issue with much that was written about rave by newspaper journalists. As Thornton illustrates, there were substantial differences in the way in which rave was treated by the mainstream press and the subcultural media that sprung up around the rave scene. At the height of rave, during the late 1980s, when the popular press was featuring stories with headlines such as 'Rave to the Grave' and 'Killer Cult', alluding to several fatalities associated with Ecstasy use, the subcultural press was busy analysing such reports and illustrating how and why they served to misrepresent acid house music, the use of Ecstasy and the essential nature of the rave event. Similarly, in the early 1990s when the damning reports of the mainstream press gave way to more positive representations such as 'Bop to Burn: Raving is the Perfect Way to Lose Weight', the subcultural press was again quick to respond. *Torch* magazine, for example, wrote 'the *Sun* knows absolutely fuck all about what's happening in the Rave scene, just as they knew fuck all in 1988 and 1989' (Thornton, 1994: 183).

According to Thornton, by ridiculing both the mainstream press's representation of rave and engaging in a critical analysis of journalists' accounts, the subcultural press communicated its own particular set of values and beliefs about rave culture to a young readership for whom rave had become part of their lifestyle. The subcultural media associated with rave culture thus provided an alternative platform for debate, allowing those involved in the rave scene to evaluate this scene on their own terms and to situate their personal feelings towards rave culture within the forms of alternative discourse that the subcultural press made available.

The internet

So far in this chapter the emphasis has been upon 'traditional' media, notably television, niche magazines and underground publications such as zines. In recent years, however, the potential for audience participation in media processes has been enhanced considerably through the development of 'new media' technology. New media defines a range of digital products such as mobile phones, camcorders, and PCs, together with computer generated communication forms, notably email and the internet. New media forms have also had a significant impact on the nature of everyday life, further blurring the boundaries between public and private space and offering more rapid forms of communication between individuals in regionally and globally diffuse locations. The internet in particular has played a key role in fostering such new forms of communication. Uses of the internet range from the establishment of fan-sites for the exchange of information about topics such as music, film and sport, to trans-local correspondence between globally diffuse new social movements and other groups involved in DiY politics.

The perceived effect of internet communications on processes of interaction and resultant forms of collective association is effectively captured in the notion of the 'virtual community', a term coined by Rheingold to describe 'webs of personal relationships in cyberspace' (1994: 5). A key feature of the virtual community, it is argued, is its ability to transcend both geographical and temporal boundaries, providing individuals with the freedom to engage in new forms of collective association beyond the confines of their own immediate physical locality. Thus, as Healy notes: 'No longer limited by geographical happenstance to the interactions that might develop in a town or neighbourhood ... individuals can free themselves from the accidents of physical location to create their own virtual places' (1997: 60). The fact of such 'virtual' communication between individuals has led some theorists to rethink the notion of individual identity (Bassett, 1991; Jones, 1997). According to Bassett, internet communications, particularly those which occur within Multi User Domains (MUDS), facilitate the creation of virtual identities in which the basic attributes of identity, name, gender and appearance, can be adapted or entirely discarded. As Bassett observes, individuals, 'may play with multiple subjectivities by "morphing" (transforming) between different identities ... Or they may build a relatively stable alternative identity' (1991: 538).

More critical readings of the internet, however, suggest that while it may indeed offer channels for new forms of communication and interaction, this, in itself, does not amount to the existence of a community. This view is succinctly expressed by Lockard who suggests that: 'To accept only communication in place of a community's manifold functions is to sell our common faith in community vastly short' (1997: 225). A similar concern is expressed by Wilbur who considers the characteristics of online communication to be so far removed from those underpinning face-to-face communication as to render the very notion of a virtual community highly problematic. Thus, he argues: 'Any study of the virtual community will involve us in the difficult job of picking a path across a shifting terrain, where issues of presence, reality, illusion, morality, power, feeling, trust, love, and much more, set up roadblocks at every turn' (1997: 20).

The respective arguments of Lockard and Wilbur are supported by the findings of recent empirical studies on uses of the internet in everyday life. Such work suggests a high degree of continuity between online and offline identities, arguing that, while the internet may indeed facilitate new forms of trans-local communication, the physical, everyday communities of internet users remain an important aspect of their perception and use of the internet. This is clearly illustrated in Miller and Slater's study of internet users in Trinidad:

Trinidadians ... seemed highly aware, whenever they were online, that they were meeting the rest of the world as Trinis. They might be aware of this in either a nationalistic, patriotic sense (they were Trinidadians encountering other countries) or through a broader sense of the cultural specificity of their tastes, ways of doing things and communicating things. (2000: 86)

Other studies reinforce this notion of a strong continuation between on- and offline communication. For example, Wakeford (1999) identifies strongly gendered patterns of internet use, while the results of a study by Facer and Furlong suggest that interest in and use of computer technology by young people 'is patterned along socio-economic lines' (2001: 459). According to Facer and Furlong, the daily lives of young people from low income backgrounds who have no ready access to a computer at home are far less computer-centred than young people from higher income backgrounds who are likely to be computer literate and make use of PC technology on a daily basis. Indeed, for those young people with ready access to and knowledge of computer technology this becomes a significant form of cultural capital informing the way they are perceived by others in their offline, everyday lives (see Drotner, 2000).

The internet also offers individuals considerable opportunities for hands-on creativity and participation in cultural production. As Abbott notes, internet users quickly realised the value of 'the World Wide Web as a cheap, adaptable and far-reaching publishing medium. Web sites now routinely include not just text and images, but sounds, speech, music, animations and video' (1999: 111). The variety of uses to which website technology has been put adds a significant new dimension to our understanding of the ways in which individuals interact with media in the course of their everyday lives. Across a range of activities, including music, sport and DiY politics, the internet plays a central role. Kibby (2000), for example, notes how websites are often established by fans of obscure music artists as a means of both establishing and perpetuating the cult status of these artists. Such websites often feature chat rooms which enable geographically dispersed fans to interact online and exchange information and personal knowledge about particular groups and performers in whom they all share an interest.

Music websites allow fans to construct 'virtual scenes' in instances where face-to-face interaction between fans is prevented by geographical distance. An example of this is provided in Bennett's (2002, 2004) study of the 'Canterbury Sound', a term briefly used by the British music press in the late 1960s to describe a number of groups with Canterbury connections, such as Soft Machine and Caravan. During the mid-1990s the term was revived through a series of dedicated Canterbury Sound websites, which gave rise to a new generation of fans. According to Bennett, the internet has allowed geographically dispersed Canterbury Sound fans to effectively build a music scene from scratch. Canterbury Sound fans use the internet as a means of discussing the relative merits of different groups and artists, applying their musical knowledge in the creation of a 'history' of Canterbury music, and speculating as to the 'Englishness' of the music and its status as a distinctive 'local' sound.

Borden's study of contemporary skateboard culture reveals a parallel creative use of the internet in conjunction with another form of new media, the digital video camera. As Borden notes, many skaters now post video clips of their own skating moves on skater websites together with 'textual descriptions, choreographic codes using the ASCII character set [and] still photographs' (2001: 118–19). In this way, skaters both illustrate their individual prowess and pass on their skill and abilities to others. Borden suggests that such creative use of the internet is also an important community-building device for skaters. Thus, he observes: 'The overall effect [of the internet] is to make it easier for skaters to disseminate material globally, certainly compared to their access to commercial magazines or videos' (ibid.: 119). The result of this, according to Borden, is to make skateboarding both a global and a local phenomenon. Skaters exchange images and information about skating style and technique on the internet but operationalise these resources in the context of their own local environment. As such, local groups of skaters experience an on-going dialogue between their own creative synergy and a global skating community. According to Borden:

> [The skating] community is knitted through a continual exchange and re-experiencing of a lexicon of skate moves. The image becomes not only a locally lived but, simultaneously, a globally reproduced and exchanged phenomenon, part of modernity's intensification of global communication and simultaneity. (ibid.: 126)

The capacity of the internet for weaving together global and local dialogues in this way can also be seen in relation to the rise over the last decade of 'new social movements', forms of direct action which reject mainstream political ideologies and adopt alternative or DiY strategies (see McKay, 1998). As Atton observes, new social movements now routinely make use of the internet 'as the primary channel for autonomous communication' (2002: 133). By-passing traditional media, to which such groups in any case have very limited access, the internet offers new social movements the potential 'for sociality, community, mobilization, knowledge construction and direct political action' (ibid.). According to Atton, in addition to facilitating global communication between locally dispersed movements and action groups, the internet also provides a vehicle for more equal participation in debate and decision-making processes. Thus, argues Atton, by allowing individuals to voice their opinions more readily, the internet 'weakens the vanguardist conception of a social movement, where an elite employs authoritative forms of discourse' (ibid.: 149). Atton further suggests that the internet opens up avenues for challenging authoritative accounts of events, notably the 'eyewitness report[s]' or documentary accounts often used by news and press agencies (ibid.).

The value of global internet communications for new social movements is further illustrated in Smith's account of the 'Battle of Seattle', a mass protest staged against the Third Ministerial Meeting of the World Trade Organization in Seattle during November, 1999. As Smith observes, organisers of the demonstration:

> ... ma[d]e extensive use of Internet sites and electronic list serves to expand communication with dispersed constituencies and audiences. These communication networks allow[ed] organizers to almost instantaneously transmit alternative media accounts and images of protest to contrast those of mainstream corporate outlets. Alternative electronic media networks also rapidly disseminate[d] information about resistance against economic globalization in the global South, such as the Mexican student strikers. (2001: 15, see also Welsh, 2000)

The internet has also been effectively used by small scale, local protest groups movements seeking to gain wider global support. Zapatista, an organisation in the Chiapas region of Mexico, an area characterised by severe poverty despite the abundance of rich natural resources, has successfully used the internet to secure greater global awareness of their campaign against socio-economic policies in the region. As Froehling explains: 'Zapatista supporters on the Internet could produce news about the Zapatistas at a low cost and rapidly circulate it' (1999). Moreover, notes Froehling, while the mainstream Mexican media have effectively functioned as an instrument of state control, by using the Internet Zapatista 'could circumvent this control' (ibid.)

Conclusion

This chapter has considered a number of examples of ways in which individuals draw upon media and new media forms in the course of their everyday lives. Beginning with a consideration of contemporary television programmes such as soap operas and game shows, it was noted how such programmes facilitate the creative engagement of audiences, for example, through likening the scenes and scenarios in soaps to their own everyday lives or positioning themselves as game show participants. This was followed by a look at various forms of print media. Starting with professionally produced niche media magazines it was demonstrated how the content of these magazines reflects changing lifestyle sensibilities of late modern individuals, in some cases cutting across or reflexively addressing traditionally gendered notions of identity and lifestyle. Attention then focused on underground publications and zines, in particular the way in which this type of publication facilitates forms of resistance to discourses generated by the mainstream press, for example in relation to underground and alternative music scenes. Finally, the chapter examined the role of the internet as a medium of communication in contemporary everyday life. Beginning with a critical assessment of the concept of 'virtual community', this was followed by a consideration of how the internet has facilitated more ready communication between globally dispersed groups of individuals whose interests range from leisure activities such as music and skateboarding through to new social movements and DiY politics.

FIVE Fashion

Fashion is an ontological domain; in and through an interaction with fashion *subjectivities* are literally made and worldly relations established between clothes and bodies. In everyday speech ... we speak of the 'body' that is *subject* to the clothes that literally enclothe it with a significance. (Gill, 1998: 43)

Of the many commodities and leisure resources through which individuals in contemporary society construct and play out identities in the course of their everyday lives, fashion plays a central role. According to Storry and Childs, 'the way that we dress can serve either to confirm or to subvert various facets of our identities, such as our gender, race, class and age' (1997: 171). As this observation suggests, by assembling particular items of fashion in particular ways, and through experimentation with dress and appearance, late modern individuals create personal images, designed both to situate the self and send out culturally-coded messages to others. Thus, fashion embodies a range of symbolic values which are collectively understood within and across different social groups. A central feature of such image creation is the enhancement or negotiation of previously rigid demarcators of identity, most notably in relation to gender, race and ethnicity, class background and age.

The possibilities that fashion affords for the construction of such 'personalised' identities have led to claims that it constitutes 'a celebration of individualism' (Mort, 1996: 16), a form of conspicuous consumption through which individuals display their individuality and uniqueness in the context of contemporary mass urban societies. Arguably, however, another way of understanding fashion is as a means of forging new forms of 'collective' identity. Thus, being increasingly less constrained by the structural experience of class, gender and ethnicity, individuals create new cultural alliances based around reflexively articulated lifestyle preferences.

Within this process, fashion and visual appearance play a considerable part in informing notions of commonality. Thus, as Langman notes, the cultural alliances formed by late modern individuals are generally the product of 'shared patterns of cultural consumption [including] tastes and fashion [rather than] more traditional forms of community' (1992: 60).

This chapter examines the significance of fashion and style in the context of everyday life. Beginning with an examination of the everyday significance of fashion, the chapter then examines grounding analyses of fashion in the work of late nineteenth century sociologists Simmel and Veblen. This is followed by an in-depth consideration of the ways in which fashion caters for an increasingly diverse and sophisticated range of consumer sensibilities in late modern society. Themes covered in this part of the chapter include, youth, feminity, masculinity, retro and ethnic fashions.

Fashion as an 'everyday' resource

Fashion provides one of the most ready means through which individuals can make expressive visual statements about their identities. As Entwistle observes, the 'tension between clothes as revealing and clothes as concealing of identity' has been noted by theorists of fashion for a number of years (2000: 112). This aspect of fashion, argues Entwistle, is particularly relevant in the context of 'the modern city [where] we mingle with crowds of 'strangers' and have only fleeting moments to impress one another' (ibid.). In contemporary urban settings, fashion is a key resource through which individuals are able to present themselves to others, the relative anonymity and pace of life in the late modern metropole calling for highly visual and relatively instantaneous means of asserting one's identity. As various fashion theorists note, the creative use of fashion items can be used to portray a range of images centred around identity politics depicting, for example, wealth and status (Veblen, 1994 [1924]; Simmel, in Frisby and Featherstone, 1997), power and success (Rucker et al., 1999), or an underground or bohemian status (Wilson, 1998; Szostak-Pierce, 1999). As Finkelstein observes: 'In everyday life, fashioned appearances [are interpreted] as literalizations of the wearer's character, sexual preferences, economic success and educational attainment' (1999: 376).

In addition to informing the external gaze in this way, however, fashion in late modernity also provides a source of highly personalised pleasure. Moreover, such pleasure comes not only from the visual aspects of fashion, but also from the cut and feel of the clothing itself, this contributing significantly to the individual's phenomenological experience of the everyday. Thus, according to Finkelstein: 'Fashionability can involve highly sensualised experiences. The feel of fabric can evoke private pleasures. Being clothed in a desirable ensemble can feed the individual's fantasies of developing an alter ego' (1996: 58).

Both interpretations of fashion's significance in everyday life point to the high level of personal investment in fashion items by individuals in late modern society. This chimes with the writings of contemporary cultural theorists such as Featherstone (1991) and Chaney (1996) concerning the creative competence of individuals in using the cultural resources of late modern cultural life. According to Chaney, 'fashion literally displays the exercise of taste, an alignment to a sensibility. In the personal choices we make from public vocabularies (that is, fashions), we exercise and display sensibilities that inform and organise choice and taste' (1996: 132-3). Developing this theme, Langman suggests that such individual competence in using fashion, together with other accessories of late modern life, have resulted in a pluralisation of the self; a self which is 'differentially expressed and experienced depending on context' (1992: 67). According to Langman, the reflexive subjectivity facilitated by fashion becomes multiply articulated to present a range of different identities within and across the various spaces and territories that characterise everyday life.

Such personal investment in fashion has also been made possible by the fashion industry itself which, during the last fifty years, has become increasingly more expert in its reading of consumer tastes and the ways that such tastes correspond with particular lifestyle sensibilities. Indeed, as Entwistle notes: '"Lifestyle" marketing has subtly altered the way in which not only fashion, but such commodities as food are produced, distributed, marketed and sold' (2000: 225-6). This aspect of the contemporary fashion industry is supported by a sophisticated range of fashion magazines that communicate 'desirable images' to an increasingly heterogeneous consumer base (O'Shea Borrelli, 1997: 149). According to Breward, such is the effectiveness of the contemporary fashion industry in marketing fashion as a barometer of lifestyle and taste, that it has created a new international language of style. Fashion, suggests Breward 'has become a kind of contemporary Esperanto, immediately accessible across social and geographical boundaries. Fashion change in this context can be reduced to a shorthand for ... cultural experience or 'lifestyle' (1995: 229).

Breward's view is qualified by other theorists who, while conceding the relatively universal nature of fashion, emphasise the continuing importance of local variations in fashion sense and the importance of local knowledges and sensibilities that determine the meanings attached to fashion in particular social contexts (Brydon and Niessen, 1998). Similarly, Eicher and

Sumberg (1995) note that the increasing prevalence of trans-local fashion trends is often emphasised at the expense of considering the continuing popularity of ethnic and national dress styles. Indeed, as will be considered later in this chapter, in recent years some forms of ethnic dress have themselves become trans-local fashion statements, serving as an affective link between displaced communities of African and Asian diasporas (Kahn, 1993; Tulloch, 1993). This supports Eicher and Sumberg's view that: 'Many fashions in dress exist simultaneously in complex industrial societies where heterogeneity, rather than homogeneity, is found' (1995: 300). The fact of ethnic dress being transformed into items of fashion in this way also clearly problematises the dominant equation of fashion with 'styles emanating from an acknowledged fashion center, such as Paris' (ibid.).

Fashion then, provides individuals with a key means through which to manage their identities in the context of everyday life. As Entwistle notes, although individuals are aware of both the ritualistic and often highly deceptive qualities of the dressed body, this 'does not stop us from attempting to control how we look and to calculate our appearance' (2000: 113). Clearly, fashionable clothing is not the only way through which individuals attempt to construct themselves at a visual level; equally important in this respect are other visual attributes, such as hairstyle (Zdatny, 1997) and makeup, together with items of jewellery. Similarly, partly as a result of the impact of youth cultural styles such as punk (Hebdige, 1979) and goth (Hodkinson, 2002), forms of body modification such as tatooing and piercing are now increasingly prevalent aspects of the fashioned body (Sweetman, 2004). In many ways, such examples of body modification produce an even more striking statement of identity than items of clothing because of their permanence on the body. Indeed, as Hardin notes, tatooing has become a significant resource for marginalised groups such as ethnic minorities, gays and lesbians. According to Hardin, 'by marking the body of one who has been placed outside the social order because of his/her body, one can challenge the very legitimization of that order' (1999: 85).

As the above interpretations of fashion illustrate, like other consumer items in late modern society fashion allows for a high degree of creativity on the part of individuals in the construction of their identities and the presentation of such identities in everyday life. Indeed, as Barnard observes, the cultural 'meaning' and significance of fashion is as much down to the collective creativity of consumers as the intended statements of fashion designers. As with other forms of manufactured items and goods in late modern society, once items of fashion enter the public sphere they are inscribed with a new range of meanings which reflect the everyday cultural circumstances of consumers. Thus, as Barnard comments, while fashion designers may often have a clear perception of the meanings which they intend their clothes to articulate, individuals 'appropriate the meanings of garments and adapt them to their own intentions' (1996: 71). This view supports Fiske's (1989a) observation that the act of consumption is an act of cultural production (see Chapter 3). According to Barnard, the fact of consumer inscribed meaning in fashion garments is clearly illustrated in an everyday context through the differences of opinion which emerge concerning the relative quality and appeal of particular garments. Thus, he argues:

> Since there are disagreements about the meaning of garments or collections, and since there are alternative interpretations of works, sometimes coming from the designers themselves, sometimes coming from the wearers of the garments, meaning cannot simply be a product of the designers intentions. (1996: 71)

Fashion, then, serves as a potent visual symbol in society, one which individuals use in an attempt both to assert their individuality and, at the same time, to align themselves with particular social groupings. As such, fashion is a form of social power (Rucker et al., 1999). This corresponds with Cannon's observation that individuals use fashion 'to indicate to themselves and others whether they think they belong with another individual or group, or whether they consider themselves another's equal or superior' (1998: 24). Such considerations of the role of fashion garments in society are central to some of the earliest work on fashion, that is the work of Simmel and Veblen.

Simmel and Veblen on fashion

The first sustained attempt to consider the cultural significance of fashion in everyday life was made by Simmel in his essay *The Philosophy of Fashion* (see Frisby and Featherstone, 1997). Central to Simmel's interpretation of fashion is an acknowledgement of its function as a means through which individuals in the emergent cosmopolitan centres of western Europe were able to satisfy the dual desire for conformity and differentiation, which, according to Simmel, is a key characteristic of the human condition (see Hamilton, 2002). Simmel suggests that, through buying and wearing fashionable clothes, individuals both signal their awareness of social trends, and concomitant notions of collective acceptability, while simultaneously creating an individual identity through which to distinguish themselves from the urban mass:

> Fashion is the imitation of a given pattern and thus satisfies the need for
> social adaptation; it leads the individual onto the path that everyone travels,
> it furnishes a general condition that resolves the conduct of every individ-
> ual into a mere example. At the same time, and to no less a degree, it sat-
> isfies the need for distinction, the tendency towards differentiation, change
> and individual contrast. (in Frisby and Featherstone, 1997: 189)

Simmel further suggested that such collective individual responses to
fashion were circumscribed by wider issues of power and status, fashion
becoming a visual indicator of established power relations deeply embedded
in the social strata. According to Simmel, fashion became, in effect, a
visual statement of wealth and status, a way in which individuals demonstrated their membership of a particular social group, and their distance
from groups who held a lower social position. For Simmel then, fashion
played a key role in reproducing class relations: '... fashion signifies a
union with those of the same status, the uniformity of a social circle char-
acterized by it, and, in doing so, the closure of this group against those
standing in a lower position which the higher group characterizes as not
belonging to it' (ibid.).

A similar view is presented by Veblen, whose work on fashion and
other aspects of late nineteenth-century consumer culture centred around
the emergent American leisure class (see also Chapter 3). Veblen's work is
significant as it represents an early acknowledgement of the way in which
individuals, rather than remaining rigidly located in a particular socio-
economic group, could become socially mobile through the acquisition of
wealth, thus enhancing their social status. In his analysis of the significance
of fashion for the leisure classes, Veblen demonstrates that a key feature of
expensive fashion garments was the very definite message they were
intended to convey concerning the wearer's attainment of a status removed
from that of working, professional and other occupational classes:

> Elegant dress serves its purpose of elegance not only in that it is expensive,
> but also because it is the insignia of leisure. It not only shows that the
> wearer is able to consume a relatively large value, but it also argues at the
> same time that he consumes without producing. (1994 [1924]: 105)

Veblen's work on fashion is also characterised by a sophisticated understanding of the shared aesthetic value placed by consumer groups on
items of fashion. Thus, according to Veblen, conspicuous consumption of
fashion and other items involves collective displays of wealth and 'good
taste', such displays being not merely projected outwards to other social
groups but also inwards towards members of the same group. As such,
conspicuous consumption serves as an internal bonding for the group, a

collective celebration of their shared social position which is played out, and thus continually re-emphasised, on the surface of the body. In Veblen's analysis then are the foundations of an approach that interprets fashion goods as aesthetically inscribed resources, collectively consumed by individuals whose primary rationale for purchasing particular ranges and types of garments is their use in the articulation of shared lifestyle statements.

Fashion and youth

Youth has been a particularly prominent object of study in research on the collective significance of fashion and style. As historical studies have illustrated, youth's 'revolt into style' (Melley, 1970) is not a new phenomenon. Roberts's account of the Salford Scuttlers, a nineteenth-century gang based in the north-west of England, is telling in this respect. As Roberts notes, the Scuttler 'had his own style of dress – the union shirt, bell-bottomed trousers, the heavy leather belt, pricked out in fancy designs with the large steel buckle and the thick, iron-shod clogs' (1971: 123). A similar example can be seen in Fowler's account of the Napoo, a Manchester-based gang during the inter-war years who wore 'a highly distinctive uniform borrowed from American gangster films [which consisted of] a navy blue suit, a trilby and a pink neckerchief' (1992: 144). Following the Second World War, the combined effect of technological advances, increased affluence and demographic changes resulted in youth becoming a highly lucrative target for the consumer industries whose mass production of fashion items and other consumer goods led to the formation of a series of style-based youth cultures, particularly in the case of working-class youth who were among the most affluent consumers of the post-war period (see Chambers, 1985; Bocock, 1993).

Early work on post-war style-based youth cultures argued that items of fashion were being symbolically transformed by working-class youth and used in strategies of resistance. The most well-known exponent of this approach is the Centre for Contemporary Cultural Studies (CCCS) at the University of Birmingham (see also Chapter 1) who produced several interpretations of style-based youth resistance. According to Phil Cohen (1972), the collective appropriation of selected items of fashion by young working-class 'subcultures' related to their need to retain a sense of community, which, Cohen argued, was being threatened by post-war re-housing programmes that broke up traditional working-class communities. Cohen's theory of style-based resistance is developed in subsequent CCCS studies focusing on specific youth cultures. Clarke's study of skinhead culture argues that the skinhead style represents 'an attempt to re-create through the "mob" the traditional working class community as a substitution for the real decline of the latter' (1976: 99). Similarly, Jefferson suggests that the style of the teddy boy directly reflects his '"all-dressed-up-and-nowhere-to-go" experience of Saturday evening'(1976: 48). The relative affluence of the teddy boys allowed them to 'buy into' an upper class image – the Edwardian suit revived by a group of Saville Row tailors in 1950 and originally intended for an upper-class market. Jefferson argues, that the teddy boys' 'dress represented a symbolic way of expressing and negotiating with their symbolic reality; of giving cultural meaning to their social plight' (ibid.: 86). Finally, Hebdige claims that the mod style was a reaction to the mundane predictability of the working week and that the mod attempted to compensate for this 'by exercising complete domination over his private estate – his appearance and choice of leisure pursuits' (1976: 91).

The concept of youth fashion as a means of facilitating visual 'shock tactics' was further developed in Hebdige's (1979) *Subculture: The Meaning of Style*. Centring around the UK punk rock scene of the mid to late 1970s, the book draws heavily on the semiotics theory of Barthes (1972) and Saussure (1974). This is most clearly evident in Hebdige's interpretation of the punk style which, he argues, mirrors the socio-economic turmoil of late 1970s Britain – the increasing joblessness, the rediscovery of poverty and the onset of economic depression. According to Hebdige, the increasingly dysfunctional nature of British society was mirrored in punk's 'spectacular transformations ... of commodities, values, common-sense attitudes, etc.' on the site of the body (1979: 116). Thus, observes Hebdige:

> Objects borrowed from the most sordid of contexts found a place in the punks' ensembles: lavatory chains were draped in graceful arcs across chests encased in plastic bin-liners. Safety pins were taken out of their domestic 'utility' context and worn as gruesome ornaments through the cheek, ear or lip ... Hair was obviously dyed (hay yellow, jet black, or bright orange with tufts of green or bleached in question marks), and T-shirts and trousers told the story of their own construction with multiple zips and outside seams clearly displayed. (ibid.: 107)

The work of the CCCS represents an early acknowledgement of the aesthetic value for youth of fashion and attendant commodities as resources in the symbolic negotiation of everyday life. Where the CCCS work fundamentally fails is in its rather crude interpretation of the cultural relationship between visual style and identity. Thus, the assumption made is that the selective appropriation of items of fashion by youth subcultures serves only to accentuate, albeit in a more visually spectacular way, traditional, class-based habits and sensibilities (Bennett, 2000).

More recent work has attempted to recast the relationship between youth, style and identity by arguing that, rather than accentuating the fact of class in a pre-determined structuralist sense, youth fashions allow for far more reflexive expressions of identity. This new perspective on the meaning of youth style is effectively captured by Muggleton's (2000) notion of 'post-subcultural' youth,[1] which suggests that young people in the twenty-first century pursue a far more individual agenda both in their choice of style and the personal image they wish to create through their use of style. A similar view is expressed by Polhemus who argues that if youth styles were once broadly indicative of class-based subcultural membership, the rapid succession of youth fashions over the last fifty years, combined with the growing number of 'retro' fashions now available in both high street and more alternative clothing outlets, has given rise to new pick and mix fashion sensibilities among young people. According to Polhemus:

> We now inhabit a Supermarket of Style where, like tins of soup lined up on endless shelves, we can choose between more than fifty different styletribes. Jumbling geography as well as history, British punk circa 1976 sits on the shelf next to 1950s American Beatnik or late Jamaican Ragga ... In the end, in the mix, the possibilities are unlimited: an Armani suit worn with back-to-front baseball cap and 'old school' trainers, a 'Perfecto' black leather jacket worn with tartan flares, a Hippy caftan worn with rubber leggings, DMs and a Chanel handbag. (1997: 150)

A criticism that can be made of such postmodern accounts of youth style and fashion is that in their attempts to deconstruct earlier structuralist accounts they simultaneously deconstruct the notion of style as a collective sensibility per se. Certainly, youth styles no longer appear to routinely cohere around readily identifiable images based on spectacular forms of dress – a notable exception here being the 'goth' image, (see, Hodkinson, 2002). Nevertheless, recent research suggests that, despite their apparently more neutral appearance, youth fashions still appear to be inscribed with a semiotic function which ascribes wearers to particular groups. Thus, as Miles notes, contemporary young people invariably demarcate their individuality by comparing themselves with 'other "types" of consumers' (2000: 138). Still, evidence suggests that the relationship between visual image and group identity is now less arbitrary. This point is illustrated by Szostak-Pierce in her description of a group of techno fans in the US: 'On display was not a group style of dress but a mixture of vernacular style unique to each individual. Dress style was influenced by other lifestyle choices outside weekend raving' (1999: 147). At the same time, however, a new array of culturally embedded signs appear to have come into effect, with the result that, in the context of contemporary youth, much can still be ascertained about the individual from basic patterns of consumption, particularly in relation to fashion. This is illustrated by the following observation from Miles based on empirical research carried out on consumption patterns among young people in two UK cities during the 1990s. As part of the research, the respondents were asked to study pictures of young people and describe their lifestyle preferences based on the image portrayed in the pictures:

> Though my respondents acknowledged that it was an impossible task to accurately associate particular consumer goods with pictures of individuals, and thereby draw an accurate picture of what those people are like, they did find it easy to generalise to this end. Their experience of consumer culture was such that they were able to make judgements about individuals according to the clothing they were wearing. (2000: 138–9)

Thus, according to Miles, contemporary young people appear to be experts in reading cultural indicators, 'putting together a jigsaw of consumer goods' in order to ascertain a person's lifestyle preferences and likely relationship to others (ibid.: 138).

Fashion and femininity

During the mid-1970s, feminist theorist Angela McRobbie (1980) argued that a key problem with research on youth cultures was its failure to consider style-based patterns of resistance as these related to the lives of teenage girls (see also McRobbie and Garber, 1976). In her subsequent pioneering work on fashion and culture, McRobbie demonstrated how, though their appropriation of fashion garments, young women produced strategies of resistance that were equally as subversive as those produced by their male counterparts. Thus, for example, commenting on female members of the UK punk rock scene, McRobbie notes how 'punk girls salvaged shockingly lurid lurex minis of the sort worn in Italian 'jet-set' films of the mid-1970s. They reinstated the skinny-rib jumper and plastic earrings ... [and] ... tarty fishnet stockings' (1994: 147). According to McRobbie, however, it is not merely such overtly alternative expressions of female identity that function to subvert dominant, patriarchal notions of femininity. On the contrary, she argues, female fashion styles which, on the surface, appear to conform more closely with conventional notions of female attractiveness, and their designation of women as objects of desire, articulate pleasure in one's own body and appearance. This observation is reinforced by Carter who notes how the mass production of fashion and style designed to conform with dominant modes of femininity is only one aspect of the process through which feminine identities are constructed. Equally important, argues Carter, is the 'deconstruction, appropriation, subversion and reassemblage' of fashion commodities by female consumers themselves (1984: 198). A similar point is made by Partington who argues that:

> In trying to impose certain standards of taste on consumers [which conform to dominant ideological values] the design profession and the marketing industries [have] created the opportunity for the roles of 'good consumption' to be broken, inadvertently allowing consumers to produce unexpected meanings around fashion goods. (1993: 147)

Partington goes on to suggest that, while marketing strategies are designed to train female fashion consumers into particular patterns of consumption which correspond with dominant ideological values relating to 'femininity and domesticity' (ibid.), the actual effect of such strategies has been to facilitate 'the consumer's active use of an increasingly complex "language of clothes" to express differences' (ibid.: 148). A significant aspect of this more active involvement in the creation of the feminine image, argues Partington, has been a transformation of women's role as the object of the male 'gaze'. No longer are women simply passive recipients of the male gaze. Rather, through allowing them to 'manage' their bodies (Craik, 1994) fashion provides women with the means by which to actively invite and direct the male gaze. Thus, as Partington observes, 'femininity' is transformed from a socially proscribed given into '"simulation", a demonstration of the representations of women – a "masquerade"' (1993: 156).

Partington's view is developed by Craik who argues that when considering the significance of the visual statements made by women through their fashion choices, the desire to satisfy the requirements of the male gaze can be regarded as only one, and perhaps not the most important, factor governing women's dress sense. According to Craik:

> The separation between sex, gender and sexuality runs through codes of dress and decoration in complex ways. Furthermore, understandings of these distinctions are not necessarily shared by women and men ... evidence suggests that the model of the 'male gaze' as the basis of codes of looking and ways of seeing may be just one arrangement. In terms of dress behaviour, there may be multiple understandings of allusion to sexuality. Despite the rhetoric that women dress to please men, other evidence suggests that women primarily dress to please other women. Further, there is no clear pattern as to whose 'eyes' women view other women through. (1994: 56)

As Craik suggests here, the function of female dress is not simply dominated by the need for women to look physically attractive as defined by the conventions of patriarchy. On the contrary, in selecting a wardrobe of clothes and dressing in particular ways, female consumers may also adhere to the requirements of a female gaze, defined by issues of dress sense and taste in choosing items of clothing. Fiske is similarly critical of the view that the fashion sensibilities of women are entirely circumscribed by the conventions of patriarchy. Fiske challenges this view by suggesting that, through the creative use of fashion garments, women are able to take control of their own bodies, determine their 'look' and thus exert influence over the way in which others see them: 'The pleasure of looking good is not just the pleasure of looking good for the male, but rather of controlling how one looks and therefore of controlling the look of others upon oneself' (1989b: 34). This notion of women effectively asserting control over the way they are seen by others through their choice of dress is supported by Ganetz. According to Ganetz, such reflexive awareness of the dressed body in public spaces is a centrally defining feature of women's fashion sense. Thus, she argues: 'Women view themselves "from the outside", which means they can spend hours putting on and taking clothes off in order to find the right combination for that particular occasion and those particular people. Women not only *see* themselves, they also see themselves being seen' (1995: 78).

Research during the late 1990s revealed that new expressions of femininity in fashion were also beginning to make an impact on the workplace, notably in businesses. In such male dominated contexts, conventional wisdom had held that, in order to succeed, 'women should adopt male props or symbols' (Rucker et al., 1999: 61). As a study by Rucker et al. illustrates, however, a more liberal outlook in business settings, resulting from the increasing prevalence of women in more senior positions has begun to emerge. Thus, rather than opting for business suits, women are now more prone to wear individually selected items of clothing, combining, for example, a blazer, skirt and jumper. Similarly, instead of the dark colours typically worn by men, women preferred a wider variety of colours, including brighter colours such as red and purple. As Rucker et al. discovered, women in business settings have developed a competence in choosing sets of clothes that display their power and status in the workplace while simultaneously providing scope for the display of femininity.

Fashion and masculinity

As Finkelstein notes: 'In contemporary society, a frequent complaint is that men are left out of the fashion rush' (1996: 61). Indeed, prior to the mid-1980s there was considerable justification for this comment. While women and younger consumers of both sexes were well provided for by the fashion industries, the range of fashions produced for men beyond the age of twenty-five was decidedly narrow. To some extent, the shortage of fashion products available for men was dictated by established conventions of masculinity which tended to equate 'fashion with women', regarding them as 'the fashionable gender of the species' (Craik, 1994: 176). In contrast, men who displayed an interest in clothing and visual appearance, beyond a purely functional meaning, were seen as effeminate. Thus, according to Craik, while women's fashions were produced with the aim of 'achieving a look' ... men's appearance has been calculated to enhance their active roles' (ibid.: 176).

Prior to the mid-1980s the most noticeable advances in male fashion were made in the youth market. Moreover, it was in the domain of youth that the most strident challenges to dominant modes of male sexuality were evident. As Entwistle observes, during the early 1970s:

> ... glam rock bands such as Roxy Music as well as performers such as David Bowie challenged some of the standard conventions of masculine self-presentation. Their exaggerated costumes, elaborate hair and dramatic make-up were the antithesis of conventional sobriety associated with masculinity. Later on, in the 1980s, the emergence of new bands associated with the 'New Romantic' movement similarly challenged some of the most potent taboos in male dress. Pop stars such as Boy George wore obvious make-up, nail varnish, hair ribbons and skirts, provocatively playing with conventions, not just of gender, but sexuality too. (2000: 175)

Although such experiments with fashion challenged dominant notions of male gender and sexuality at the level of youth and youth culture, their impact on mainstream male fashion sensibilities was nominal. During the mid-1980s, however, a rapid expansion of the male fashion market took place. Within a short period of time a new and dramatically increased range of clothes was available for men. According to Nixon, this expansion of the male fashion industry reflected a widening range of male identity roles in society. Nixon also suggests that such changes in the design and availability of male fashions produced 'a shift in the visual languages of maleness' and had the effect of sexualising the male body (1992: 155). A similar view is put forward by Craik who suggests that '[c]hanging conventions of men's fashion ... re-worked attributes of masculinity [and] transformed male bodies into objects of the gaze, of display and decoration' (1994: 203).

The shift towards a greater range of male fashion garments during the mid-1980s was initiated with the arrival of 'designer wear', a range of clothing characterised by particular brand names often conspicuously displayed on external labels. The kudos of designer clothing was considerably enhanced through its endorsement by film and TV stars, notably in the popular 1980s US crime drama *Miami Vice* whose leading actors sported a range of smart-casual designer wear. The rise of the designer market was a product of two inter-related factors. First, it reflected the fashion industry's perfection of a new 'commercial language' designed to appeal to a male market (Mort, 1996: 9). This involved the nurturing of an 'aesthetic' sensibility with respect to the desire for and purchase of fashion clothing (ibid.: 121). A central aspect of this was the promotion of what were deemed to be desirable male images that could be achieved through the acquisition of a suggested range of clothing. As Mort observes, the crucial message sent out to consumers and potential consumers of designer wear by advertisers and fashion journalists was that fashion could no longer be interpreted merely as 'the clothing one wore, it was a state of mind, "an attitude, a complete lifestyle"' (ibid.: 121).

The new commercial logic of fashion inherent in the marketing of designer wear had a marked effect on the high street clothing stores. Both established menswear retailers, notably Burtons, and new high street chains, such as Next and Top Man, used window displays and advertising campaigns designed to sell a particular range of clothes to their male clientele. According to Nixon: 'This approach to menswear put a premium on a relatively restricted range of clothes, while organising these into loose collections. The marketing ethos here was about presenting a fairly tightly integrated "lifestyle" package' (1997: 177). The 'lifestyle' message of designer wear was further reinforced through 'niche' magazines, such as *The Face* and *GQ*, which catered specifically for a 20–30 something readership (Thornton, 1995; see also Chapter 4). Nixon suggests that such magazines played an important role in the 'articulation of forms of knowledge concerning style, and definitions of taste and lifestyle' (1992: 162). Nixon further observes how these magazines established what he refers to as 'a repertoire of looks', each carefully crafted to produce a certain image and collectively presented as a range of image 'options' to the reader (ibid.: 1992). According to Nixon, 'masculinity is [here being] consciously put together through the assemblage of clothes and haircut; attention is focused on the production of a particular "look". Beyond this is the incitement to participate in rituals of adornment; the putting together of an "appearance"' (ibid.).

The second factor underlying the rise of the designer clothing market was the declining status of youth as the primary consumer group in contemporary society (Cashmore, 1984). The rise in youth unemployment during the early 1980s meant that fashion producers had to look for new markets. The more affluent 25–45 age group became the new target for the fashion industry. As Savage explains:

> This age bracket is employed, often 'up-scale', and has already been trained to consume in the period of teenage's greatest outreach. The consumers of those products marked teenage in the commodity marketplace are now ... not teenaged but middle aged. (1990: 167)

Savage goes on to consider how this new marketing campaign was consolidated through a global advertising campaign during the mid-1980s in which the emphasis was on nostalgic references designed to appeal to the ageing baby-boomer generation. As Savage observes, slickly produced TV and cinema advertisements using musical and visual references from the 1950s and 1960s chimed with 'a new "life-style" marketing fantasy' designed to allow the baby boomers to hold on to their youth by preserving its spirit of freedom and adventure through the air of nostalgia such advertisements were purposely designed to create (ibid.). As an illustration of this, Savage refers to an advertisement for Levi 501 jeans, the popular 1950s button-down fly design re-introduced during the mid-1980s:

> This TV advertisement, shown on both sides of the Atlantic, showed a young man – with a fifties DA topping the perfect body – walking into a launderette in an unspecified present from any time within the last thirty years ... To the strains of 'I Heard It Through The Grapevine' – a 1968 'classic' meant to signify taste, authenticity, and the community of a shared past – the young man strips to his boxer shorts and basks in the gaze of the male and female onlookers ... As a Levi's spokesperson notes, 'The campaign captures the atmosphere of the 1950s in a 1980s style, effectively "air-conditioning" the past and achieving a dramatic and compelling crossover of image, music and fashion'. (ibid.: 165)

If the use of sophisticated advertising campaings to sell male fashion products corresponds at some level with shifting perceptions of men and male identity in contemporary society, this has also involved the challenging of more deeply ingrained discourses concerning male dominance and superiority. This point is effectively illustrated in Finkelstein's examination of an advertisement for men's business suits that made use of Bauhaus architectural imagery. According to Finkelstein, the effect of the advertisment was to produce a confused message. Thus, on the one hand, the juxtapostion of the architecture and the suit suggests that 'both are naturalised sites of masculinity' (1996: 363). Simultaneously, however, the unconventional and short-lived era of Bauhaus architecture is suggestive of the suit as symbolic of a more 'radical masculinity' (ibid.).

secondhand and retro-fashions

Just as 1980s saw the rise of the designer market, it was also the decade in which secondhand and retro-fashions started to become increasingly popular. There had been a steady trade in secondhand clothing before the 1980s, but this was generally restricted to older people and those with little money to spend on clothes. Similarly, throughout the 1960s and 1970s urban market stalls had provided a source of secondhand clothing for hippies, artists and others with avant garde tastes (McRobbie, 1994). During the 1980s, however, the demand for secondhand clothing broadened considerably due to increasing unemployment. Similarly, university and college students with little money to spend began to frequent secondhand clothing shops. The initially economically motivated trend in secondhand clothes buying among young people soon developed its own conventions of style (McRobbie, 1994), becoming in effect an alternative fashion statement. For one thing, it quickly became clear to students and other young buyers that the clothing on offer in secondhand outlets was often of a superior quality, both in terms of materials used and craftsmanship, to the current fashion clothes offered by high street chain stores. Moreover, an imaginatively assembled wardrobe of secondhand clothing offered a much sought after opportunity for individuality and distinctiveness as compared with what many young people saw as the bland and characterless dress options offered by the designer clothes shops and other high street stores.

Another significant feature of the secondhand market was the possibilities it offered young people for 'dressing-up' and 'dressing-down', experimenting with visual identities that transcended boundaries of class, age and gender. As McRobbie has noted, the subversive potential of secondhand style had a noticeable effect on young women whose appropriation of male clothing items was used to challenge dominant stereotypical ideas concerning desirable feminine appearances. McRobbie also cites a number of female role models, including punk singer Patti Smith and actress Diane Keaton (famous through her role in the Woody Allen film *Annie Hall*), whom, McRobbie argues, were instrumental in 'alert[ing women] to the feminine potential of the male wardrobe [and making] the do-it-yourself look attractive' (1994: 149).

The appropriation of retro-fashions, particularly those associated with the 1970s, is often equated with a tongue-in-cheek sensibility based around *irony* and *play*, a view reinforced by retrospective media accounts which routinely reduce the popular culture of the 1970s to a series of stereotypical images of platform boots and sequinned jackets (synonymous with the glam rock image of 1970s groups such as Slade and The

Sweet) or white flared trousers and medallions (images borrowed from the 1978 film about disco dancing *Saturday Night Fever* starring John Travolta). Such ironic usage of 1970s retro-fashion is most commonly seen during *70s Nights*, night-club events which mimic the 1970s dis-cothecque setting by playing hits of the decade and encouraging the clientle to dress in 1970s fashions. According to Gregson et al., in the con-text of the *70s Night* and similar events, such as bad taste parties (see Beattie, 1990), '70s fashion[s are] constructed ... as items of "apparel", as "outfits" that are motivated by the desire to produce bad taste' (2001: 5). This, in turn, suggest Gregson et al., plays a key role in the way that 1970s fashions are received and understood by the clientele of such events: 'The appropriate mode of appreciation here ... is about laughter: the wearing here is not about clever, knowing citation, but about fun, laughter and collectivity of "abject humiliation"' (ibid.).

This type of self-mocking 'anti-fashion' sense fits well with Grossberg's observation that contemporary youth tend 'to keep everything at a dis-tance, to treat everything ironically' (1994: 53). However, according to Gregson et al. the appropriation of 1970s retro-styles cannot uniformly be read in terms of such ironic and self-mocking sensibilities of style. Thus, they argue, a distinction needs to be made here between two distinct modes of appropriation which they term 'carnivalesque' and 'knowing-ness'. The carnivalesque mode of appropriation refers to that associated with the non-serious response to 1970s styles typically observed at 70s Nights. According to Gregson et al. this form of appropriation can be regarded as 'a theatrical form of fancy dress cum burlesque inspired by and thought to accompany the meanings (cheese and kitsch) inscribed in certain musical forms/genres of the period' (2001: 11). At a deeper level, they argue, playfulness effected through such non-serious appropriations of 1970s clothing may be seen as a collective attempt to suspend the pres-sures and responsibilities of the adult world. Thus, they argue 'this par-ticular wearing of the 70s is about a particular version of carnival, one grounded in re-imagined worlds of safe, childhood play' (ibid.: 12).

The second mode of appropriation identified by Gregson et al., that of 'knowingness' is informed by a more conventional range of fashion sensibilities. As Gregson et al. observe, 'knowing' consumers of 1970s retro-fashions tend to cite criteria such as quality of materials used and relative exclusivity of garments as informing their consumption choices. Furthermore, note Gregson et al., knowing consumers wear 1970s fash-ions 'as part of their routine, everyday dress rather than temporarily [as is the case with carnivalesque consumers of 70s clothing]' (ibid.). Indeed, through this example, Gregson et al. illustrate the complexity of late modern fashion sensibilities, the same resources being used to very different ends by different groups of consumers. Thus, through wearing 1970s fashions in everyday contexts, knowing consumers seek to articulate the 'authentic' rather than the 'ironic' qualities of such fashions. In doing so they utilise 1970s fashions 'as a means of demonstrating individuality, knowingness, knowledgeability and discernment, as an expression of their cultural capital, and as a way of constructing their difference from others' (ibid.: 16).

A similar sensibility can be identified with the bohemian look, a style of dressing that also involves the careful selection of clothing that does not conform with the mass-produced appearance of contemporary fashion items. As Wilson notes, the appearance of bohemians in western society coincided with the industrial revolution, the bohemian style of dress symbolising a form of resistance to industrialisation and the rationalised process of mass production to which it gave rise. According to Wilson: 'Bohemians used dress to signal inner authenticity and theatrical display *simultaneously*. To be a bohemian was to find an aesthetic expression for a sincerely felt alienation from the world of industrial capitalism' (1998: 239). During the course of the twentieth century, argues Wilson, bohemian qualities have been evident in a range of anti-establishment youth movements, from the beatniks of the 1950s and the hippie counter-culture of the late 1960s, through to more contemporary youth cultures such as punks and New Age Travellers. Each of the latter has been characterised by a collective desire to break with mainstream conventions and to create an alternative image based around a look that is out of step with late modern consumerist fashion sensibilities.

A further attempt to subvert contemporary fashion sensibilities is the movement referred to as 'deconstruction fashion', a style inspired by similar developments in architecture, graphic design and media which share a commitment 'to the undoing of modernist cultural forms' (Gill, 1998: 26). 'Deconstruction fashion' is characterised by a recycling of old clothing, and pieces of material, to produce new garments. Typically this involves the use of mismatched fabrics and the reversing to the outside of conventionally hidden 'mechanics of dress structure' such as darts, seams and zippers (ibid.: 27). According to Gill, the simultaneous act of creation and destruction is the key to understanding the personal feeling of authenticity that 'deconstruction fashion' supplies to the garment maker and, subsequently the wearer: '... the garment maker is simultaneously forming and deforming, constructing and destroying, making and undoing clothes. This biodirectional labor continues in dressing and wearing clothes, as clothes figure and disfigure the body, compose and decompose' (ibid.: 28).

Fashion and ethnic identity

Fashion also plays a significant role in the articulation of ethnic identity in contemporary everyday settings. As Back notes, ethnic identity, as with other forms of social identity, can no longer be regarded as '"real" or "essential"' but is rather a 'multi-faceted phenomenon which may vary through time and place' (1993: 128). A major factor informing the construction and articulation of ethnic identities through fashion has been cultural displacement. Forced to relocate to different parts of the world due to a variety of reasons, including slavery, poverty, and religious or political persecution, displaced ethnic minority groups invariably utilise cultural resources, such as dress and music, as a means of marking out new cultural spaces for themselves. This is particularly common among the youth of ethnic minorities.

During the 1970s, innovative work by Dick Hebdige (1979) examined how second generation members of African-Caribbean immigrant communities in Britain pioneered a series of stylistic innovations as a means of asserting a new form of black identity in the face of an urban environment which appeared increasingly hostile and exclusionary. Hebdige considered how a succession of stylistic innovations, beginning with the 'rude boy' look – a style which appropriated Italian 'sharp' suits, short-brimmed hats and dark glasses – sought to articulate a new expression of blackness on the streets of Britain. By the early 1970s, black youth style in Britain had evolved a new and far more radical look, modelled on the visual style of the Jamaican Rastafarian movement. This image become popular in a pan-Caribbean context due to its adoption by reggae artists such as Bob Marley and Peter Tosh (see Hebdige, 1987). Whereas earlier stylistic innovations of African-Caribbean youth in Britain had been readily adopted by white youth, for example in the case of mods and skinheads who both modelled their visual style on the look of the rude boy (Hebdige, 1979; see also Tulloch, 1993), the Rastafarian look was much more difficult for white youth to emulate. Thus, as Hebdige observes: 'The difference around which the whole Rasta style revolved was literally inscribed on the skin of black people and it was through appearance that this difference was to be extended, elaborated upon, realized' (1979: 43).

According to Price, from the point of view of African-Caribbean youth, the Rasta look 'helped to inject a much needed sense of ideological and cultural solidarity' (1981: 134). Rastas in Britain began to fashion an image which was, in keeping with the reggae artists whose music they listened to, more 'African'. Synthetic materials, such as mohair and terylene, were replaced with more 'natural' fibres such as wool and cotton. Similarly, while earlier black styles had drawn on western fashion items, the rasta look was distinctively non-western in appearance. For example, the short-brimmed hat was replaced by the 'tam', a roughly woven, loose fitting hat designed to be worn over dreadlocks, themselves a strong symbolisation of the rejection of western ideals. According to Cashmore, dreadlocks:

> ... were an element in redefining the black man to himself; to demonstrate that Rastas were prepared to go against the ideological grain and respond to white definitions with counter-definitions ... The appearance of locks celebrated blackness: made its quality and possession esteemed and positively valued. (1983: 158–9)

The significance of dreadlocks mirrors that of black pride as this manifested itself in the US during the early 1970s. As Mercer notes 'once "locks" were popularized on a mass scale – via the increasing militancy of reggae, especially – their dread logic inscribed a beautification of blackness' (1987: 424). A similar point is made by Willis who suggests that dreadlocks '[transpose] the difference already immanent in the acceptable openess of dark skin into open symbolic struggle (1990: 92).

Similar processes of ethnic identity construction facilitated through the appropriation of fashion and style can be seen in relation to other ethnic minority groups. Thus, for example, in her study of dress patterns among young women of Asian ethnicity in Britain, Khan identifies substantial changes during the last thirty years in attitudes towards the wearing of traditional dress. As Kahn observes, during the 1960s and 1970s attempts by mothers to impose traditional dress on their daughters created a high level of generational conflict: 'As a result, young women tended not so much to reject their culture as to keep it discreetly to themselves. British on the streets, Asian at home; one behaviour at school, another at home' (1993: 68).

Khan then goes on to describe how developments in the ensuing years functioned to change such perceptions of dress and tradition on the part of young Asian women. First, British-Asians travelling to the Indian subcontinent on holiday or to visit family became aware of a 'creative fashion explosion', centring around a new range of 'vivid imaginative clothes that explored and celebrated Indian roots' (ibid.). At the same time, a new generation of British-Asian women had absorbed the sensibilities of female independence prevalent in Britain and consequently felt less need to adhere to the constraints of tradition. Finally, the growth in number and strength of anti-racist groups galvanised a 'new consciousness' among young Asians (ibid.).

According to Khan, each of these factors were, in their own ways, responsible for significant changes in the way that young Asians began to view their culture and heritage. No longer were these regarded merely as a point of generational contention. Rather, they became important issues in the question of cultural identity. From the point of view of young Asian women, the issue of identity was played out stridently on the surface of the body. Fashion clothes modelled on traditional styles became a strong visual statement of a new sensibility of 'Asianness'. As Kahn explains, such fashions:

> ... found ready acceptance [among young female Asians] ... here were clothes that could take in both East and West, that didn't involve them in a choice between two different words, and that mirrored their confidence in presenting themselves on their own terms as Westernised Asian women. (ibid.: 70)

A similar sensibility is evident in Dwyer's study of young British-Muslim women where a number of respondents 'rejected the fixed meanings of "Asian" and "Western" clothes and attempt[ed] to offer new meanings which challenge[d] the "traditional"/"modern" dichotomy' (1998: 57). Such selective appropriation of fashion and style on the part of members of ethnic minorities and the reflexive identities to which they give rise are key to understanding the nature of ethnic identity in late modern, multi-ethnic societies. In late modernity, ethnic identities are as individually constructed and multiply staged as other forms of social identity. Tulloch (1993), for example, notes how contemporary black British youth, as with Muggleton's (2000) white post-subcultural stylists, draw from a range of black fashion and style in the creation of individual identities. Similarly, in examining the significance of hairstyle in the framing of ethnic identity, Willis suggests that:

> Young black people may choose and shift between many different available hairstyles, drawing on diverse sources for symbolic resources and stylistic inspiration, such as books, magazines of museums, as well as particular stars in music, fashion, film or sport. (1990: 93)

Conclusion

This chapter has examined the significance of fashion as a key resource through which individuals in late modernity construct their identities and position themselves in relation to others. As with other consumer products, it has been illustrated how, on entering the public domain, fashion items cease to be purely commodities and take on a range of everyday meanings. Such meanings derive in part from consumers themselves who inscribe fashion items with forms of significance grounded in everyday experience. A central aspect of the cultural work performed by fashion at an everyday level is its communication of visual messages about the status of the individual. It has been illustrated how fashion can serve a number of different roles in this respect. Thus, fashion can function as a symbol of power and a means to communicate wealth and individual success. Alternatively, it can be used as a means of signifying rejection of such status, with particular styles or ensembles of clothing displaying a commitment to bohemian or other alternative value systems. Similarly, retro and secondhand fashions are used to experiment with and modify identity, as evidenced, for example, in the 'dressing-up' or 'dressing-down' of individuals as they symbolically negotiate issues of class, economic and educational status. Fashion also facilitates strategies for the negotiation of other structurally proscribed identities, notably in relation to gender and ethnicity where, as this chapter has illustrated, particular features of one's identity can be modified or emphasised through the creative use of fashion garments.

Note

1. Although Muggleton was the first to offer a developed theory of 'post-subcultural youth', the term itself was first used by Redhead (1990).

SIX Music

At the level of daily life, music has power ... Music may influence how
people compose their bodies, how they conduct themselves, how they
experience the passage of time, how they feel – in terms of energy and
emotion – about themselves and others, and about situations. (DeNora,
2000: 16–17)

As the above observation from DeNora implies, to speak of the significance
of music in everyday life is to go considerably beyond issues of music-making
and the creativity of musicians. On the contrary, music informs everyday
life at a number of levels, 'participation' in music being effected as much
through consumption practices as through active involvement in process of
production (Bennett, 2000: 60). This aspect of musical life has been most
thoroughly investigated with regard to stylistic responses to music, particularly in relation to the young. Since the mid-1950s, genres of popular
music from rock 'n' roll onwards have inspired a range of visually distinctive styles through which young fans have both shown their attachment
to a particular music and marked themselves out from the wider society
(Hebdige, 1979; Chambers, 1985). However, the appeal and significance of
music in everyday life is by no means restricted to youth, nor to 'popular'
music. Research has illustrated how a variety of styles of music are actively
'used' by audiences in the context of their everyday lives. This chapter
addresses such everyday uses of music, examining a number of ways in
which music can be understood as a symbolic resource for late modern
individuals.

Music and the 'everyday'

In the context of contemporary society, music forms an integral part of
our everyday soundscape, featuring in a diverse array of social contexts

including fitness centres (DeNora, 2000), airport departure lounges, shopping malls and pubs/bars (Bennett, 1997). Similarly, the development of the personal stereo during the early 1980s facilitated a new way of consuming music, the personal listening choice of the individual providing a soundtrack for his/her phenomenological experience of the everyday world (Bull, 2000). Technology has also led to a significant re-ordering of the artist/audience divisions in music performance contexts. From underground dance music scenes, where computer technology has redefined what it means to be a 'musician' (Negus, 1992) to Karaoke bars, where audience and performers are essentially interchangeable (Drew, 1997, 2001, 2004), technological advances have had a considerable impact on the role and significance of music in everyday life.

The pervasive use of music in advertising and the growth of the retro market over the last twenty years has also seen a broadening of the relationship between music and lifestyle. Like fashion (see Chapter 5), music is now effectively used to articulate an increasingly diverse series of lifestyles within contemporary society. Similarly, music has also played a significant role in the construction and articulation of ethnic identities (see Stokes, 1994), while recent globally mediated musics such as rap and bhangra have given rise to new forms of trans-local diasporic communities whose shared experiences of displacement, racism and social exclusion have led to the forging of new forms of mutual identification and solidarity, the latter being symbolically realised through the common appropriation of musical texts (Gilroy, 1993).

Frith has suggested that what makes music special is 'the way in which it seems to make possible a new kind of self-recognition [and] frees us from the everyday routines and expectations that encumber our social identities' (1987: 144). In their appropriation and use of musical texts, individuals also symbolically engage with the everyday, the conventions of play, pleasure and protest associated with collective participation in music, facilitating a symbolic negotiation of everyday life in contemporary social settings. This point is reinforced by Grossberg who argues that an understanding of music 'requires asking what it gives to its fans, how it empowers them and how they empower it. What possibilities does it enable them to appropriate in their everyday lives?' (1986: 52). Although Grossberg is concerned here primarily with rock music and youth culture, his observations can be related to the role of music in everyday life more generally. Recent research illustrates how a whole range of musical styles, from rock (Weinstein, 2000) through jazz (Lopes, 2002) and folk (MacKinnon, 1994) are actively operationalised by audiences as a means of making sense of their everyday lives and positioning themselves in everyday contexts. As DeNora observes: 'Music is a device or resource to which people turn in order to regulate themselves as aesthetic agents, as feeling, thinking and acting beings in their day-to-day lives' (2000: 62).

Scene, community and subculture

A common way of mapping music's everyday significance has been through the use of one of three basic theoretical models, 'scene', 'community' and 'subculture'. What each of these models has in common is an attempt to understand the 'cultural' properties of music, that is, how particular styles of music are appropriated by groups of individuals and used as a means of collectively distinguishing themselves from other social groups.

Scene

An early attempt to map the cultural significance of music using a scene perspective is Becker's (1951) study of professional jazz musicians. According to Becker, central to the jazz music scene is the notion of a distinction between musicians and their audience:

> The musician is conceived of as an artist who possesses a mysterious artistic gift setting him apart from all other people. Possessing this gift, he should be free from control by outsiders who lack it. The gift is something which cannot be acquired through education; the outsider, therefore cannot become a member of the group. (in Denisoff and Peterson, 1972: 249)

Becker notes how jazz musicians consolidated their felt sense of collective association and scene membership through reference to non-musicians as 'squares', the latter bespeaking a range of characteristics inherent in the non-musician including an inappropriate understanding of music: 'The square is thought of as an ignorant, intolerant person who is to be feared, since he produces the pressures forcing the musicians to play inartistically' (ibid.: 252). More recent applications of the scenes perspective have cast 'scene' as encompassing a broader range of musical and extra-musical practices (see, for example, Bennett and Peterson, 2004). Within this context a variety of individual investments in music find collective forms of articulation and expression; scene membership covers a wide spectrum of activities which, in addition to performance, also includes production, promotion, journalism and consumption (Lopes, 2002).

The significance of music scenes in everyday life is argued by some to be accentuated by their embeddedness in local circumstances. For example, Shank's (1994) empirical study of the local music-making scene in Austin, Texas, maps the continuities between local networks of social relationships and the building and maintenance of the local music scene. Similarly, Cohen's (1991) study of the local music scene in Liverpool argues that the basic attitudes and outlook of local musicians towards music-making is inherently bound up with their socio-economic circumstances. Thus, observes Cohen:

> ... in a city where the attitude was that you might as well pick up a guitar as take exams, since your chances of finding full-time occupation from each were just the same, being in a band was an accepted way of life and could provide a means of justifying one's existence. (1991: 2)

Other work on scenes has questioned the extent to which they can be understood as purely local phenomena. Straw suggests that music scenes transcend particular localities 'reflect[ing] and actualiz[ing] a particular state of relations between various populations and social groups, as these coalesce around particular coalitions of musical style' (1991: 379). This observation is supported by Hodkinson (2002, 2004) whose work on the goth scene demonstrates how this is maintained by trans-local networks of fans, musicians and entrepreneurs. Finally, Peterson and Bennett (2004) note how increasing access to the internet has given rise to 'virtual' music scenes made up of fans whose interaction takes place purely or primarily in online contexts such as chatrooms and Email-lists.

Community

Community has been applied to the study of music in two main ways. First as an means of addressing the way in which locally produced musics become a means through which individuals identify with a particular city, town or region and their place within it. Thus, as Lewis notes: 'People look to specific musics as symbolic anchors in regions, as signs of community, belonging, and a shared past' (1992: 144). This point is reinforced by Dawe and Bennett who suggest that: 'Music is a particularly potent representational resource ... a means by which communities are able to identify themselves and present this identity to others' (2001: 4). The second application of community to music focuses on the significance of community as a symbolic construct, that is, as a means through which individuals who lack the commonality of shared local experience attempt to cast music itself as a 'way of life' and a basis for community. A pertinent example here is the significance attached to rock music by the hippie counter-culture of the late 1960s. As Frith observes: '"Community" became something that was created by the music, that described the musical experience. This was the ideology that became central to rock' (1981: 167). A similar sensibility of community is apparent in the use of music as a bonding device for followers of indie (independent) music.[1] According to Fonarow, central to indie music is 'an emotional feeling of community and connectedness' between musicians and their audiences (1997: 364). At a performative level, this community spirit is accentuated through the shortness and simplicity of indie songs and the emphasis on small venues, factors which indie musicians and their fans use to collectively articulate their sense of authenticity and distinctiveness from fans of more obviously 'commercial' and 'packaged' chart musics (Bennett, 2001a).

Subculture

The third and perhaps most widely used conceptual model in the study of collective responses to music is 'subculture'. Originally introduced by the Chicago School as a means of providing sociological explanations of crime and deviance, in the early 1970s subculture was adopted by cultural theorists at the Birmingham Centre for Contemporary Cultural Studies (CCCS) researching youth cultural groups of post-war Britain such as teddy boys, mods and punks (Hall and Jefferson, 1976; Hebdige, 1979; see also Chapters 1 and 5). Although the CCCS used subculture more directly in relation to youth style rather than music, post-CCCS work on youth culture has increasingly applied subculture to the collective appropriation and use of music itself. For example, in her study of heavy metal Weinstein suggests that the collective consumption of heavy metal music in the context of live concerts does much to affirm the metal subculture, its collective values and sense of community. In effect, the heavy metal audience asserts a collective ownership of the music. Thus, as Weinstein observes:

> The songs performed by the band embody the values of the subculture. The ones that the band selects are not randomly chosen from its repertoire, particularly if it has released several albums. Concert favorites are those giving voice to subcultural themes by idealizing them. (2000: 218)

A further example of music's 'subcultural' significance is provided in Sardiello's account of Deadheads (fans of psychedelic rock group The Grateful Dead). As Sardiello notes, within the highly complex 'Deadhead' subculture which grew up around the band, a number of fans, described as hardcore Deadheads, deemed it necessary to attend as many concerts as possible. These fans organised their lives around the touring schedule of the band, taking on 'transient jobs, such as restaurant work, so they can travel' and thus retain their membership of the Deadhead subculture (1998: 132).

Music and youth

During the 1950s, youth became an obvious target for the emergent post-Second World War leisure industries. Being in full time employment but still living in parental homes, 16–21 year olds were among the most afflu-ent of post-war consumers (Bocock, 1993). The consequent boom in 'youth' products had a significant impact on youth leisure, while also altering the status of youth:

> Leisure was no longer simply a moment of rest and recuperation from work, the particular zone of family concerns and private edification. It was widened into a potential life-style made possible by consumerism. To buy a particular record, to choose a jacket or skirt cut to a particular fashion, to mediate carefully on the colour of your shoes is to open a door onto an actively constructed style of living. (Chambers, 1985: 16)

As Chambers illustrates here, through their appropriation of music and associated stylistic products, young people simultaneously acquired new sensibilities. Music, and the related 'accessories' of youth, became part of a lifestyle project, a means of articulating a series of identity statements designed to mark off 'youth' from the parent culture. The relevance of music in this respect is evident in the responses of young people to the first actively marketed 'youth' music, rock 'n' roll. According to Bradley, rock 'n' roll became a soundtrack for a youth rebellion, a means of 'resisting certain widespread discourses about what was possible and permissible' (1992: 125). During screenings of the first rock 'n' roll film, 'Rock Around the Clock' in 1956, young audiences danced in the aisles of cinemas and ripped out seats (Street, 1992). The resultant banning of the film in Holland led to street protests as young people 'demonstrate[d] for their right to see the film' (Mutsaers, 1990: 307).

The relationship between rock 'n' roll and its young audience was fur-ther enhanced by the image and demeanour of rock 'n' roll performers themselves. As Frith (1983) observes, post-war pop idols such as Elvis Presley and the Beatles were both the same age and from the same socio-economic backgrounds as the young fans who bought their records and attended their concerts. Thus, these artists were readily adopted as role models by young audiences. The apparent 'naturalness' of the association between rock 'n' roll performers and their audiences was further accentuated by their representation in the media. In an account of Elvis Presley's early TV appearances, Shumway notes how 'the audience becomes part of the show ... the film cut[ting] between shots of Elvis and shots of the audience ... whose response tells us of the excitement the performer is generating' (1992: 127).

As the above observations begin to reveal, key to an understanding of the significance of rock 'n' roll and subsequent genres of post-war popular music for young people is their role in the establishment of new cultural territories for young people within the context of everyday life. Such territories became crucial sites for the formulation of collective 'youth' identities through which young people could symbolically negotiate their disempowered status in society. According to Grossberg:

> Rock emerged as a way of mapping the specific structures of youth's affective alienation on the geographies of everyday life, and the specific differences of youth's social identity on the grid of socially defined differences. Rock was a response to a certain kind of loneliness and uncertainty: it was about the ways in which youth itself offers new possibilities of identification and belonging through the construction of temporary mattering maps. For youth inhabited a place in the social order which demands that they live according to someone else's maps, someone else's dreams, someone else's trajectories. (1992: 179)

This interplay between popular music and the cultural sensibilities of youth intensified during the 1960s and 1970s when rock music became more overtly political. The hippie movement of the late 1960s attempted to harness the cultural power of music as a means of changing the world order, rejecting the technocratic tendencies (Roszak, 1969) of capitalist society and opting instead for an alternative lifestyle based around rural communal living (Webster, 1976; see also Chapter 8) and experimentation with Eastern religion and mind altering drugs, notably LSD[2] (Hall, 1968). Indeed, the collective investment made in the power of music as a means for social change was perhaps more prominent in the late 1960s than in any other era of post-war popular music before or since. As Eyerman and Jamison observe: 'Movement ideas, images, and feelings were disseminated in and through popular music and, at the same time, the movements of the times influenced developments, in both form and content, in popular music' (1998: 108).

A decade later the punk rock scene in Britain mobilised a similarly significant form of youth resistance directed against the downturn of the British economy and the apparent refusal of the British establishment to acknowledge the deepening socio-economic crisis in the country. Punk music, angry and discordant, resonated with the mindset of young punk followers whose visual image incorporated a satirical defacement of imagery associated with the national culture, notably the British flag and pictures of the Queen. According to Chambers:

> Through their music and stylistic commitment, [punks] suggested and enlarged the spaces for subversive cultural 'play' ... Punk proclaimed the necessity of violating the quiet, everyday script of common sense. It proposed a macabre parody of the underlying idealism of 'Englishness' – that dour pragmatism that sees no future beyond the present, and no present except that inherited, apparently unmodified, from the past. (1985: 185)

A more contemporary example of the resonance between musical significance and socio-economic circumstances can be seen in the case of 'extreme' metal, whose dialogic engagement with urban problems and diminishing life chances for young people has generated a global following for this metal subgenre (Harris, 2000). Writing about the appeal of extreme metal, Kotarba suggests that this can be largely attributed to 'the ability of the narrative to collectively conceptualize individual experiences of growing up' (1994: 143), while Harrell goes further, defining extreme metal as an 'unofficial expression of industrialism's emotional isolation and violence' (1994: 91). This point is developed by Berger (1999) who maps a series of continuities between the aggressive and disturbing tonal textures achieved in extreme metal music and the everyday experiences of extreme metal musicians and fans. Thus, according to Berger, the frustration and anxiety associated with socio-economic dislocation and the onset of risk and uncertainty (Beck, 1992) in the daily lives of these young people finds an expressive voice in extreme metal music. As Berger observes:

> [Extreme] metal's heaviness and affects have not sprung from the pristine individuality of the composer's soul; they have been constituted by the practices of social actors operating within numerous contexts, including the development of pop metal and the deindustrialization of Britain and the United States. The participants' exploration of grim emotions has not occurred as some autonomous aesthetic project but is used to serve the broader purposes of casting away obstacles, motivating the self, and clearing a path for action. (1999: 272)

Berger's interpretation of extreme metal's cultural significance illustrates how the popularity of this style among young audiences relates to its correspondence, both lyrically and musically, with their everyday experiences of the risks and uncertainties associated with post-industrial society. Extreme metal moves its audience at a visceral level, providing a collective platform for them to experience emotions of anger and frustration 'without having to suffer the consequences' (ibid.)

For over half a century then, music has been a key resource for successive generations of young people, facilitating the articulation of a form of everyday politics. Given youth's disempowered status, music and attendant stylistic resources have functioned as one of the few accessible means of articulating an oppositional stance and establishing an alternative cultural space. Moreover, while many instances of youth *resistance* are short-lived, with even radical forms of music such as punk and grunge ultimately being appropriated by the mainstream music industry (Hebdige, 1979), the role of music as a 'voice' for youth has proved to be one of continual development and change. In every generation, emergent styles of music have reflected at some level the socio-economic circumstances of youth.

Music and ethnic identity

Music also plays a significant part in relation to ethnic identity as this is constructed, articulated and experienced in the context of everyday life. As noted in Chapter 5, patterns of migration and resultant socio-cultural displacement have led ethnic minority groups to seek ways of culturally relocating themselves in new surroundings. Music has proved to be a very important cultural resource in this respect. As Stokes observes: 'The musical event, from collective dances to the act of putting a cassette or CD into a machine, evokes and organises collective memories and present experiences of place with an intensity, power and simplicity unmatched by any other social activity' (1994: 3). The key function of music, according to Stokes, lies in its ability to readily articulate a collective sense of cultural identity. Inscribed in the musical text are a range of cultural referents which are instantly brought to life through the act of performance, dancing and singing. Participation in this musicalised enactment of collective cultural identities plays a highly important role in the lives of displaced ethnic minority groups.

If music provides an important underpinning for the articulation of particularised expressions of ethnic identity in given regional and urban settings, then it also performs an important bridging function, symbolically connecting diaspora populations. Significant here is the work of Gilroy (1993) which illustrates how the commercial appropriation of ethnic minority musics from the US and the Caribbean and their transformation into globally mediated popular music styles has given rise to trans-local expressions of ethnic identity. Examining this process in relation to reggae music, Gilroy notes how, due to its appropriation and marketing by the global music industry, reggae ceased 'to signify an exclusively ethnic, Jamaican style and derived a different kind of cultural legitimacy both from a new global status and from its expression of what might be termed a pan-Caribbean culture' (1993: 82). This point echoes that of Hebdige (1979) who considers how reggae, in conjunction with the Rastafarian image of leading reggae artists such as Bob Marley, was locally reworked by African-Caribbean youth in Britain during the mid-1970s as a means of establishing a cultural space for themselves and symbolically resisting the racism and social exclusion to which they were subjected on a day-to-day basis (see also Chapter 5).

In more recent times, rap music has been similarly reworked by the youth of ethnic minorities in cities around the world. Originating in the Bronx district of New York during the early 1970s as part of an African-American street culture known as hip hop, which also included break-dancing and graffiti (see Rose, 1994), rap became globally popular during the early 1980s due to the huge commercial success of rappers such as Ice T and Run DMC. As with reggae, key to rap's early appeal was its significance as a new urban soundtrack for the disenchanted youth of African-diasporic communities. Back (1996) notes how the early rap scene in London was dominated by black British artists who took their inspiration from the African-American rap music being played on the radio and MTV but reworked this to suit a British context. Similarly, black French rap artist MC Solaar, through asserting the thematic and aesthetic distinctiveness of his music from that of African-American rappers (see Huq, 1999), has also contributed to rap's profile as a global soundtrack for the youth African-diasporic groups. Significantly, however, rap also began to appeal to a wider global youth audience from a variety of different ethnic backgrounds. In Germany, for example, Turkish and Moroccan youth combined the sounds of commercial African-American rap with the traditional music of their parent cultures, often adding Turkish or Moroccan lyrics (Bennett, 1999, 2000; Kaya, 2001). The thematic content of these lyrics generally focused on local issues such as problems experienced by non-German nationals in obtaining German citizenship and the resurgence of fascism in Germany. As Bennett notes, young rappers from Turkish, Moroccan and other ethnic minority backgrounds in Germany 'began to make the realisation that, as with African-Americans, theirs was a 'distinct mode of lived [ethnicity]' which demanded its own localised and particularised mode of expression' [Gilroy, 1993: 82] (2000: 140).

Parallel instances of localised rap music can be seen in Bjurström's (1997) research on rap and ethnic minority youth in Stockholm and in Mitchell's (1996) work on Maori hip hop culture in Autearoa/New Zealand. In each case, young rappers have taken 'the basic tenets of the rap style [and] reworked [these] in ways that incorporate local knowledges and sensibilities, thus transforming rap into a means of communication that works in the context of specific localities' (Bennett, 2001b: 93–4).

Music has played a similarly important role in enabling the youth of South Asian minorities across Europe and other parts of the world to establish a cultural space for themselves. During the early 1980s, young Asian musicians in London, Birmingham and other British cities developed a fusion music which combined bhangra, a traditional Punjabi folk music, with aspects of western popular music. According to Banerji and Baumann, 'bhangra-beat', as this style became known, 'was exactly what the new generation wanted. Young, fresh, lively and modern, it was as genuinely Indian as it was recognisably disco' (1990: 142). In the early 1990s bhangra-beat was superseded by a series of post-bhangra Asian styles that drew on new electronic dance music forms such as house and techno (Bennett, 2001b). From the point of view of South Asian youth, bhangra provided a means of cultural expression that they had hitherto been denied due to both parental pressure and also because of stereotypical images attached to South Asian ethnic minorities by white Britons. As Huq observes, from the point of view of mainstream white British society, South Asians were 'considered unhip ... submissive, hard-working, passive and conformist' (1996: 63).

From the point of view of young South Asians themselves, this process of exclusion was exacerbated through their own contradictory experience of living in Britain. Despite being distanced from the pre-emigration values of their parents (Baumann, 1997) and more readily familiar with the everyday cultural sensibilities, 'styles, speech and consumption patterns' of the urban localities in which they had grown up, young South Asians still found it hard to integrate into everyday British cultural life (Bhachu, 1991: 408). Bhangra and post-bhangra styles thus became a resource for the forging of a new 'Br-Asian' identity in response to the contradictory position that young South Asians continued to find themselves in, their integration into everyday British cultural life being blocked by prevailing racist stereotypes (Kaur and Kalra, 1996). As Kaur and Kalra observe, Br-Asian signified a new cultural territory for South Asian youth, positioned between the cultural sensibilities of their parent culture and those of white Britain. This new Br-Asian youth culture also contested the cultural and religious divisions that characterised its parent culture, arguing that such tensions 'do little to resolve the marginalization, exclusion and hostility to which Asians in Britain are subjected' (Bennett, 2001b: 112). According to Kaur and Kalra, bhangra and post-bhangra styles function as 'an accessible and universal forum for articulating this dynamic social flux' (1996: 218).

Music and pub culture

While the everyday significance of music has been most readily noted in relation to more overtly socio-political contexts, involving issues of power, resistance and cultural identity, music also plays an important role within a range of more mundane everyday settings. One such setting is the 'pub' (that is, public house) or bar. Many pubs have at least one jukebox, while many others have televisions tuned into MTV or comparable music channels. The pub has long served as an important setting for the collective enjoyment of music. An illustrative example of this is Pickering's account of Juniper Hill, a nineteenth-century public house in rural Oxfordshire where patrons 'gathered nightly to consume a very moderate amount of ale, to discuss local events, work and politics, to tell stories and to sing' (1984: 481). The tradition of pub singing continues to the present day. For example, many pubs, particularly those which cater for an older clientele feature a resident pianist or organist, whose repertoire of old-time standards is designed to encourage 'sing-songs' (Finnegan, 1989).

Pubs are also favourite venues for folk clubs, weekly music events made up of regulars who take it in turn to sing folk songs with other members of the audience joining in. Significantly, although folk clubs draw on the age-old practice of pub singing, the folk music scene itself has a relatively recent history, emerging from the folk revival of the 1950s and 1960s (MacKinnon, 1993). In its early stages of development, the British folk club scene in Britain attempted to 'reinvent' a folk music tradition, a project which necessarily involved a nostalgic and highly romanticised view of the past. At the heart of this attempt was an ideology borrowed from the American folk revival movement (see Frith, 1983) which stressed the organic, and thus 'authentic', nature of folk music as compared with the artificialness of commercially produced pop music. In recent years, however, this emphasis on recreation of past traditions has become less important and folk clubs are now primarily regarded as spaces for 'live, accessible, small-scale music-making' (MacKinnon, 1993: 66).

Pubs also serve as important venues for the production and consumption of more contemporary music styles, notably rock and pop. As a number of studies illustrate, much of the appeal of rock and pop performances in pub venues centres around the intimacy of the pub setting and the ready forms of interaction between performer and audience. Moreover, in some cases, pub venues have become key spaces for celebrations of local identity which are articulated through the performances of local bands. Thus, as Bennett notes:

> ... as a primary locus for forms of local social exchange, the pub, perhaps more than any other venue in which music is featured, acts to particularise processes of musical production and consumption, particularly in cases where band and audience are already linked by common local roots. In the context of the pub venue, local musicians and their audiences become highly attuned to the commonality of social experience which bonds them together, this in turn playing a decisive role in framing the politics of performance and reception. (2000: 169)

Bennett develops this observation in ethnographic work on local pub rock performers and their audiences in the northern English cities of Hull and Newcastle. As Bennett observes, in the case of each setting, local performers and audiences were known to each other outside the performance context. As such, their shared everyday local experiences became an integral part of the performance. In-jokes, drawing upon locally understood anecdotes and the particularities of local dialect were often exchanged between artists and audiences during performances. Moreover, such was the bond between artist and audience, that songs performed 'would often be associated primarily with the local band or singer that performed [them] rather than with the original artist' (1997: 101). In Newcastle, this bonding between local musicians and their audience assumed a heightened level with the 'Benwell Floyd', a local Pink Floyd tribute band, successfully enmeshing the band and audience's shared sense of attachment to their locality, the district of Benwell in Newcastle, with a common love of Pink Floyd music. Again, the intimacy of the pub venue acted as a facilitator of this interaction between local and musicalised dialogue between band and audience:

> ... each of the [Benwell Floyd's] performances becomes simultaneously a celebration of musical taste and a celebration of regional place, vernacular and musical discourses being simultaneously interwoven. Similarly, the name of the band itself constitutes a dually articulated cultural statement combining as it does a statement of musical taste with one of regional identity. (Bennett, 2000: 191)

A further example of such vernacularisation of popular music texts in the pub setting is provided in Björnberg and Stockfelt's study of *Skansen*, a local bar in the north-east Danish town of Skagen. The focus of this study are Sussi & Leo, a local pop-cover duo whose weekly performances in *Skansen* earned them a form of local cult status. Björnberg and Stockfelt attribute this to the way in which Sussi & Leo's performances extend beyond a simple musical event to articulate a shared feeling of community between themselves and pub regulars:

> ... the musicians were part of a larger 'affinity group', a 'charmed circle of like-minded' makers of an activity in which the music-making was the foremost public facet, but only one of several essential components. In this activity, the perpetuation and nightly widening of the affinity group in itself appears to be one of the most important constituents. (1996: 142)

The significance of the pub venue as a space in which musicalised and vernacular discourses become interwoven has been further illustrated in recent years through the increasing popularity of Karaoke events, during which pub patrons are invited to take to the stage and sing songs of their choosing accompanied by specially produced backing tracks. Karaoke originated in Japan in 1972 when the proprietor of a bar in the city of Kobe decided it was economically more viable to arrange backing-tape accompaniment for the singers he hired rather than pay for bands (Drew, 1997). As Drew explains: 'Soon customers wanted to take turns at the microphone themselves ... As it caught on among amateur singers, Karaoke bars opened throughout Japan' (ibid.: 450).

Within a short time, Karaoke had become a global phenomenon. Drew (2001, 2004) identifies several distinct patterns of participation in Karaoke events which, he argues, relate to the particular setting in which Karaoke is staged. Thus, he suggests, in transient spaces, such as hotel bars and airport lounges, Karaoke participants tend to exhibit a sense of release and abandon, safe in the knowledge that within such settings they are relatively anonymous. In local pubs or bars, however, a very different Karaoke sensibility is evident, one which engenders a sense of community between 'regulars' for whom participation in Karaoke is part of a wider social scene. According to Drew: 'Performers themselves often highlight the coherence and support of the Karaoke crowd ... As this social world develops around Karaoke, performers increasingly relate to one another as colleagues or team members' (1997: 460).

In some ways, Karaoke events function in a similar fashion to the performance of folk music in pub settings. The musical event is small scale and relatively accessible; anyone who wishes to can contribute to the evening's entertainment through singing a song of their choosing. This in turn ensures that the barriers between performer and audience are broken down, those on the stage being interchangeable with members of the audience. Moreover, Karaoke extends this sense of accessibility through offering participants in Karaoke events a special form of ownership of the text. Thus, individuals can interpret songs in particular ways, bringing something of themselves to the music. As Fornäs observes:

> Users of Karaoke have the opportunity not only to be listening meaning-makers, but also to be singing sound-makers and to see and hear their own voices in the hybrid audio-visual fabric that results ... [They] sing in styles and to recordings over which [they] have no autonomous control, but [their] voices can nonetheless express something unique and make each perfor-mance special. (1994: 97)

As with the performance of folk music in pubs then, it could be argued that Karaoke constitutes a further example of how pub and bar settings offer spaces for small-scale and accessible music-making opportunities.

Music and urban soundscapes

Another way of understanding music's significance in everyday life is as an element of urban soundscapes. Thus, it is argued, late modern indi-viduals increasingly experience music as part of the wider urban experience, music being heard in the street, in shopping centres, public transport ter-minals, in restaurants and so on. As Lanza observes, 'moments of Muzak synchronicity ... occur at different times of the day, from place to place, city to city, state to state, and country to country, when the music com-ing out of an elevator, office, airport or department store seems suddenly to be playing our song' (1994: 59).

This spontaneous association with and appropriation of musical texts in urban spaces in turn has a bearing on the ways in which individuals experience those spaces, both influencing individual perceptions of place and enhancing the reflexive dynamic through which individuals locate themselves in particular places. Thus, according to DeNora: 'Within social spaces ... prominent music may allude to modes of aesthetic agency – feeling, being, moving, acting – and so may place near-to-hand certain aesthetic styles that can be used as referents for configuring agency in real time' (2000: 123).

Technology has also played its part in informing the way that music is experienced in everyday contexts. In particular, the invention of the per-sonal stereo during the early 1980s provided a new level of musicalised experience, the musical space of the individual listener merging with the public spaces through which the listener passes and temporarily resides during the course of the day. Research on the personal stereo has suggested that a key part of its appeal is the way in which it facilitates a new level of personal management of everyday life through allowing individuals more freedom in terms of choosing the soundscape which accompanies their daily activities. In an early study of the 'Walkman', the first commercially marketed personal stereo, Hosokawa offers the following observation:

> The practical meaning of the walkman [sic] is generated in the distance it poses between the reality and the real, the city and the urban, and the particularity between the others and the I. It decontextualises the given coherence of the city-text, and at the same time, contextualises every situation which seemingly does not cohere with it. (1984: 171)

Central to Hosokawa's interpretation of the Walkman is an understanding of its aesthetic value in the formulation of everyday narrative. Pickering and Green have suggested that: 'Songs constitute ways of handling the empirically experienced world ... supporting or challenging "how things are"' (1987: 3). The Walkman, and more recent personal stereo formats, such as the minidisk player and the IPod, allow for a more ready and dramatic transposition of song narratives, as selected by the individual listener, into the narrative of the everyday. Scenes and scenarios witnessed and experienced by the individual at the everyday level, are organised and made sense of in relation to his/her personalised music programme, which becomes a soundtrack for the everyday. This idea is developed by Bull who discusses a range of uses to which the personal stereo is put in what he terms the 'management' of everyday life. Thus, argues Bull, many personal stereo users use music as a means of structuring the time spent engaged in everyday activities such as, for example, the journey from home to work. According to Bull:

> Users can either package time into segments, moving towards the journey's end, or concentrate on mood maintenance that overcomes the journey time. Users sometimes record the same piece repeatedly onto the same tape or repeatedly rewind to listen to the same piece in order to achieve this level of time suspension. (2000: 56)

Alternatively, suggests Bull, the personal stereo facilitates the use of music as a way of modifying his/her experience of the outside world: 'The use of personal stereos replaces the sounds of the outside world with an alternative soundscape which is more immediate and subject to greater control' (ibid.: 78). Furthermore, argues Bull, personal stereos may also offer the listener a new level of sensory experience in relation to the everyday.

The experience of listening to a personally selected programme of music while immersed in everyday urban settings introduces a new aesthetic dimension into the relationship between aural and visual stimuli. As Bull observes: 'The use of personal stereos greatly expands the possibilities for users to aesthetically recreate their daily experience ... Personal-stereo users often refer to their experiences as being 'cinematic' in nature' (ibid.: 86). Thus, the personal stereo offers users an opportunity to negotiate the mundane predictability of the everyday by observing it through a cinematic lens, the factual and fictional blurring together and allowing for alternative narratives of the everyday to be engaged in by the listener. From the point of view of the personal stereo user, this cinematic experience of everyday life via musical texts is enhanced through his/her previous exposure to film and television, where the associative qualities of music are often creatively exploited to achieve effect. Thus, for example, contemporary urban street dramas will often make use of rap music, whose pre-formed association with street culture creates a particular sort of experience for the audience (Watkins, 1998).

Music and advertising

A further way in which music enters the vocabulary of the everyday is through its use in advertising. In particular, and as Kaplan (1987) notes, since the launch of MTV in 1981 the tie-ins between music and advertising have become increasingly more seductive, with a whole range of youth lifestyle products being packaged in commercials designed to fit seamlessly within MTV's 24-hour music programming. However, the use of music in advertising was a selling strategy long before the launch of MTV. Moreover, it is not only youth who have been targeted by commercials featuring music. Since the early 1970s, a wide range of lifestyle products for all ages have been promoted in advertisements which have used music as a key selling point. The music used in such advertisements has ranged variously from rock and easy listening to country and even classical music – celebrated examples including the use of 'Morning' from Grieg's 'Peer Gynt Suite' in an advertisement for Nescafé and the adoption of Orff's atmospheric 'Carmina Burana' in the promotion of Old Spice aftershave.

Critics sometimes decry the use of classical music in this way, suggesting that its reduction to a selling strategy denudes the music of its artistic integrity. However, it is clear that such commercial use of classical music can have a broadly opposite effect, raising the status of both the music and the performer considerably. For example, the BBC's decision to use Italian opera singer Luciano Pavarotti's rendition of Puccini's

'Nessun Dorma' as theme music for coverage of the 1990 World Cup in Italy resulted in the song going to number one in the charts and elevating Pavarotti to the status of a popular music performer. The following year Pavarotti gave a free concert in London's Hyde Park before 10,000 people. Media coverage of the event suggested that many members of the audience were those previously deterred from opera by its elitist aura and high ticket prices (see Storey, 1997).

Chart songs have also been frequently used in advertisements. Indeed, a number of chart songs, for example The New Seekers' 'I'd Like To Teach The World To Sing' and Babylon Zoo's 'Spaceman', became hits because of their use in advertisments. Even 'serious' pop artists such as Madonna have apparently suffered no loss of artistic integrity through their music being featured in advertisements (Savan, 1993). Similarly, contemporary popular music artist Moby, effectively consolidated his reputation as a critically revered songwriter and composer with his 1999 album 'Play', a record that received a great deal of publicity when several of its tracks were featured in stylish television commercials. According to Strinati (1995), the successful combination of music and advertising in this way relates to a new commercial logic that reflects a more astute understanding on the part of advertising companies as to how individuals relate to mediated images. Thus, in the media-saturated context of late modernity, individuals are more apt to apply their own meanings to images, to construct their own relationship between the sign and signified (Baudrillard, 1993). This has led to a new way of advertising products which centres around the creative juxtaposition of images and sounds. Thus, according to Strinati:

> ... advertisements used to tell us how valuable and useful a product was. Now, however, they say less about the product directly, and are more concerned with parodying advertising itself by citing other adverts, by using references drawn from popular culture and by self-consciously making clear their status as advertisements. (1995: 232–3)

One notable exception to this trend in advertising is the use of 'classic' rock and pop hits from the 1950s to the 1970s in stylish advertisements for products aimed at affluent baby boomer audiences. As Frith observes:

> What is striking about ... advertisers' use of music is that the tracks they choose are those that were, as hits, the most 'meaningful', in terms of youth culture, soul, emotion, or 'art'. Most agencies don't use rock songs simply as a lazy way of reaching the 'popular' audience; tracks are selected for *what* they stand for. (1990: 90)

A pertinent example of this is the use of Steppenwolf's 'Born To Be Wild', made famous through its use as the title track for the 1969 counter-cultural road movie *Easy Rider* (see Denisoff and Romanowski, 1991), in a 2001 advertisement for the Ford Cougar. The advertisement features original *Easy Rider* co-star, Dennis Hopper, as the driver of the Ford Cougar. Through the use of state-of-the-art digital editing, the present day Hopper is joined on the road by Billy, the character he portrays in *Easy Rider*, on his chopperised Harley Davidson motorcycle in a direct reference to the film. This juxtapositioning of the past with the present is specifically designed to appeal to the ageing baby boomer consumer by alerting them to the product – the car – through the medium of memory and nostalgia. The choice of the 1960s icon, Hopper, is significant in providing a link between 'then' and 'now'. As Frith notes, this style of advertising involves the playing back of 'old rock values – brash individualism [and] youthful rebellion ... as memories and longings that can only be reached by spending money on other goods' (1990: 90).[3]

Music and generation

At the level of the everyday, it is clear that this circulation of images and references from the 1960s contributes not only to a feeling of nostalgia among members of the baby boomer generation but also plays a significant part in how they construct their present-day identities. According to Ross:

> ... an entire parental generation [is] caught up in the fantasy that they are themselves still youthful, or at least more culturally radical, in ways once equated with youth, than the youth of today ... It is not just Mick Jagger and Tina Turner who imagine themselves to be eighteen years old and steppin' out; a significant mass of baby boomers partially act out this belief in their daily lives. (1994: 8)

In this sense, argues Ross, baby boomers indulge in an over-romanticisation of the 1960s as a 'golden age' of youth culture, which is then used as a means of assessing and evaluating the rebelliousness and 'authenticity' of contemporary youth cultures (Bennett, 2001b). In the sphere of popular journalism this has resulted in a number of searing attacks on contemporary youth who are accused of being passive and disaffected (Young, 1985; Forrest, 1994). This alleged characteristic of youth is notably addressed by Young though his assertion that:

> The term 'youth culture' is at best, of historical value only, since the customs and mores associated with it have been abandoned by your actual young person ... The point is that today's teenager is no longer promiscuous, no longer takes drugs, and rarely goes to pop concerts. He leaves all that to the over-25's ... Whatever the image adopted by teenagers now, it has to have one necessary condition: it must have nothing to do with being a teenager. (1985: 246)

More recent research, however, suggests that rather than uniformly serving to accentuate generational divisions in this way, music may also perform a bonding role between parents and siblings. In a review of a concert by Pink Floyd at Earl's Court in 1994, journalist Adam Sweeting wrote: 'IT ISN'T JUST [sic] the 30-to-50-somethings who are flocking Floydwards. There's a new generation of listeners in their teens and twenties, who have been brought up to revere the Pink Floyd imprimatur by parents or older siblings' (1994: 8).

Sweeting's observation is supported by Bennett's study of the Newcastle Pink Floyd tribute band the 'Benwell Floyd'. Noting that most members of the band were in their teens or early twenties, Bennett asked where they had initially acquired their liking for Pink Floyd music. The band members' responses were suggestive of an informal music education in the family home through which musical tastes were handed down from one generation to the next. Thus, as the band's drummer commented: '[Pink] Floyd have been up that long ... they've been making records since 1967, they're still doing it now ... so there's that wider audience ... I've been brought up with 'em me ... my brother's always loved 'em since being a young lad and I've always liked 'em from being a young lad' (Bennett, 2000: 180).

According to Bennett, this resonance between musical taste and family life results in a highly particularised series of meanings. Music, in this case the music of Pink Floyd, provides a sonic underpinning, and immediately accessible point of reference, for treasured family memories from childhood to adulthood. As Bennett observes, when the Benwell Floyd performs live and family members are present in the audience, the performance becomes in part:

> ... a celebration ... of musicalised moments which have accumulated over the years and which have made the performance possible. When the band and their families sing the words to certain Pink Floyd songs, they are collectively reliving the memories which, for them, have become woven into the understanding of such songs. Similarly, the performance of certain musical phrases can also elicit collective meanings which, for particular family groups, have become embedded in such phrases. (ibid.: 181)

Music and dance

A crucial yet often overlooked aspect of individuals' involvement with music at the everyday level is dance. Dance is perhaps the most accessible form of musicalised expression providing as it does a means for the physical embodiment of music. As Hanna observes: 'Dancing is a unique way to convey messages of identity: generational difference, gender, ethnicity, and social class. Messages in motion are also about desire and fantasy, defiance and anger' (1992: 176).

Throughout history, dance has accompanied music in a wide range of contexts from ritualistic practice through to occasions of pleasure and emotional release (Thomas, 2003). The latter interpretation of dance has become increasingly prominent during late modernity, genres of popular music from the post-Second World War period onwards giving rise to forms of dance which, on the surface at least, appear relatively spontaneous. Such forms of dance, from the 'twist' and 'jive' styles of rock 'n' roll through to the more loosely structured dance styles observed in contemporary dance music clubs, are often perceived as a radical departure from the rule-bound conventions of, for example, ballet where 'the body [is viewed] as an instrument which must be trained to conform to the classical movement vocabulary' (Novack, 1990: 31). As Hanna notes, however, all forms of dancing, irrespective of how spontaneous they may appear, employ particular structures to which all dancers adhere. At the collective level, argues Hanna: 'Structures are a kind of generative grammar, that is, a set of rules specifying the manner in which movements can be meaningfully combined' (1992: 31).

According to Bradley, the significance of dance as a collectively understood form of musicalised expression, embodying a set of attendant cultural sensibilities, has extended as dance has become, ostensibly, more individualised:

> ... paradoxically, the decline of dancing styles which involve frequent or constant contact between partners, and exact, pre-determined patterns of movements, and the rise of 'free' styles with little formal patterning, signify not an individualization but a collectivization. Each dancer enjoys a direct relation – through the synchronization of his or her movements to the music, and is thus part of a collective (comprising the musicians, the dancer and the other dancers present) whose visible sign is the diverse but unified crowd on the floor. (1992: 114)

Recent studies of contemporary dance support Bradley's observation. Moreover, in addition to identifying particular systems of rules inherent in such dance styles, these studies also demonstrate how each style incorporates particular strategies of resistance to pressures and restrictions imposed on individuals in the course of their everyday lives. For example, in his work on slamdancing, a style of dancing common in punk and indie scenes where dancers deliberately slam into each other often falling to the floor as a result, Tsitsos illustrates how this style of dancing is collectively understood as a symbol of punk rebellion against the mainstream:

> Slamdancing ... mirrors punk ideologies in the symbolic breakdown of order which seems to occur in the pit.[4] The fast, counter-clockwise motion of dancers turns the pit into a swirl of seemingly chaotic motion. Although slamdancers themselves do follow customs which prevent the pit from denegrating [sic] into actual chaos, the pit, when viewed from the outside, looks like a lawless realm. The enemy for punks is the mainstream, and slamdancing allows punks to present the threat of chaos while still maintaining unity among themselves in the pit. (1999: 407)

Research on styles of dancing in contemporary dance music clubs have illustrated similar forms of resistant strategies enacted through the practice of dance. At one level, the significance of dance in the club context has been examined in connection with the patterns of drug taking also associated with clubbing (Melechi, 1993). Thus, just as hippies during the late 1960s were argued to engage in a dance style that 'evoked and accompanied the experience of giving up control and losing oneself in the drug experience', so contemporary clubbers are deemed to engage in dance practices designed to help them attain a heightened level of experiential awareness (Novack, 1990: 39). Thus, according to Melechi: 'The subcultural tradition of sex, desire and romance has moved to a different plane of pleasures as the combination of dance, music and Ecstasy slides the body into an amphetamine bliss and the jouissance of cyber-space' (1993: 35).

A more detailed exploration of how contemporary clubbers are able to subvert the mundane sequence of the everyday through the moments of pleasure and jouissance they achieve through dance is provided by Malbon. Unlike Melechi, Malbon considers such qualities of dance in the clubbing environment to be available to all, irrespective of whether drugs are used or not. According to Malbon, the act of dancing itself can lead to the achievement of altered states of awareness:

> ... through understanding where and how to use one's body, a sensation of momentary introspection (or extasis) may be experienced ... In this way dancing offers both to individual clubbers and the group of which they are a part 'the chance to become something else "for the time being" or ... to rebecome what they never were'. (Schechner, 1981: 3, quoted in Malbon, 1999: 100–1)

Finally, McRobbie notes how dance provides a form of resistance for women against the patriarchal conventions that continue to prevail in late modern society. McRobbie argues that the act of dancing 'carries enormously pleasurable qualities for girls and women which frequently seem to suggest a displaced, shared and nebulous eroticism rather than a straightforwardly romantic, heavily heterosexual "goal-oriented" drive' (1984: 134). Pini examines McRobbie's contention in relation to rave and contemporary dance club culture, arguing that, given the more liberal conventions that pertain in such settings, the resistant qualities identified by McRobbie in relation to dance take on an enhanced meaning. Thus, argues Pini, in the dance club setting women 'feel freed from traditional associations of dancing with sexual invite' and able to engage in 'open displays of physical pleasure and affection' (1997: 166, 167). According to Pini, 'rave represents the emergence of a particular form of 'jouissance', one which is more centred on the achievement of physical and mental transformation and one which is probably best understood as a non-phallic form of pleasure' (ibid.: 167).

Conclusion

This chapter has examined the role of music in everyday life. The chapter began with a consideration of key theoretical frameworks which have been applied when studying the everyday use of music – scene, community and subculture. The chapter then went on to consider the significance of music in relation to youth, noting music's importance both as a cultural resource in the construction of identity and as source of empowerment. This was followed by a look at music's role in relation to diaspora populations, particularly the way in which music helps link such populations through its communication of a commonly understood message and also acts as a means through which diasporas forge new cultural spaces. In the second part of the chapter, a range of less widely covered aspects of musical life were considered. In the pub and club setting, it was demonstrated, music plays an important role both as a background sound and through facilitation of creative participation, for example, joining in with sing-songs or volunteering to take part in Karaoke sessions. It was also noted how music's role in relation to the everyday has been further enhanced through the introduction of the personal stereo, the latter allowing the individual to create a personal everyday soundtrack. The role of music was also considered in relation to advertising, where, it was illustrated, the choice of music can significantly add to the impact of a particular advertisement, not only commercially but also aesthetically.

The relationship between musical taste and generation was then examined. It was noted how music may act as a source of conflict or as a bridging device between generations. Finally, the importance of music in relation to dance was considered. Of the many different ways in which music impacts upon everyday experience, it was argued, dance is significant in that it provides a key way in which individuals embody musical texts, the rhythms and beats of musical styles providing a basis for the expressive movements displayed by individuals through dance.

Notes

1. 'Indie' is short for 'independent music' a term first applied to small-scale UK independent record labels and the bands they signed during the post-punk period. Although the concept of 'indie' has been problematised due to its appropriation by mainstream record labels, where it is used simply as a marketing strategy (see Negus, 1992), it retains a currency among musicians and fans (see Street, 1993; Bennett, 2001a).

2. LSD (Lysergic Acid Diethylamide) is a synthetic hallucinogenic drug developed by Swiss chemist Albert Hoffman during the 1930s.

3. For a more extensive discussion of popular music and nostalgia, see Bennett (2001b).

4. Tsitsos is referring here to the 'mosh pit', an area of the dance floor directly in front of the stage used in punk and indie clubs for slamdancing amd moshing.

SEVEN Tourism

From the mid-twentieth century onwards, tourism ceased to be the pursuit of a wealthy minority and became a more widely experienced and accepted form of leisure and recreation. To a large extent, this was due to break-throughs in technology which gave rise to more efficient and cost-effective forms of transport and made long-distance travel accessible for an increasing number of people (Urry, 1995). This, in turn, gave rise to a greater variety in the forms of travel and tourism available as travel companies sought to cater for as wide a range of tourist tastes and preferences as possible. By the late twentieth century, tourism had became a major global industry, with new resorts, theme parks and other tourist attractions appearing in various locations around the world each year. Moreover, in the case of those countries most deeply affected by de-industrialisation, the impor-tance of tourism has taken on an added significance. In Britain, for exam-ple, post-industrial cities, such as Liverpool, Manchester and Leeds, have effectively re-invented themselves in recent years, remnants of their industrial heritage and other aspects of local history being transformed into tourist attractions (see, for example, Cohen, 1997; Gold and Gold, 2000). Such innovations have both boosted local economies and facilitated urban regeneration, giving these cities a new sense of purpose in the early twenty-first century.

In addition to its economic importance, however, tourism also has a significant aesthetic value in the context of contemporary societies. As with the other forms of leisure and consumption considered so far in this book, tourism offers its own particular possibilities for the aestheticisa-tion of everyday life (Featherstone, 1991). Such is the diversity of tourist destinations and forms of tourism now available, that it has become a central component of 'lifestyle' (Chaney, 1996), linking with a range of other aesthetically informed values, notably body consciousness, diet, and personal interests in subjects such as language, art, dress, and so on. In choosing for a particular tourist destination, and a particular way of experiencing that destination, individuals make statements about themselves in much the same way as they do through their other leisure and consumption choices. Ways of 'being' a tourist often correspond to the broader identity politics of individuals, the aesthetic preferences that inform the sensibilities of the tourist being consistent with those that inform their other everyday life rituals and practices. This chapter examines the significance of tourism both as a leisure pursuit and as a further way of understanding the relationship between leisure and lifestyle in contemporary society.

The development of tourism

As Wearing and Wearing note, tourism 'is essentially a modern western phenomena [sic] ... being closely related to the emergence of modernity with the concomitant emphasis on economic viability' (2001: 143; see also MacCannell, 1976). Indeed, until the latter half of the twentieth century tourism was possible for a small elite class of people only, for whom it was 'a mark of status' (Urry, 1995: 130). Among the members of this elite, trips to exotic overseas locations became a form of conspicuous consumption (Veblen, 1994 [1924]) on a par with the wearing of expensive fashion garments and eating out in exclusive restaurants. As the twentieth century progressed, however, developments in sea and air transport made tourism a more widely accessible leisure pursuit. Similarly, during the 1960s the introduction of cheap package holidays to Spain, Greece and other Mediterranean resorts meant that overseas holidays became a possibility for working-class and lower-middle-class families, for whom such a luxury had been hitherto unaffordable (Urry, 1995: 130).

The economic impact of tourism has been considerable. In Britain, there are some 400 million international arrivals a year (compared with 60 million in 1960), and between three and four times that number of domestic tourists worldwide. International tourists are increasing by 4–5 per cent per annum and spend $209 billion a year, generate around 60 million jobs, and fill 10.5 million hotel beds. The number of tourists to the Mediterranean (the world's most popular tourist destination) is predicted to rise to 760 million by 2025 (see Urry, 1995: 174–5).

During the course of the twentieth century, tourism became increasingly rationalised, a paramount example of this being the development of 'amusement parks' and 'theme parks' (Ritzer and Liska, 1997). Such facilities boast the advantage of having all their tourist attractions, together with other important amenities, such as hotel accommodation and catering, situated on a single site and thus easily accessible. Similarly, vital infrastructural utilities, for example, electricity and water supply, food distribution and waste removal are strategically positioned so that they are out of sight, thus ensuring the 'smooth running' of the theme park without interrupting the tourist experience (Bryman, 1999a: 104). The result, according to Ritzer and Liska, is a safe and essentially 'predictable' experience for the tourist: 'there are no midway scam artists to milk the visitor; there are teams of workers who, among their other cleaning chores, follow the nightly parades cleaning up debris ... theme parks work hard to make sure that the visitor experiences no surprises at all' (1997: 97).

Tourism and late modernity

As illustrated above, the latter part of the twentieth century saw dramatic developments in tourism, so that it became an activity enjoyed by an increasing number of people. Indeed, such is the normalcy of tourism for members of contemporary western societies that it has become a largely taken-for-granted part of life. As Urry observes: 'Being able to go on holiday, to be obviously not at work is presumed to be a characteristic of modern citizenship which has become embodied into people's thinking about health and well-being' (1995: 130). If tourism is engaged in by greater numbers of people, then it has also become an increasingly specialised pursuit to the extent that it now takes a variety of forms, for example, visits to beach resorts or theme parks, adventure holidays, as well as cheaper options such as backpacking. Each of these forms of tourism illustrate an increasing plurality of tastes and preferences in society. As individuals become more differentiated due to the exercise of consumer choice, so they demand different types of tourist experience.

A number of theories have been put forward in an attempt to explain the aesthetic significance of tourism for late modern individuals. Initial interpretations of tourism's appeal saw it as a 'culturally sanctioned escape [route] for western travellers' (Wearing and Wearing, 2001: 150), that is, a means through which individuals could temporarily transcend the mundane predictability of their normal everyday existence. Cohen and Taylor (1976) argued that, from a westernised point of view, tourism and travel provided a means towards the cultivation of self-consciousness against a backdrop of an increasingly technocratic existence that hampered such development in a normal everyday context.

The tourist gaze

In more recent years, such 'escapist' interpretations of tourism have been replaced by a series of explanations that reposition the tourist as a more active participant in the creation of the tourist experience. This conceptualisation of the tourist is effectively captured in Urry's (1990) notion of the 'tourist gaze'. According to Urry, in contemporary media-saturated societies, individuals' perceptions of particular countries and regions are shaped, first and foremost, through the media-generated images they receive, the latter becoming, in effect, a primary form of experience, creating a series of impressions of place (see also Chaney, 2002a). A broadly similar point is made by Alneng through his observation that: 'Daydreaming of potential destinations precedes every act of voluntary travelling. The building blocks of these everyday-dreams are large-scale repertoires of images and narratives provided by what Appadurai has labelled "mediascapes"' (2002: 464). As such, tourism becomes a means to fulfilment, that is to say, an activity undertaken by individuals with the expectation that their preconceived images of a place will be brought dramatically to life. Thus, argues Urry, tourists 'seek to experience "in reality" the pleasurable dramas they have already experienced in their imagination' (1990: 13).

According to Urry, the tourist gaze leads to what he terms an 'emphemerality of experience' (1995: 177). As with other objects and images in contemporary society, tourist places come to be regarded by tourists as commodities, whose appeal turns on the temporal enjoyment they offer the visitor. As Urry observes:

> Everyone in the 'West' is now entitled to engage in visual consumption, to appropriate landscapes and townscapes more or less anywhere in the world ... To be a tourist, to look on landscapes with interest and curiosity (and to be provided with many other related services), has become a right of citizenship from which few in the 'West' are formally excluded. (ibid.: 176)

This desire to visually consume places has produced a reciprocal effect on local tourist industries who now actively market rural and urban sites in much the same way that other consumer commodities are marketed. In the US, for example, features such as wilderness trails, 'Wild West' experiences, Disneyland and the Johnson Space Center function to preserve particular pre-formed impressions of the US that overseas tourists take on holiday with them. Similarly, the northern English city of York, in addition to boasting a series of high profile tourist attractions, notably the Jorvik centre (an interactive museum built on the site of the original Viking settlement Jorvik from which the city of York developed), has over the years introduced a range of smaller, more discrete, attractions such as the 'Guy Fawkes'[1] pub, designed to correspond with the tourist's expectations on visiting a world famous city brimming with history. Indeed, such is the intensity of this marketing of place to tourists that conflicts of interest have arisen between tourist expectations and locals, for whom experience of a place will often be qualitatively different. As Eade notes, although local tourist industries strive to present 'certain representations of urban space' to outsiders, locals bring their own meanings and interpretations to bear on their space (2002: 138). Thus, observes Eade: 'The attempt to fix, to establish uniqueness, is challenged by the dynamic and the fragmentary' (ibid.). Moreover, such conflicts of socio-spatial interest are not restricted to urban centres, but increasingly prefigure the way in which rural spaces are consumed and interpreted. This is illustrated in Hetherington's study of Stonehenge, an ancient monument in south-west England. As both a place of significant archaeological importance and the site for the gathering of New Age Travellers and others with new age interests, the meaning and significance of Stonehenge is contested, the monument functioning to 'legitmize different sets of practices and individualized lifestyles' (1992: 89). For the tourist, the significance of Stonehenge lies in the clues it is seen to provide concerning the culture and customs of Ancient Britain. For the Traveller, Stonehenge's perceived links with Ancient Britain feed into and help to maintain a 'neo-pagan spiritual revival' (ibid.: 88). In both cases, Stonehenge is being partly fictionalised, the tourist and the festival-goer both constructing a particular narrative of the monument based on their own opinion of what Stonehenge represents.

According to some theorists, the key impact of the tourist gaze is its mythification of place. In recent decades the redefinition of tourist spaces as mythscapes has become more pervasive due to the influence of global media, notably film and music. An illustrative example here is Fruehling Springwood's study of Japanese tourists' romanticisation of America's agrarian mid-west. According to Fruehling Springwood, immersion in particular filmic and televisual texts has equipped Japanese tourists with 'prior ways of imagining "America"' (2002: 177). This in turn has resulted in a desire among Japanese tourists to visit those mid-west locations in which popular films like *Field of Dreams* and television programmes such as *Little House on the Prairie* are set. A similar form of touristic pilgrimage is documented in Grazian's (2003) study of Chicago blues clubs. As Grazian observes, in addition to mythologising Chicago as 'home of the blues' tourists to the city invariably seek out 'classic' clubs and venues in the city in an effort to experience 'the blues' in its *authentic* surroundings. Such a practice involves having prior knowledge based on a musical, and sometimes literary, knowledge of the Chicago blues scene, its history and development.

Another factor that has had a significant impact on the nature of the tourist gaze in recent years is the rapid development of photographic technology. As such technology has advanced, so the tourist's demand for sights and landscapes to photograph has also changed. Thus, for example, advances in colour photography has resulted in a higher demand for travel to 'unspoilt' and visually striking locations, places free from urban sprawl, pollution, motorways, power stations and derelict land (Urry, 1995: 176). Similarly, the increasing possibility of high quality night photography has created demand for images that can be photographed after dark. Consequently, a range of urban features, from churches and historic buildings to statues and ornamental fountains are now routinely floodlit at night to enhance the aesthetic enjoyment of the tourist and feed their desire for high quality holiday photographs. According to Crawshaw and Urry, such is the ease of access to relatively cheap and easy-to-use photographic equipment in late modernity that photography has become an integral and even 'ritualistic' aspect of tourism. Crawshaw and Urry suggest that photography has become a means by which tourists can position themselves within an unusual or foreign landscape and begin to impose some kind of order on their experience. The landscape is ritualistically transformed into a series of scenes and scenarios to be captured on camera and thus owned and preserved by the tourist:

> … photography is a socially organised set of rituals. It involves a set of rules and roles which people take up in new or special environments. A sense of being out of place can be offset by following a set of photographic rituals. It involves a repertoire of actions when confronted by the 'other' – an other which may be awesome, threatening, mysterious. (1997: 183)

Tourist encounters

A further way of understanding the aesthetic significance of tourism is offered by Crouch et al. through their concept of 'tourist encounters'. In keeping with more general theories of the individual in late modern society as an active agent, reflexively engaging with the everyday and making sense of everyday practices and surroundings on his/her own terms, Crouch et al. argue that key to understanding the tourist experience is accounting for how this is responded to and made sense of at the individual level. Thus, they observe:

It is ... possible, and useful, to think of the tourist as 'doing tourism'. Tourism may become verbalized, thus active, agentive, through the tourist. It is also subjective, with the tourist making his or her own sense of what is going on, drawing upon, among other things ... their own resources in encountering the world. Agency and subjectivity are thus crucial constituents of process, in this case of being a tourist. (2001: 254)

According to Crouch et al., then, the 'tourist encounter' is a two-way process. On the one hand it encompasses the external stimuli that greet the senses – new sights and sounds, unusual and exotic smells and so on. On the other hand the tourist encounter is also forged by the body itself, or rather the way the body responds to and transforms its new surroundings. The aesthetic value of the tourist encounter is precisely the way that it involves the individual subject, the movement, positioning and general disposition of the body, and the personal subjectivity this expresses, being a necessary component of the tourist encounter and one that makes it specifically meaningful for the individual:

Rather than simply the body being the receiver of inscriptions – a naked body on a beach, or wearing a particular costume – it expresses, it acts, it turns, touches, moves or remains still, conveys meaning of the self. The body, expressive, inscribes space with significance. The places that tourists use are walked over, discovered with both feet, leaned against, reached, rested on, enjoyed and endured. (ibid.: 260–1)

Crouch et al. thus suggest a more complex relationship between the tourist, the tourist site and the host community than that envisaged in Urry's (1990) concept of the tourist gaze. Thus, rather than regarding places as things to be 'consumed', tourists form a sensual and corporal bond with their new environment, the latter facilitating a form of situating practice. A similar argument is put forward by Wearing and Wearing who argue that tourism involves the transformation of 'self', both on the part of the tourist and those who belong to the host community as each attempt to adapt to and accommodate each other's presence in the tourist site. According to Wearing and Wearing, 'the selves of tourists and hosts [are] predicated on a subjective, cumulative, non-essentialist, but embodied and emotional, "I" which constructs and reconstructs the tourist experience in interaction with significant others' (2001: 152). The notion of locals modifying their identities in accordance with the expectations of the tourist gaze is central to work by Filipucci on the residents of Bassano, a tourist town in Northern Italy. As Filipucci observes, through annual street events such as the local carnival, residents of Bassano engage in a spectacular celebration of their regional heritage and local tradition. The carnival thus becomes 'an intersubjective field' in that it allows both locals and tourists to engage in constructing narratives of place. Thus, in fulfilling the desires of the tourist gaze, locals also indulge their own desires by presenting the carnival as an event in which the past is dramatically brought back to life and 'something essentially "local" is displayed' (2002: 75).

Tourism and the carnivalesque

The concept of carnival also assumes a more metaphysical resonance in some contemporary academic writing on tourism, a number of theorists equating tourism with Bakhtin's (1984) notion of the 'carnivalesque'. In this sense, tourism becomes a means through which individuals can temporarily reinvent themselves, playing with identities and engaging in forms of 'carnivalesque' behaviour impermissible in their normal everyday lives. Thus, as Chaney observes, 'holidays or tourist sites have commonly legitimated transgressions and indulgencies comparable to medieval precedents' (2002a: 146). This interpretation of tourism is central to a study by Shields which argues that tourist resorts are liminal spaces, that is 'in-between' places where individuals can momentarily disengage with their more normal, everyday identities and experiment with new selves and ways of being. Shields uses the example of the 'beach' which he describes as a 'locus of an assemblage of practices ... behaviours and patterns of interaction outside the norms of everyday behaviour, dress and activity' (1991: 75).

A further dimension of this 'carnivalesque' tourist sensibility is seen in Sánchez Taylor's study of sex tourism among white, western women in the Caribbean. As Sánchez Taylor notes, such women construct the Caribbean as an exoticised space in which they can engage in forms of behaviour that are not permitted in their home environment, including the soliciting of physically attractive men for sex. Moreover, argues Sánchez Taylor, the ability to command sex with local men for money in this way offers these women a sense of empowerment which is often missing in their day-to-day lives at home:

> ... being able to command 'fit' and sexually desirable bodies which would otherwise be denied to them reaffirms female tourists' sense of their own privilege as 'First World' citizens ... Their economic power and their whiteness means that they are not treated as local women but respected and protected. Their bodies are also valued over local women's bodies and they are offered a stage upon which they can simultaneously affirm their femininity through their ability to control local men and reject the white men who have rejected them. (2001: 760)

Tourism and lifestyle

While each of the above theoretical approaches goes some way towards uncovering the aesthetic significance of tourism in late modernity, it could be argued that key to a broader understanding of tourism's role in the context of everyday life is the continuity between the aesthetics of tourism and those which inform other aspects of daily life practice. This view is supported by Chaney who suggests that in the early twenty-first century tourism must be seen as an aspect of lifestyle, an activity bound up with other lifestyle choices and preferences. According to Chaney, contemporary tourism embodies 'a self-consciousness of performance ... consistent with the reflexivity of lifestyle consciousness' (1996: 134). A similar view is expressed by Craik who suggests that in the context of late modernity, 'tourism has somewhat *converged* with leisure and cultural consumption' (1997: 121).

Applying this interpretation to different forms of contemporary tourism, the relationship between tourist activities and broader lifestyle preferences can be clearly observed. Indeed, as Pritchard (2001) observes, the marketing strategies of the contemporary tourist industry are now firmly orientated towards particular target audiences. For example, the classic Mediterranean package holiday, combining a warm, sunny climate with more 'familiar' options in terms of food, drink and entertainment, caters particularly well for what Hannerz refers to as 'anticosmopolitans', those people who 'travel for the purpose of home plus' (1990: 241). On the other hand, adventure holidays, such as white water rafting and canoeing, cater for those with a preference for more 'hands on', sporty and, ultimately risky activities. Moreover, such holidays demand by definition an element of pre-existing skill and experience in the chosen activity, thus connecting with the everyday hobbies and interests, that is, general lifestyle orientation, of those who opt for this sort of tourism. Similarly, the increasing demand for 'alternative' tourist options bespeaks a reflexive awareness, and often accompanying cynicism, on the part of many individuals regarding the increasing commercialisation of tourism. Such tourists thus seek out holiday options which promise a more 'authentic' tourist experience than those offered by mainstream, high street travel agencies. 'Backpacking', a form of DiY tourism supported by budget hostels, long-distance rail-travel cards and round-the-world air tickets, makes it a particularly appealing travel option for students and other young people with limited financial resources (see, for example, Desforges, 1998). Finally, in recent years, the growing popularity of dance music and club culture (Thornton, 1995) on a global level has given rise to a new form of youth travel termed 'dance tourism' (see, for example, Carrington and Wilson, 2002; Saldanha, 2002). Taking advantage of the cheap travel options established to suit the young budget traveller, dance music fans organise their overseas trips with a view to visiting particular cities reputed for their dance clubs, or to attend dance music festivals. The rest of this chapter examines several forms of contemporary tourism which illustrate the relationship between tourism and lifestyle in late modern society.

Anti-cosmopolitans and post-tourists

As the increasing number of purpose-built and essentially uniform holiday resort complexes in diverse parts of the world readily illustrate, a major concern of global tourism is the accommodation of tourists, primarily from developed parts of the western world, in surroundings that boast an exotic location while at the same time offering familiar home comforts, notably choice of food and drink, but also perhaps television, newspapers and forms of entertainment that comply with the taste and expectations of the tourist. Indeed, as Hannerz observes, for many tourists

> ... travel is ideally home plus ... There is no general openness ... to a somewhat unpredictable variety of experiences; the benefits of mobility are strictly regulated ... Much present-day tourism is of this kind. People engage in it specifically to go to another place ... the 'plus' often has a lot to do with facts of nature, such as nice beaches. (1990: 241)

However, it is not simply such stereotypical 'sun resorts' that facilitate anti-cosmopolitan tourism. On the contrary, a whole range of holiday options now exist where the tourist is able to enjoy the experience of 'home-plus'. A particularly successful venture in this respect is the 'theme park'. As Rojek observes, theme parks are 'organized around serialized spectacles and participant attractions. Common features include fantastic and bizarre landscapes, exotic regions and "white knuckle" rides' (1993: 137). As Rojek's description implies, the theme park is intended to provide a 'total experience', the needs and wishes of the tourist being catered for entirely on-site.

The world's first official 'theme park', Disneyland, was opened in 1955 in California by children's cartoon mogul Walt Disney. Although intended to act as a vehicle for Disney characters, such as Mickey Mouse and Donald Duck, as well as the various Disney films adapted from popular children's stories including Snow White and Sleeping Beauty, Walt Disney's vision was 'to create an environment which adults would be just as keen to visit as children' (Bryman, 1999b: 31). So rather than pitching the entertainment value of Disneyland exclusively at the level of the child's imagination, Disney sought ways of fashioning the attractions that would also appeal to the everyday sensibilities of adults. As Bryman observes:

> ... Disneyland was conceived as a celebration of America's past and as a paean to progress ... The former element allowed Walt Disney to lace many of the attractions and environments with heavy doses of nostalgia that he thought would have a direct appeal to adults. (ibid.: 31)

This fashioning of multi-media attractions to appeal to the tastes of respective generations, from childhood to old age, has remained central to the rationale of theme parks, and has seen them grow in number and variety since the mid-twentieth century. Theme parks now constitute a major form of tourism. In addition to the original Disneyland and the other Disney theme park variations, Disney World (Orlando) and Disneyland Paris (formerly Euro Disney), other popular theme parks include Sea World and Universal Studios (both in Los Angeles, see Bryman, 1999a). In attempting to account for the popular appeal of theme parks, a number of theorists have suggested that this can be put down to an increasingly prevalent sensibility which they refer to as 'post tourism'. Like the non-cosmopolitan, the post-tourist's desire is for a holiday that offers home comforts – in which the exotic exists only for its entertainment value rather than something that fully envelops the tourist and dominates the holiday experience. Some theorists link post-tourism with the onset of particular postmodernist traits in contemporary society, notably the increasing dominance of simulations. Thus, according to Ritzer and Liska:

> ... it could be argued that people living in a post-modern world dominated by simulations increasingly come to want, nay insist on, simulations when they tour ... In such a world, the tourist would not know an authentic experience even if one could be found. [Moreover], living on a day-to-day basis with simulations leads to a desire for them when one becomes a tourist. Accustomed to the simulated dining experience at McDonalds, the tourist is generally not apt to want to scrabble for food at the campfire, or to survive on nuts and berries picked on a walk through the woods. The latter may be 'authentic', but they are awfully difficult, and unpredictable in comparison to a meal at a local fast-food restaurant or in the dining room of a hotel that is part of an international chain. Most products of a post-modern world might be willing to eat at a campfire, as long as it is a simulated one on the lawn of the hotel. (1997: 107)

Although perhaps accurate in its description of the simulated nature of the tourist experience in this way, Ritzer and Liska's account positions the post-tourist as a cultural dupe, characterised by an uncritical acceptance of the tourist experience. As Rojek points out, however, such a reading of the post-tourist is inaccurate in a way analogous to early readings of mass media audiences (see Chapter 1). Rojek argues that far from being taken in by the simulated delights of 'McTourism', 'the post-tourist is [entirely] aware of the commodification of the tourist experience' and simply treats it as a game to be played (1993: 177). Moreover, there are clear benefits in this as far as the post-tourist is concerned. Thus, whereas MacCannell suggested that 'staged authenticity' undermined the tourist search for 'truth and beauty', for the post-tourist such staged authenticity is both anticipated and favoured as it functions to produce an essentially risk-free environment (1976: 103). In the post-tourist experience then, one finds an apparently paradoxical combination; on the one hand, a desire for a 'range of [travel] experiences and direct encounters with locals' – on the other, a distinctly anti-cosmopolitan sensibility and willing acceptance of the stage-managed nature of tourist encounters (Featherstone, 1995: 120). As Featherstone observes, for post-tourists:

> ... the ease with which they can now travel to the more exotic and remote parts of the world amounts to a step into a tourist reservation in which they enjoy 'home plus' ... Some of those post-tourists are not at all worried that what they are presented with is a simulation of local culture; they are interested in the whole paraphernalia of the 'behind the scenes' and the construction of the performance and the set ... Such staged simulations of localities can vary from reassuring clear cartoon-style parodies (the Jungle Cruise in the Magic Kingdom), to small-scale 'walk-in, see and touch' simulations of the key buildings and icons which in the popular imagination are taken to represent a national culture ... to whole heritage industry efforts to preserve and restore full-scale living and working examples of the past. (1995: 120–1)

An effective illustration of how more remote and inaccessible parts of the world are now increasingly catering for post-tourists is offered by Nuttall in his work on the 'packaging' of Alaska. As Nuttall explains, Alaska is 'marketed as a land of superlatives and extremes, where nature can still be experienced as raw and untouched' (1997: 226). Tourism in Alaska is organised in such a way that the variety of expectations that tourists bring with them to the region can be relatively easily realised. Trips to areas of outstanding natural beauty, visits to local Native-American communities, whale-watching tours and even the possibility of consummating a marriage under the *aurora borealis* are easily accessible to the tourist. It is clear then, even if they may seem to be wholly different tourist pursuits, the 'wild frontier' of Alaska and the hermetically sealed pleasuredome of the theme park are packaged and presented to the tourist according to the same principles of late modern rationalisation. Moreover, according to Nuttall, a concerted effort is made to ensure that the image of Alaska presented to the tourist is crafted in a way that excludes those aspects of the region that tourists wish to ignore. Discussing this process in relation to the plight of the Alaskan Native communities, Nuttall notes how:

> ... tourists visiting Alaska are looking to experience authentic and traditional Native culture, and do not want to be presented with lectures on social problems and how Alaskan villages are ravaged by unemployment, alcoholism and substance abuse. Some things are worthy of the tourist experience while there are other things that they cannot see. (1997: 231)

A similar example is provided in Spark's study of 'Brambuk', a cultural centre established by Aborigines in Victoria, Australia. Originally intended to draw attention to the destruction of Aboriginal culture by white settlers, the centre finally succumbed to pressure from the regional government to tone down the content and exhibits of the centre in order to make it more 'acceptable' to tourists. As Spark observes:

> Presenting images that are less confrontational ... the new Brambuk promotes a simplified version of a supposedly authentic Aboriginality. This change reflects the power of the tourist industry and the Victorian government to shape representation and mobilize a way of looking at places that romanticizes and objectifies them. (2002: 38)

As the above examples illustrate, post-tourism encompasses a range of very different tourist experiences. Central to each of these however, is an understanding on the part of tourists and local tourist industries that the tourist experience offers a risk-free environment. For the post-tourist, an enjoyable tourist experience is contingent on the provision of home comforts together with a range of 'stage-managed' attractions from which undesirable images and encounters have been systematically removed. Such stage-management of the tourist experience can now be achieved routinely across a range of different tourist settings, including those in more exotic and remote parts of the world.

Alternative-tourism

If theme parks and related forms of 'staged' tourism cater for a post-tourist sensibility which, as demonstrated above, is increasingly prevalent in late modernity, alternative tourism denotes an altogether different kind of late modern tourist sensibility. Rejecting what they consider to be commercial and sensationalised tourist attractions associated with 'post-tourist' destinations, individuals opting for alternative tourism strive for what they deem to be more 'authentic' tourist experiences. As MacCannell notes, this type of tourist sensibility is characterised by a 'desire to share in the real life of the places visited, or at least to see that life as it is really lived ... "to get off the beaten path" and "in with the natives"' (1976: 96–7). MacCannell's observation is supported by Hannerz's concept of cosmopolitanism. According to Hannerz, cosmopolitans 'loathe being taken for tourists [and] want to immerse themselves in other cultures, or in any case be free to do so. They want to be participants, or at least do not want to be too readily identifiable within a crowd of participants, that is, of locals in their home territory' (1990: 241).

As MacLeod notes, alternative tourists regard themselves as being wholly different, in personal taste and general outlook, to more 'mainstream' tourists, a statement which is often articulated through their visual appearance: 'The overall appearance is one of casualness: sometimes a statement of individuality, often a statement of freedom – a sort of structured anti-conventionality' (1997: 132). According to MacLeod, alternative tourists actively seek out destinations whose lack of an established infrastructure of tourist facilities make them unattractive to 'less adventurous visitors' (ibid.: 129). Alternative tourists will also attempt to integrate into the local culture of their chosen destination as much as possible: 'As well as favouring accommodation belonging to local people, "alternative" tourists have a greater tendency to shop locally ... They also [eat] in local restaurants and dr[i]nk in local bars' (ibid.: 140). Similarly, alternative tourists will often attempt to integrate into the local community by, for example, learning the local language and attempting to converse with the locals, and showing an interest in aspects of local culture and tradition.

As illustrated above, 'alternative tourism', although a form of contemporary leisure practice arrived at through a personal decision to reflect in the activity of tourism a series of aesthetic values, translates into a collective form of resistance against more 'mainstream' forms of tourism and the commercial, capitalist interests that lie behind this. Thus, in choosing to become 'alternative tourists', individuals transform their personally held beliefs into a collective lifestyle statement which is communicated through a shared set of beliefs and practices relating to tourism as an activity that involves, respect for and interest in the host culture. Thus, observes MacLeod:

... the conscious decision of certain individuals to be regarded as 'alternative' tourists ... demonstrates a merging of the personal identity with the social identity. A person's intimate sense of self, of private identity or reality can become reflected or absorbed into a group which shares similar interests. This phenomenon indicates how personal and social identities can become combined in a tangible manner, where a person's privately felt emotions and opinions can be articulated by a group. (ibid.: 138)

In addition to a desire to step outside the sphere of 'commercial' tourism and the staged authenticity that prevails there, alternative tourism can also be seen as a quest on the part the individual for personal enrichment. As Craik observes, 'tourist experiences embody aspects of self-improvement, education, discovery and individualism' (1997: 126). In the case of alternative tourism, these aspects of the tourist experience possess a particularly high currency. Reneging against the 'package holiday' or theme park experience embodies a more deep-felt resistance on the part of the individual towards the commodification of everyday life in late modern society per se. The sense of reflexively enacted detachment from, and rejection of, the 'packaged' tourist experience is thus deeply inscribed in the aesthetic of alternative tourism. Indeed, in establishing such critical distance between themselves and 'mainstream' tourists, alternative tourists reflexively enact what Rojek refers to as a tourist/traveller distinction, placing themselves firmly in the latter category:

Tourists are presented as lacking initiative and discrimination. They are unadventurous, unimaginative and insipid. For them, travel is akin to grazing – they mechanically consume whatever the tour operator feeds them. Their presence coarsens the quality of tourist sights ... The polar opposite is the traveller. The traveller is associated with refined values of discernment, respect and taste. (1993: 175)

The critical stance assumed by alternative tourists in relation to those who opt for 'home plus' package holidays and similar 'tourist trap' locations raises another important aspect of the tourist/tourism relationship. Thus, like other aspects of late modern leisure and consumption, the practice of tourism is seen to manifest a series of pluralistic and competing sensibilities. In this way, not only the practices of tourism but also the spaces in which such practices occur become contested. Thus, while alternative tourists express distaste at commercialised holiday resorts, and also abhor the infringement of their own 'out of the way' holiday destinations by 'mainstream' tourists with seemingly little respect for the local culture, ultimately both types of tourist are engaging in a form of identity politics in which use of space becomes a feature in the metaphorical construction of self. This again relates back to the embeddedness of tourism within the sphere of late modern mass culture and the pluralising effect of mass culture on everyday life. Tourists, sensibilities of space and place, however constructed and articulated, correspond neatly with wider consumerist sensibilities and the differing lifestyle strategies to which such sensibilities give rise. Thus, as Chaney observes:

> What and how a [tourist site] represents will differ between visitors and locals, but then neither of these categories will be homogenous, so that meaning is dispersed, existing on a number of dimensions simultaneously, and subject to change through succeeding waves of expectations. The problem of meaning in tourism is part of a broader change in popular culture towards industries of mass entertainment in which commercially provided culture has become more important in everyday life, and yet, almost paradoxically, 'culture' has lost its unity and coherence and become more problematic. (2002b: 194)

Backpacking and DiY tourism

As the tourist industry has expanded to meet the varying aesthetic demands of different types of tourist, it has also adapted to suit the financial resources of the individual tourist. In addition to expensive 'luxury' and mid-range tourist options, there also exist a number of low budget opportunities. The possibility of low budget travel and cheap holiday accommodation options is particularly appealing to young people, who, for the most part, are happy to forego the luxuries enjoyed by the more affluent tourist and view travel as a form of adventure in itself. Indeed, from the point of view of the young, low budget travel often has an appeal all of its own. The introduction of inter-rail cards, which offer unlimited travel for fixed periods of time in a particular country or countries, and round-the-world air tickets offer young people the possibility of organising their own travel and choosing destinations according to their own preferences. As Desforges (1998) observes, such low budget, DiY travel options are particularly appealing to young people taking a 'year out' from education or those between short-term employment contracts or 'McJobs'.

The popularity of low budget youth travel is such that it has now become an accepted part of youth lifestyles in contemporary society. Bell, for example, notes how, in contemporary New Zealand, post-School/University travel for young people has effectively become an expected part of growing up, a rite of passage on the way to adulthood.

According to Bell, the 'OE', or 'overseas experience', is viewed by 'many young adults and their parents ... as a valid alternative education. Beyond the actual physical flight to the other side of the globe it is a spiritual journey of discovery of the world and of the self' (2002: 144). The alternative educational qualities associated with the OE encompasses a range of learning experiences, from individual independence and self-sufficiency to personal enrichment and transformation engendered through travelling to a foreign location. The OE thus becomes a way through which young New Zealanders reflexively engage with their identities, reassessing and remaking themselves in the light of their encounters and experiences abroad. As Bell observes, such remaking of identity applies both to themselves as individuals with specific tastes and preferences, and also to their national identity and the place of that identity in the wider world.

> Once away, the young New Zealander stops being an insider in a taken-for-granted culture, and becomes and outsider somewhere else. On OE there is the liberty to reconstruct themselves. OE transcends the intellectual and spiritual limitations of staying in a small New Zealand town, or even an over familiar city. A huge world of options and experiences has suddenly opened. During their absence they also develop an 'outsider' view of New Zealand. They can now claim a far larger vision than those who stayed at home. (ibid.: 147)

In a similar fashion, Desforges suggests that youth travel often facilitates a way for young people to develop their personal biography through what he terms 'collecting places'. According to Desforges, this describes: 'A "framing" of the world in which knowledge and experiences can be gathered or "collected" through travel' (1998: 178). Experience of the world is gained by experiencing different places and committing those experiences to memory to be recounted again at a later date. Collecting places thus involves building a representation of the world based on experiencing difference, that is, places which are 'different' from home: 'Difference is defined by the traveller as something which can be known, understood and experienced through travel' (ibid.: 178–9). The process of collecting places is analogous to Urry's (1995) notion of 'consuming places'; a place must have a series of presenting aspects which are relatively easy to access, and which give the feeling of having experienced a place to the full. Thus, as Deforges observes: 'travellers represent destinations as containing a number of collectable places, for example to 'do' Peru for some means using a popular division of the country into desert, mountain and rainforest as the basis for a trip' (1998: 179).

Desforges goes on to suggest that the practice of 'collecting places' constitutes a form of cultural capital (Bourdieu, 1984). Young travellers recount a trip not simply in terms of places visited, but using a broad ranging narrative including, for example, accounts of personal development, increased knowledge of the world, broadened horizons, and new ways of looking at other cultures:

> The main way travellers convert 'collecting places' into cultural capital is through a narrative of personal development and authoritative knowledge about the world. Audiences can conspire with this narrative, even gaining cultural capital themselves through sharing a respect for travel. (Desforges, 1998: 189)

The concept of 'collecting places' is also central to a study by Alneng of western backpackers in Vietnam. According to Alneng: 'Tourism does not begin with the act of touring, but with the construction of a world picture that renders the world "tourable"' (2002: 485). Alneng then goes on to consider how the practice of collecting places is informed by media images, the latter interweaving fact and fiction to create particularly seductive fetishisations of place, suggesting particular 'ways' in which places *must* be experienced by the tourist. In the case of Vietnam, suggests Alneng, popular perceptions of young backpackers who tour the country are dominated by images of 'war', drawn both from actual documentary footage and Hollywood films. This phantasmic visualisation of Vietnam is further enhanced through the way in which backpackers often tour the country, for example using local transport services rather than those organised specially for tourists, despite the discomfort and danger associated with this.[2] Similarly, the local tourism industry supports such tourist expectations through a variety of museums and other attractions focusing on aspects of the Vietnam War. Alneng argues that the backpacker's 'doing' of Vietnam in this way can be seen as both a celebration of the country's Disneyfication and an uncritical 'adhere[nce] to Cold War paranoia and Hollywood mythologization of a monolithic evil communist foe' (ibid.: 475). This said, however, it is also possible to argue that the experience of 'doing' Vietnam's war-tourism route may function to subvert dominant western perceptions of the war, much of what is on display relating to the human cost in terms of civilian lives lost during the war. In this sense then, the practice of collecting places is changed, the initial images of place being altered or adjusted by the actual experience of a place, albeit through the ideological lens of the local tourist industry.

Conclusion

This chapter has focused on the significance of tourism as an aspect of everyday life in late modern society. Beginning with an overview of the factors that gave rise to the development of tourism as a mass leisure pursuit during the mid-twentieth century, the chapter then went on to consider a number of key theoretical perspectives that have been used to explain the cultural significance of tourism for late modern individuals. In each case, it was noted how the cultural significance of tourism can be linked with a range of other trends in late modernity, notably the dominance of media images, the latter giving rise to particular tourist expectations of different urban and rural spaces, and the commodification of tourism in ways that correspond with other aspects of leisure and lifestyle in contemporary society. The second part of the chapter developed this interpretation of tourism by looking at three distinct tourist sensibilities – anti-cosmopolitan/post-tourism, alternative tourism, and DiY tourism – and how each of these forms of tourism corresponds with a broader range of lifestyle politics.

Notes

1. This pub was renamed the 'Guy Fawkes' during the early 1990s. The building in which the pub is housed is the birthplace of the famous conspirator Guy Fawkes, executed in 1606 for his role in attempting to blow up the Houses of Parliament in protest at the monarchy's attempts to claim authority over the Church. Fawkes and his fellow conspirators were arrested in the Palace of Westminster on 5th November, 1605. The event is marked each year on 5th November with the British tradition of Bonfire Night.

2. Elsrud (2001) suggests that such experiences are integral to a discourse of risk and adventure prevalent among long-term and seasoned backpackers. According to Elsrud, for backpackers the trading of experiences involving risk and adventure is central to the construction and narration of identity.

EIGHT Counter-Cultures

Throughout the second part of this book it has been illustrated how the increasing development of global media and consumer industries has directly corresponded with a diversification of lifestyle tastes and preferences in late modern society. As the studies discussed in Chapters 4 to 7 demonstrate, however, research focusing on the significance of lifestyle for our understanding of late modern identities has, for the most part, been restricted to an examination of mainstream consumerist activities, notably, media use, fashion, music consumption and tourism. Significantly, and somewhat paradoxically, however, late modernity has also witnessed the development of a growing range of counter-cultures – 'alternative' lifestyle strategies and sensibilities which actively reject the beliefs, customs and cultural practices that centrally define contemporary late modern societies.

In particular, the last two decades have been characterised by a revival in ideologies, and practices associated with the pre-modern, notable examples being new-ageism, witchcraft, paganism and the 'back-to-the-land' movement. Each of the latter embody a range of assumptions concerning quality of life, care of the environment, and health of body and mind, all of which are deemed to be jeopardised by the increasing reliance on science and technology in late modern societies. Similarly, the belief in folklore, legends, supernatural phenomena, UFOs and metaphysical concepts such as out-of-body experiences, life after death and reincarnation all bespeak at some level a rejection or distrust of rational-scientific explanations and the faith invested in such explanations by technologically advanced societies. Alongside such pre- and anti-modern beliefs, seemingly more mundane activities, such as organic farming, vegetarianism and alternative therapies and medicines also reject at some level late modernity's emphasis on technological and scientific modes of production.

While some forms of 'pre-modern' practice and belief are exercised at an individual level and combined with more conventional lifestyle tastes and preferences, others demand greater levels of commitment, often involving the adoption of a radically alternative set of lifestyle practices, as is the case, for example, with New Age Traveller groups who reject urban living in favour of a rural, semi-nomadic way of life. This concluding chapter examines a number of examples of pre- and anti-modern practice and the alternative lifestyle strategies they engender. The chapter considers how such beliefs offer an alternative range of ideological and political discourses through which individuals can position themselves in the context of everyday life. It is also illustrated how many such alternative lifestyle strategies, while opposing the rationalised nature of late modern society, often continue to demonstrate a reliance upon and acceptance of late modern consumerist practices which, as repeatedly shown in previous chapters of this book, are now a centrally defining aspect of everyday life in contemporary society.

Technocracy and the counter-cultural revolution

Fear and distrust of technological advancement has long been an aspect of human history. For example, in mid-nineteenth-century England the Chartist and Luddite movements regaled against rapid industrialisation and the concomitant shift from traditional ways of life based around agriculture to new commercial values based around waged factory labour (Peel, 1968). In the case of the Luddites, resistance to industrialisation was particularly extreme, involving the destruction of new mechanised threshing machines used by farm labourers in the English countryside (Thompson, 1984).

Protests against capitalism and its reliance on science and technology continued into the twentieth century, taking on a more global character fostered, ironically, by improved systems of communications. Such protests also became more elaborate, resisting not only technological advancement itself but the ideological mindset it was deemed to have imposed on the dominant culture. An important catalyst for more contemporary shows of resistance against the rational-scientific logic of capitalism was the counter-culture of the late 1960s, a movement that took much of its inspiration from the mass produced and globally distributed musics of artists such as The Beatles and Jimi Hendrix (Bennett, 2001b). According to Reich (1971), the defining characteristic of the counter-culture was a generational shift in consciousness, the younger generation adopting new lifestyle values which openly contested those of the parent culture.

Central to the ideology of the counter-culture was a rejection of the technocratic principles of advanced western societies. According to Roszak, a technocracy is 'that social form in which an industrial society reaches the peak of its organizational integration. It is the ideal men usually have in mind when they speak of modernizing, up-dating, rationalizing, planning' (1969: 5). The counter-culture's reaction against technocratic tendencies in society took a variety of forms, including a back-to-the-land philosophy, encapsulated by rural communes (Webster, 1976), and an experimentation with hallucinogenic drugs, meditation and other forms of spiritualism drawn from Eastern religions (Hall, 1968; Willis, 1978). According to Willis (1978), a key aspect of the counter-culture's rationale in using drugs was to disrupt the rationalised organisation of time as experienced in western industrialised society and achieve another level of consciousness through heightened sensory awareness of sound and colour. This desire for heightened awareness, and concomitant withdrawal from the dominant concerns of everyday life in industrial society – work, family commitments, personal gain etc. – was also central to the counter-culture's interest in forms of meditation and spiritualism based around religious practices of the Far East. Thus, as Hall observes:

> The sacred books of Eastern religion and mysticism, the erotic code-books, the figures of the Buddha and of Karma, fragments of Eastern Philosophy, the adoption of the kashdan, the simulated orientalism of Leary's ritual LSD 'performances', the music of Ravi Shankar, the sitar, the looping and winding dances, the Buddhist chants of Allen Ginsberg – all these are elements in the eclectic orientalism of Hippie life, representing a return to contemplation and mystical experience. (1968: 8)

Although in itself a relatively short-lived phenomenon, the counter-culture served as a catalyst for a range of subsequent movements based around alternative lifestyles and belief systems, including organic farming, alternative medicine and healing practices, and a global interest in environmentalism and green politics. While the basic commodities of such alternative lifestyles are now successfully marketed much like any other product, as evidenced for example by the growing number of alternative clinics and wholefood supermarkets, such commodities are effectively weaved into lifestyle projects which retain a critical, and often physical, distance from what are regarded as more 'mainstream' consumer lifestyles. In addition to such mundane examples of alternative lifestyle, the 1990s saw the rise of more radical forms of opposition to contemporary society's reliance on and investment in technology and rational scientific explanations. Again, several of these movements have their roots in the counter-cultural activity of the late 1960s (see McKay, 1996).

The 'back-to-the-land' movement

Increasing concern about threats to the natural environment from industrial pollution and the vast amounts of waste produced through urban living has resulted in a series of 'back-to-the land' movements. The rejection of urban life central to each of these movements is directly linked with the rural commune movement of the late 1960s.

According to Webster the neo-greenism underpinning the commune movement articulated an 'anti-technological bias', a collective rejection and 'dropping out' of technological society based around both disillusionment and fear of its eventual consequences (1976: 128). Thus, argues Webster:

> The eschatological basis of the rural theme also takes the form of the 'end-of-the-world' both *experientially* (the drop out experiences *his* or *her* urban middle-class world ending) and through the imagery of environmental pollution, ecological catastrophe, racial strife, war and the 'demonic' technocratic system that supports it. The commune becomes here a 'saving remnant' and ritually and practically anticipates the paradise that will come after the demonic reality has passed away. (ibid.)

The 'back-to-the-land' ideology inscribed in the commune movement is preserved in contemporary movements such as Earth First, which, according to Plows, 'challenges [the] dominant paradigm, the structure/values/structure spiral which promotes and perpetuates exploitative unsustainability, and terms it "progress" [and] development' (1998: 159). Similarly, a diverse range of activities, from independent farming – which rejects industrial farming in favour of using organic methods – to the reclaiming of derelict land, each, in their own way, articulate a 'back-to-the-land' aesthetic, stressing the importance of respect and appreciation of the natural environment. As with the communes, the more radical examples of contemporary 'back-to-the-land' movements involve a complete rejection of the ideologies and practices that underpin late modern urban living and the adoption of a rural or semi-rural nomadic lifestyle (McKay, 1996).

Such a sensibility is exemplified by groups of young people known as New Age Travellers who, as Hetherington notes, share 'an identification with nomadism that is seen to be more authentic than the sociality of modern industrial societies' (1998: 335). According to Martin, the collective nomadic aesthetic of New Age Traveller groups involves a conscious distinction between themselves and those 'who live in houses which are seen as artificial and alienating environments' (2002: 82). Indeed, such is the investment of the New Age Traveller culture in this back-to-the-land philosophy that its level of individual articulation has become an important mark of status among members of Traveller groups. As Martin observes, Travellers 'who live in benders (traditional Gypsy tents) are deemed more authentic than those who live in vehicles because they live closer to the earth' (ibid.: 82).

The rural lifestyle of New Age Traveller groups, and their frequent occupation of green field sites has resulted in considerable negative exposure in the mainstream press (see McKay, 1996), including a short-lived attempt during the early 1990s to make New Age Travellers the centre of a new 'moral panic' similar to that created around the mods and rockers during the mid-1960s (see Cohen, 1987). As Hetherington notes, however, occupation of land is a central aspect of the New Age Travellers' resistance against the authority of late modern rational-legal institutions. According to Hetherington, New Age Travellers collectively endorse beliefs and practices that pre-date modernity, notably 'earth mysteries' which recast the countryside as a 'sacred and mysterious place' (1998: 335):

> Earth mysteries practitioners adopt a more holistic approach that refers back to ancient folk ways of understanding and interpreting the landscape: dowsing, ley line hunting, recovering folklore and customs associated with particular sites. The earth mysteries tradition challenges the modes of understanding offered by modern science and seeks to find in the landscape forgotten practices of knowing and understanding. (ibid.)

A considerable part of the New Age Travellers' rationale for adopting a rural, nomadic lifestyle then, is an attempt to retune themselves with premodern knowledges and skills practised by an earlier race of human beings who are deemed to have been at one with the natural world.[1] At the same time, New Age Travellers constitute a grass roots protest against the way in which the countryside continues to be devastated by the building of new roads, industrial sites and shopping complexes.

'The Land is Ours' (TLIO) campaign is similarly concerned with the misuse of land by urban policy-makers. However, unlike New Age Travellers who stage their protest by rejecting urban environments for the countryside, TLIO reclaims and transforms derelict urban sites. Such sites are then made habitable through the restoration of buildings, or the building of new accommodation using environmentally friendly materials, and the reintroduction of plants and trees. TLIO has been particularly effective in areas of urban decay on the outskirts of major conurbations. For example, as Monbiot observes:

> In May 1996, five hundred Land is Ours activists occupied thirteen acres of derelict land on the banks of the River Thames in Wandsworth, highlighting the appalling misuse of urban land, the lack of provision of affordable housing and

the deterioration of the urban environment. The site was destined for the ninth major superstore within a radius of a mile and a half. They cleared the site of rubble and rubbish, built a village entirely from recycled materials and planted gardens. (1998: 175-6)

TLIO and comparable initiatives, such as the Exodus Collective (see McKay, 1996; Malyon, 1998; Bennett, 2001b), are argued by those involved to present credible grass-roots solutions for disempowered and dispossessed individuals. Faced with the prospect of being forced out of their urban environment by lack of state housing, soaring prices in the private housing sector and the expansion of consumer-centred developments, such as shopping malls and cinema complexes, these movements enable activists to claim back space for themselves in a way that allows for the practice of a neo-greenist philosophy that is not shared by urban developers and mainstream political parties.[2]

A similarly pro-active strike against the perceived neglect and abuse of the environment by government agencies and planning departments is made by the Anti-Road Protest. This is a network of activists who specialise in sabotaging the building of new roads, for example, by occupying wooded areas due for clearance and building elaborate networks of tunnels in which activists are able to hide for weeks at a time, so delaying building work until the tunnels can be cleared of their inhabitants. As this brief description reveals, such is the commitment of Anti-Road Protest activists that they are willing to adopt a subversive lifestyle strategy that involves considerable amounts of personal discomfort and risk. According to Malyon (1998), activists' commitment to the Anti-Road Protect cause is underpinned by a belief, in line with other neo-greenist movements, in the human race's one-ness with the natural environment; a unison that has only recently been obscured through modernising process and the power of the modern state.

The Anti-Road Protest's anti-hegemonic stance against the state and its rational-scientific legitimation for the destruction of the natural environment has been enhanced through the movement's adoption of a spiritual leader, Arthur Pendragon, a Druid leader who believes himself to be a reincarnation of the legendary King Arthur of ancient Britain. In a recent biographical account of his life, Pendragon and co-author C.J. Stone note the significance of King Arthur as a figurehead whose authority over the land predates that of the modern state. Writing about the Anti-Road Protest's attempts to block the building of a new bypass near the town of Newbury in south-east England, Pendragon and Stone describe how the pre-modern aesthetic of the Arthurian legend permeated the discourses used by the protesters:

There was much talk of the spirit of the land, of its magical rebirth. Of the spirit of place. Of ancient battles being replayed. Of mythical codes written into the very landscape. Of dark conspiracies on a magical level. Of earth energy and earth peoples. Of the power of rocks and stones. Of the secret places, of the magical places. Of the magical power of water. Of the ancient tribes and their ceaseless wanderings. (2003: 126)

Witchcraft, paganism and the occult

Resistance against late modernity's investment in science and technology, and the latter's apparent disregard for the natural environment, can also be seen in the resurgence of interest in pre-modern practices and beliefs such as witchcraft and paganism. Like those groups who observe a 'back-to-the-land' philosophy, witches and neo-pagans also place emphasis on the natural powers of the earth. However, unlike New Age Travellers and similar groups, witches and neo-pagans are often based in urban locations, their sense of connection with the natural world being articulated through acquired forms of practice and belief rather than a radically alternative rural lifestyle (Moody, 1974). Moreover, while various 'back-to-the-land' activist groups embrace contemporary drug culture, seeing no apparent contradiction between modern chemically produced drugs and their anti-modern philosophy, witchcraft rejects 'narcotics, hallucinogens, or any other agents that might separate rational man from his material environment' (Truzzi, 1974).

A study of contemporary witchcraft practice in the UK by Greenwood (2000) illustrates how, through the learning and performance of ancient rituals, witches seek to harness the natural powers of the earth as a means of achieving spiritual power and harmony. Drawing on the work of Giddens (1991), Greenwood argues that everyday life in late modernity exhibits a number of pathological features, among them 'personal meaninglessness' which is brought about through the 'disembed[ing] of social relationships' and a withering away of 'tradition' (2000: 118). According to Greenwood, contemporary witchcraft is viewed by practitioners as part of a healing process, as a means of engaging with the fragmentatory effects of late modernity:

... magical practice is [considered to be] a spiritual path, a route to wholeness. Magic is often viewed by practitioners as a way of healing the individual from the effects of a fragmented rationalist and materialist world – it is a re-enchantment of the self ... Magical rituals may also be seen as spaces of resistance to the ordinary everyday world where alternative identities as transformative modal states for healing ... may be worked out. (ibid.: 121)

Greenwood's notion here of magic and witchcraft providing spaces of resistance offers another example of how late modern individuals are able to draw on pre-modern belief systems and practices as a means of subverting, or at least bringing into question, the taken-for-granted forms of cultural practice that dominate late modernity. Paradoxically, however, particular everyday cultural practices and customs associated with late modernity, notably consumerism, have played a significant part in enabling those with an interest in witchcraft to gain access to knowledge and resources. Thus, the contemporary practice of witchcraft is facilitated by, for example, organisations and associations, workshops, seminars, books and dedicated internet sites. Similarly, specialist shops play a crucial part in contemporary witchcraft practice, often being the only places in which the necessary ingredients for magic rituals can be acquired. Indeed, as Moody observes, in addition to providing the 'raw materials – oils, incenses, candles, herbs, parchments, etc. – for the magical workings, [such shops also] serve as meeting places for those interested in the occult' (1974: 226). The scenario described here can be equated with that of other leisure and lifestyle activities associated with late modernity. Thus, like music and sports fans, comic collectors, rock climbers and the like who frequently use clubs, retail outlets, internet sites, and so on, as a means of findings and communicating with others who share their interest, contemporary witches use the channels of communication and meeting places familiar to them as members of late modern society to gain contact with other likeminded individuals. This point is further illustrated through Greenwood's identification of what she refers to as a 'magical subculture' based in London, a network of urban dwellers from different walks of life drawn together because of their common interest in witchcraft (ibid.: 18). Within this 'magical subculture', however, the practice of witchcraft has been woven into a strategy of resistance aimed at subverting the less agreeable aspects of late modern living while maintaining those that are deemed desirable.

A similarly 'selective' rejection of late modern ideas and practices is evident in the growing interest in paganism. Like witchcraft, pagan beliefs centre on the forces at work in the natural world. Rather than investing faith in a metaphysical god or other deity, paganism inscribes such faith physical objects present in the natural world – animals, birds, trees, streams and so on. In the context of pagan belief 'humans are portrayed as inseparable from nature, and the entire universe is imagined as interconnected through a seeming system of symbolic correspondences' (Magliocco, 2001: 66). Such beliefs are taken up and re-enacted by neo-pagan groups in an attempt to re-establish the harmonic relationship with the natural world that they deem to be absent from late modern styles of living. As with contemporary witchcraft practices, however, neo-paganism is an example of a revived pre-modern belief system which rejects the rational-scientific knowledge base of late modernity, yet selectively draws upon late modern consumer practices in the enactment of pagan beliefs and rituals. Indeed, certain cultural forms more closely associated with late modernity, notably style-based youth cultures, have, in themselves, proved to be a catalyst for the resurgence of interest in paganism. Magliocco notes how during 'the last fifteen years, tattoos and body painting have become increasingly popular in the Pagan community, in part because they have been embraced by youth culture and other communities as symbols of oppositional identity' (ibid.: 48–9).[3] The connections between the pre-modern and the late modern are further evident in the way that neo-pagans draw upon the consumerist sensibilities they have acquired as members of late modern society. As Magliocco observes, in acquiring and/or fashioning magical tools for use in ceremonies, neo-pagans often 'convert ordinary commercial items ... subverting the item's original meaning and function, or layering new esoteric meanings onto everyday objects' (ibid.: 23).

Another form of resistance to late modernity's emphasis on scientific progress and rational explanations can be seen in the resurgence of interest in the occult. As Campbell and McIver note, science has effectively driven a wedge between the rational and the spiritual, its attack on religion being such that late modern individuals feel increasingly alienated from conventional religious belief. At the same time, however, science is unable to offer an alternative set of ideas to aid individuals in their quest for spiritual knowledge and understanding. It is in response to such circumstances that the recent growth of interest in occultism must be understood. Thus, according to Campbell and McIver, from the point of view of contemporary occultists, 'occultism and only occultism can serve to heal this great breach in [late] modern consciousness. It is a claim that neither science nor religion can make, and it is a major source of its strength and appeal' (1987: 49). From the point of view of its followers then, occultism provides a means of remaining in touch with the spiritual self, and thus subverting the feelings of alienation that threaten to engulf the individual in the state of spiritual anomie to which late modernity's paradigm of rational scientific explanation gives rise.

As with other forms of anti-modern belief and practice examined here, occultism's appeal in late modernity has much to do with its status as a form of 'popular' knowledge. Like witchcraft, paganism and other forms of anti-modern belief, occultism has entered the realm of the popular through its presence in films, television programmes, popular literature, and, increasingly during recent years, the internet. Such a popularisation of the occult has prompted criticism in some quarters. Adorno (1947a, 1947b) argues that occultism's appropriation by the cultural industries denudes it of any oppositional quality towards late modernity, 'popular' occultism being regarded by the masses as simply another form of mass entertainment. Adorno's view is shared by Nederman and Goulding who argue that, through its popularisation, occultism has become merely another discursive device whereby the underlying, taken-for-granted order of the everyday is reproduced: 'The Ouija board and the crystal-ball gazer tell us who we will marry and what our occupation will be. The underlying structure of everyday life, of the social conditions under which we live, is left completely intact' (1981: 330). Thus, argue Nederman and Goulding: 'Occultism ultimately comes to the defense of what it is intended to oppose; the given material reality' (ibid.: 331).

Arguably, however, the popularisation of occult knowledge can also be interpreted in an alternative way. Thus, through its incorporation into the realm of the popular, occultism has become one of a range of alternative knowledge bases that individuals may draw upon. Indeed, as Jorgensen and Jorgensen observe, contemporary occultism is located within an 'esoteric community' that 'derives [knowledge] from almost every conceivable source, including Indian and Eastern religions, Greek mythology and philosophy, heretical visions of early Christianity, paganism, the occult, psychic phenomena and research, and an odd assortment of anomalies (monsters, UFOs, Atlantis and pyramids)' (1982: 379). Clearly, then, to speak of occult practice in contemporary society, is to speak of a practice that may incorporate and combine a range of different knowledges and beliefs, depending on the aesthetic preference and everyday experience of those who involve themselves in occultism.

As the above observation indicates, the popularisation of occultism has served to both widen its appeal and to make it perhaps, more meaningful and understandable to individuals who feel alienated from the increasingly technocratic discourse of late modernity. Such contemporary appeal of occultism is also evidenced through its considerable youth following. As Ellis observes, horror films, such as those produced by British Hammer Film Production Ltd during the 1960s and early 1970s, did much to generate a fascination among young cinema audiences with the occult. According to Ellis, a highly influential film in this respect was *The Devil Rides Out*, based on Dennis Wheatley's 1934 novel of the same name:

> ... when Hammer Studios released a film version of Wheatley's 'The Devil Rides Out' ... in 1967, it was ideally placed to introduce Wheatley's vision

of 'black magic lodges' to British teenagers ... [The film] became a huge success ... and popular publishers were quick to follow with a series of cheap reprints of Wheatley's 'Black Magic Novels'. (2000: 158)

Ellis goes on to consider how the 'packaging' of the occult for a younger audience in turn gave rise to the appropriation of such beliefs into a lifestyle statement. The articulation of this lifestyle statement at a collective level included the staging of black mass rituals, the most celebrated of which took place during the early 1970s on Halloween in Dartmoor, south-west England and modelled itself closely on a scene described in *The Devil Rides Out* (ibid.: 164).

The interest in occultism among contemporary youth also relates to occult references in rock and heavy metal music. During the early 1970s, British heavy metal group Black Sabbath's eponymous debut album contained several songs with occult references, while Led Zeppelin guitarist Jimmy Page professed an interest in the books of Alistair Crowley, a leading practitioner of black magic (see Weinstein, 2000). This in turn generated an interest among many fans of those groups in the occult. In the 1990s black metal, a more extreme form of heavy metal (see Harris, 2000), took heavy metal's association with the occult to a new level. In the most extreme cases, black metal fans desecrated churches and other holy sites, while in Norway a spate of church burnings took place. Reasons given for engaging in this activity by those arrested, and often imprisoned, for their part in church burnings vary, but some perpetrators, drawing on discourses borrowed from black magic ritual and belief, described a sense of empowerment. For example, Kristian Vikernes, a black metal fan who is now serving a prison sentence for murder, stated in a newspaper report that 'by burning down, old churches especially, [sic] the power of the building accumulated by age would be transmitted to him' (Vestel, 1999: 12).

The associations made between heavy metal and the occult have been wildly exaggerated over the years, not least of all because of sensationalised media accounts and several high profile court cases against heavy metal artists in the US (see Richardson, 1991; Bennett, 2001b) following allegations that their music led several teenagers to commit suicide. At the same time, however, it seems clear that the occult references made in heavy metal music strengthen its appeal as an oppositional music, as a means through which young fans can symbolically reject the mundane predictability of their everyday existence, or negotiate the alienating effects that many young people feel as a result of the increasing risk and uncertainty (Beck, 1992) to which they are subjected.

A less controversial, yet equally popular, form of occult practice in contemporary everyday life is astrology. As Truzzi observes: 'Unlike witchcraft or most forms of occult belief, acceptance of astrology creates little religious conflict' (1975: 908). Moreover, such is the taken-for-grantedness of astrology that it has become seamlessly interwoven into the fabric of everyday life. This is particularly so in the case of horoscope reading which now ranks as the most popular form of contemporary astrological practice. Thus, according to Truzzi, a survey during the 1960s revealed that '53% of the French population regularly read their horoscopes in the papers' while a German study conducted during the 1950s with 100,000 interviewees 'found that 30% of those interviewed believed that there was a connection between the destiny of men and the stars (ibid.: 909). As Truzzi, notes, the fascination with horoscope reading continues despite astrology's rejection by the scientific community. In its own particular way then, the reading of horoscopes also represents a means through which individuals are able to look for answers that science is unable to provide; it 'represents', along with other forms of astrological practice, 'a general metaphysical world view for its adherent', that science is unwilling to engage with (ibid.).

The supernatural

The routinised and predictable pattern of everyday life in late modernity is also frequently subverted by stories of ghosts and other supernatural phenomena. As Nelson notes: 'Psychic experiences appear to be a universal feature of all human societies' (1975: 167). In a study of supernatural belief in westernised societies, Wuthnow (1976) suggested that such beliefs were primarily held by marginalised groups as a means of empowering themselves. Emmons and Sobal (1981), however, found no such correlation between supernatural belief and marginality, arguing that individuals across the social strata express beliefs in supernatural phenomena. Indeed, Greeley goes as far as to suggest that paranormal experiences are relatively 'normal' in contemporary society in that the 'majority of the population has had some such experience' (1975: 7). For Greeley, the capacity for belief in some form of afterlife, of which ghosts, apparitions, 'and various other assorted varieties of disembodied spirits' are deemed to provide evidence, is essentially a part of human nature, linked with a universal question as to what happens after death (ibid.: 33).

Again, there is a clear continuity between interest in the supernatural and its representation in popular media and consumer culture. The popularity of television shows such as the *X Files*, whose storylines focus primarily on ordinary people's encounters with inexplicable happenings in the context of their normal everyday surroundings – often in the 'safety' of their own homes – feeds a popular fascination with the supernatural. Moreover, such fictional accounts serve as an important handling strategy for late modern individuals who, while expressing an interest in supernatural phenomena, wish to avoid the sense of embarrassment and risk of stigma often associated with a publicly declared belief in such things. This concurs with Campbell and McIver's observation that when talking about supernatural phenomena individuals often 'feel it incumbent upon themselves to express some disclaimer' (1987: 47). In this sense, displaying an interest in the supernatural with reference to a popular fictional television show such as the X Files provides a form of legitimation, in that personal interest in the supernatural can be articulated without necessarily claiming personal belief in ghosts and other supernatural phenomena.[4]

The example noted above is analogous to Laba's interpretation of how folkloric beliefs and practices are now routinely evolved and passed down through the medium of popular culture. Central to Laba's argument here is a deconstruction of the folk/popular distinction and a reassessment of folk and popular culture as participating in a perpetual form of dialogic engagement, to the extent that the one is realised in and through the other:

> When popular culture is conceptualised as a socially-based structure of symbolic forms and human activities, it can be approached not as a product of technology per se, but of the various human interactions, expressive resources and patterns of communication that support and are framed by involvement in the popular culture process. The essential connection between folkloric and popular culture is in the social sphere ... The social practice of folkloric communication is structured by the symbolic forms in popular culture and serves as a means by which individuals and groups ritualize, organize and make sense of those forms of their day-to-day experience. (1986: 16–17)

In a similar way, it could be argued, our interest in and knowledge of supernatural phenomena are legitimated through their representation in popular cultural texts. In addition to fictional accounts of the supernatural, epitomised in the ever-popular late night 'ghost stories' on television and radio, it is also the frequent subject of 'serious' documentary programmes and magazine articles, thus providing additional avenues through which everyday discussions of ghosts and other supernatural phenomena both take their lead and find legitimation.

Like witchcraft, paganism and other themes discussed, the continuing interest in supernatural phenomena in late modernity can also be perceived as constituting an important strategy for the negotiation of rational-scientific explanations and technological processes, which infrequently instil a sense of powerlessness in individuals. Thus, as Walker argues:

> Although technology is a human endeavor, for most of us the intricacies of things like microcircuitry or fiber optics or even grocery-store bar code readers are essentially outside of our immediate understanding. In such a world, where the individual may sense a certain loss of control, belief in the supernatural (itself quite possibly outside of our control) ironically returns more direct power to humans ... technology is powerless and perhaps irrelevant when juxtaposed with the supernatural ... Some occurrences cannot be explained through logical or scientific thought. (1995: 5)

In his extensive work on contemporary belief in supernatural phenomena, Ellis (2001) argues that a major part of the attraction and appeal of the supernatural is the widely held notion that it is here among us, poised to disrupt in a spontaneous and unpredictable fashion the accepted routine of our day-to-day living. For this reason, suggests Ellis, aspects of the supernatural – haunted houses, ghostly apparitions and spectres – become woven into local knowledges. Every locality, he argues, can boast particular accounts of unexplainable phenomena, such accounts becoming ingrained in local discourses, the latter being manifested in stories about 'strange goings on' that are replayed around family meal tables, between friends in local bars and so on.

According to Ellis, the situating of supernatural happenings within particular local spaces in this way serves a dual function. First, it gives locals a point to focus on when discussing such happenings among themselves and with outsiders. Second, it provides a means of negotiating the supernatural, of assigning it to a particular site or sites. Thus, observes Ellis: 'The uncanny side of life is ... concentrate[d] into culturally safe locations and channels of expression' (2001: 117). Ghost walks through older city quarters have long exploited such 'safe spaces' of the supernatural as a means of enriching the tourist gaze (Urry, 1990). However, as Ellis notes, the assimilation of the supernatural into the everyday takes a variety of forms, many of which centre around the most unlikely locations. A pertinent example of this is the alleged haunting of the local Pizza Hut in a small town in central Ohio. The haunting has become an established aspect of local folklore, with many of the town's inhabitants being able to relate stories about employees' encounters with the ghost. As Ellis observes, the way in which locals construct this ghost story range from serious belief, accompanied by a mild fear, through to scepticism and, finally, unabashed disbelief. An overarching process for each mode of attachment to the Pizza Hut ghost story, however, is the symbolic transformation of a mundane space – a chain restaurant which is basically identical to thousands of others throughout the world – into a special space, one which has become the focus for a local legend and, thus, for a locally informed mode of story-telling in the context of which individuals are permitted to collectively discuss the subject of ghosts and the supernatural, a subject which in other conversational and situational contexts is deemed to be taboo.

A further explanation for the continuing belief in ghosts and spirits in late modern society is offered by Pimple who argues that this can be put down to the crisis of religion in late modernity. According to Pimple, this crisis is due to the increasing prevalence of science and its questioning of the metaphysical premises upon which Christianity and other religions are based. With the onset of modernity, science overtook religion as a means of explaining the origins of the universe and the evolution of life on earth. From Pimple's point of view, the contemporary practice of spiritualism, that is, the communication with spirits via mediums at séances, constitutes an attempt 'to reconcile science with religion' (Bednarowski quoted in Pimple, 1995). Pimple suggests that spiritualism is based on an interweaving of religious and scientific beliefs, in that belief in spiritual forces is based not upon external faith but on their physical manifestation during séances. Thus, observes Pimple, 'to the Spiritualists and to their detractors the one great truth was empirical evidence; religious authority did not reside in a charismatic leader or in a book or in a church, but in the continued proofs offered at séances' (1995: 84).

There has also been a steady growth in the belief in life after death and reincarnation in late modern society during recent decades. While there is little scientific support for such beliefs, at the same time science is unable to offer its own explanation of what follows death. In the absence of such an 'official' explanation, individuals seek their own answers to the question, or, alternatively, construct coping strategies which help them come to terms with the inevitable fact of death. At a popular level, such interest in and demand for answers on the subject of life after death has created a ready market for mediums and clairvoyants, ordinary individuals who profess a gift for contacting and communicating with spirits that occupy the 'after-life' (see, for example, Wooffitt, 1988, 1992, 1994). The obsession with life after death has similarly led many western individuals to selectively reject the doctrines of Christianity, and to seek solace in the notion of reincarnation, a belief derived from the Hindu and Bhuddist religions which holds that those who have died will return to earth again in human or animal form. Of significance in the way that western individuals respond to the notion of reincarnation is their construction of a particular discourse of reincarnation that conforms with late modern, western sensibilities. Thus, whereas Hindu and Bhuddist versions of reincarnation hold that the individual has no influence over the form that their reincarnation will take, western believers construct a discourse of reincarnation that centres around the preservation and continuity of their reflexively derived everyday self. As Walter observes:

> Modern [western] people … are likely to use the idea of reincarnation in order to search for the self, or at the very least to affirm the indestructibility and continuity of the self … the identities people construct in either past or future lives will have significant continuity with their present identity – at the very least they will be human rather than non-human identities, and more specifically will have personalities broadly consistent with their perceived present personality. (2001: 24–5)

Walters's observation is indicative of the trend already noted in this chapter whereby all forms of ideological discourse, irrespective of their apparent fixity in doctrines of culture, tradition and even religious belief, are subject to a process of reflexive selectivity in late modern society. As with all forms of information that enter the global flow, such discourses are reworked in particular local contexts in ways that correspond with specific instances of local, everyday experience and the collective knowledges, desires and beliefs that emerge from such contexts.

UFOs and alien encounters

Stories of aliens and UFOs (Unidentified Flying Objects) are another popular topic of everyday conversation in which the 'taken-for-grantedness' of rational-scientific explanations are challenged. Accounts of UFO encounters range from eyewitness reports of strange lights in the sky, occasionally supported by live footage caught on video camera, to more harrowing stories of alien abduction. In recent years, the issue of alien abduction has received more widespread attention, and is now the subject of numerous books (see, for example, Mack, 1994) and several films, including *Communion*, based on novelist Whitley Strieber's own alleged experiences as an alien abductee (see Ellis, 2001).

According to Rojcewicz (1991) belief in UFOs and aliens reflects a continuation of beliefs that predate modernity but adapt these in ways that correspond with late modern experience. Thus, as Rojcewicz observes, stories of encounters with 'subtle beings' date back to at least the Middle Ages, during which the dominance of religion played a central role in determining the origins and nature of such beings: 'The average citizen assumed the possibility of interaction with luminous entities called "daemons", positive demons, or one's personal creative spirit' (1991: 488). Rojcewicz further suggests that accounts of aliens and UFOs are essentially a present-day version of such earlier belief in supernatural beings. A parallel view is offered by Malmstrom and Coffman (1979) who identify a continuity between reports of humanoid aliens and the deities of Ancient civilisations, many of whom were also depicted as possessing human characteristics.[5]

Significantly, however, if earlier stories of encounters with strange beings drew on a metaphysical knowledge of a world not yet conquered by science and technology, contemporary accounts of UFOs start from the context of a world dominated by scientific explanation, posing the question of life on other worlds as a means of countering the dominance of the scientific authority. Although aliens are represented as technologically superior beings, they simultaneously stand outside the world of science and technology in that they are beyond the realm of rational-scientific explanation. In this sense, argues Rojcewicz, alien beings become a form popular everyday folklore which, as with contemporary belief in phenomena such as fairies, ghosts and other supernatural beings, can be placed in the domain of the unexplainable:

> Fairylore and the emerging lore of UFOs join together the subjective and the objective, the seen and the unseen, the factual and the imaginal as part of the ongoing culturally specific formulations of our entity with the world. The scientific worldview would rob the universe of spirit and purpose; fairies and UFOs re-enchant the world, not in the way of 'glamour' or 'pishogue', but in the sense that the world and our place in it is more and not less than it seems to the eyes. (1991: 503)

This view is supported by Fox through her observation that many UFO believers justify their belief precisely by pointing to the gaps in contemporary scientific knowledge. As Fox explains, the majority of individuals believe that 'science has [not yet] uncovered all there is to know about the universe. Most of us are aware that our stock of scientific knowledge is changing and expanding. Consequently, although it does not currently include knowledge of extra-terrestrial visitors, it may someday' (1979: 26). One notable deviation from this trend among contemporary UFO believers are those belonging to particular cults and sects, for whom UFOs take on a quasi-religious significance, becoming an object of worship or a source of salvation (ibid.: 27). Indeed, in many ways such interpretations of UFOs and their occupants relate more closely with the metaphysical belief systems of pre-industrial society. Thus, as Fox observes: 'Not convinced that intelligent life exists elsewhere in the universe, some fundamentalist sects interpret UFOs as angels from God or Satan' (ibid.: 27).

Mind and body

If the contemporary backlash against modernity has produced a series of beliefs and ideologies designed to subvert the dominant rational-scientific discourse with more esoteric forms of awareness and understanding about the world, then it has also produced new discourses of health and personal well-being. A pertinent example here is the increasing turn towards alternative medicines and healthcare in recent years. As Weissmann notes, many individuals now take advantage of 'unconventional' therapies, such as 'acupuncture, chiropractic, herbal medicine, spiritual healing [and] relaxation techniques' (1996: 183). Such a trend in late modern society denotes a growing distrust of western medical science, in particular its claims to superiority over pre-modern and non-western forms of treatment and its reliance on mass produced, chemical-based drugs. According to Weissmann, proponents of alternative therapies argue that 'medical science ... has substituted its own elite values for those that would better serve' the health and well-being of individuals (ibid.: 185). Such alternative discourses of health are further propelled into the public sphere by the media which now devotes considerable space to examining the relative merits of alternative therapy as compared with conventional medical treatment (Sampson, 1996).

A further indication of shifting attitudes towards health and well-being are the changing patters in purchasing and preparation of food, in particular the increasing popularity of organic food products. Though organic farming dates back to the rural communes of the late 1960s, in recent times the market for organic produce has grown considerably due to widespread public distrust of new farming methods. In recent years this distrust has been exacerbated due to the discovery of BSE (Bovine Spongiform Encephalopathy) and its human equivalent CJD (Creutzfeldt-Jakob Disease), which are believed to have been caused through the introduction of waste parts of slaughtered animals back into the foodchain of livestock in the industrial farming process. In addition to dedicated organic food shops and 'supermarkets', a number of established high street chain supermarkets now feature a limited range of fresh and tinned organic foods, particularly fruit and vegetables. The argument for organic food is that it is produced using traditional farming methods, thus avoiding the health risks deemed to be caused by pesticides and other chemicals associated with modern industrial farming (Chaney, 1996: 124). Similarly, organically farmed products are claimed to be free from the genetic modification that is now increasingly seen in industrially produced vegetables and fruit. Another reason why organic produce has become so popular over the past decade is the belief that it is more friendly to the environment than industrially farmed products, where the use of chemical-based fertilisers and poor crop rotation damages the soil and threatens to render acres of farming land infertile for long periods of time.

The adoption of vegetarian or vegan eating habits also symbolises a rejection of the rationalised methods of late modern farming and food preparation; such rejection is dually articulated, pertaining to both issues of personal health and well-being and to what is regarded as the exploitation and mistreatment of animals (Singer, 1998). The mass slaughtering of animals for food has increased progressively with the rising prominence and appeal of fast-food outlets such as McDonalds in major cities throughout the world. In this sense, vegetarianism can be regarded as a direct 'challenge to the dominant "food ideology"' (Charles and Kerr, 1988: 4) 'of western culture ... and an attempt to translate concern into action in terms of modified food choices' (Beardsworth and Keil, 1992: 284). As Beardsworth and Keil note, the rationalised way in which meat is prepared for the dinner table in western societies is such that the whole process is concealed from public view and, by definition, from consideration:

> Currently, the killing and processing of food animals are events which are removed from public contemplation by the physical shielding provided by the walls of the specialized abattoir or processing plant ... consumers normally only encounter food animals as sanitized, packaged commodities ready for cooking and consumption. (ibid.: 286)

Vegetarianism actively attempts to deconstruct this established, and taken-for-granted perception of meat as food by refocusing attention on the fate of animals and 'conceiv[ing] of [them] as moral patients' (ibid.: 284). Indeed, in recent years, the emphasis on the rights of animals not to be used as food has taken an increasingly militant stance, signalled, for example, by the attacking of fast-food outlets during anti-capitalist demonstrations in major cities. Given the various ideological positions that have become inscribed in the act of being a vegetarian, and which encapsulate a varying combination of philosophical, moralistic and health-related issues, it is possible to see vegetarianism as a possible core element within a range of inter-linked alternative lifestyle practices. This view is supported by Warde:

The centrality of the moral elements involved in the adoption of vegetarianism is important as an expression of alternative styles of life in the contemporary UK. It is possible to think of vegetarianism as a social movement, and in that sense to see it as part of stylization, as the emergence of a group of people defined by their specialized consumption practices, in a manner consistent with notions of lifestyle politics. There is some evidence of an association between alternative diets, use of alternative therapies, health consciousness and spiritual quests. (1997: 87)

Warde also identifies links between vegetarianism and 'political, ethical or religious commitments' (ibid.: 32). Warde's findings correspond with Hanke's notion of the preparation and eating of food as a discursive practice that resonates 'with a new "urban" ideology of lifestyles' (1989: 229). According to Hanke, recent decades have seen a radical shift in the significance of food and eating away from the sphere of the domestic and into the public sphere. Food and eating now rank as highly visual social descriptors of identity and outlook, along with fashion, style and a range of other lifestyle resources used by individuals to situate themselves in particular social groups and to communicate messages about themselves to others.

Conclusion

This chapter has considered the significance of a range of pre- and anti-modern sensibilities as alternative lifestyle strategies in the context of late modernity. Beginning with a look at various neo-greenist movements, it was noted how each of these contribute, in their own way, to a growing concern about threats to the environment caused, for example, by urban development and the disposal of industrial waste. It was also noted how neo-greenist movements embrace pre-modern knowledges regarding the powers of the natural world. This sensibility is shared with witchcraft and paganism, practices which have also found a renewed level of support in late modernity due to their emphasis on the power of nature to heal the mental and physical damage done to the individual by the rigours of late modern existence. Paganism and witchcraft are also used as a means of subverting the dominance of rational-scientific explanation and its steady encroachment of the institutions of social life. Other subversion strategies employed by individuals include an interest/belief in supernatural phenomena, examples of which include ghosts, spirits and alien beings. As examined in the chapter, the latter are used by late modern individuals as a means of challenging the parameters and authority of rational-scientific explanation, the supernatural being beyond such forms of explanation. Finally, it was examined how new sensibilities of mind and body, notably alternative medicines and organic/vegetarian diets, are providing late modern individuals with resources through which to challenge the dominance of scientific methods and industrial production in another crucial sphere of everyday life, health and well-being.

Notes

1. The 'back-to-the-land' aesthetic expressed by New Age Travellers and associated groups, for example, the Anti-Road Protest, has also inspired a growing 'New Age' literature. See, for example, Pendragon and Stone's (2003) *The Trails of Arthur.*

2. Many of these movements grew out of the late 1980s British rave party scene which, through its use of rural locations and emphasis on 'tribalism' provided an impetus for the back-to-the-land philosophy preserved in the more politicised groups that followed.

3. Another link between paganism and youth culture is Robin Hardy's 1973 film *The Wicker Man* which depicts a present-day pagan community on a remote Scottish island. Since its release the film has acquired cult status, to the extent that an annual *Wicker Man* festival, featuring music from a variety of new-folk and new age artists, now takes place in the south-west of Scotland at the location where the film was made. The festival culminates with the sacrificial burning of a giant wicker man, mimicking the final scene of the film.

4. As Knight (2000) notes, the *X Files* also feeds a growing interest among late modern individuals in conspiracy theories. The appeal of the *X Files* can also be attributed in part to the fact that it draws in part on actual allegations of supernatural happenings and eye-witness reports (see Goldman, 1995).

5. The more sinister concept of abduction by aliens also predates modernity. According to Ellis (2001) recorded accounts of abduction, detailing experiences of medical examination and sensory deprivation broadly similar to those described by modern day abuctees, go back at least as far as the seventeenth century.

Bibliography

Abbott, Chris (1999) 'Web Publishing By Young People', in J. Sefton-Green (ed.) *Young People, Creativity and New Technologies: The Challenge of Digital Arts*. London: Routledge.

Abercrombie, Nicholas (1994) 'Authority and Consumer Society', in R. Keat, N. Whiteley and N. Abercrombie (eds) *The Authority of the Consumer*. London: Routledge.

Abrams, Mark (1959) *The Teenage Consumer*. London: London Press Exchange.

Adorno, Theodore W. (1990 [1941]) 'On Popular Music', in S. Frith and A. Goodwin (eds) *On Record: Rock, Pop and the Written Word*. London: Routledge.

Adorno, Theodore W. (1947a) 'Thesis Against Occultism', *Telos*, 19: 7–12.

Adorno, Theodore W. (1947b) 'The Stars Down to Earth: The Los Angeles Times Astrology Column', *Telos*, 19: 13–90.

Adorno, Theodore W. and Horkheimer, Max (1969) *The Dialectic of Enlightenment*. London: Allen Lane.

Alasuutari, Pertti (1999) 'Introduction: Three Phases of Reception Studies', in P. Alasuutari (ed.) *Rethinking the Media Audience*. London: Sage.

Allen, Robert C. (1988) 'Bursting Bubbles: "Soap Opera", Audiences, the Limits of Genre', in E. Sieter, H. Borchers, G. Kreutzner and E.M. Warth (eds) *Remote Control: Television, Audiences, and Cultural Power*. London: Routledge.

Alneng, Victor (2002) '"What the Fuck is a Vietnam? Touristic Phantasms and the Popcolonization of (the) Vietnam (War)", *Critique of Anthropology*, 22(4): 461–89.

Ang, Ien (1996) *Living Room Wars: Rethinking Audiences for a Postmodern World*. London: Routledge.

Appadurai, Arjun (1990) 'Disjuncture and Difference in the Global Cultural Economy', in M. Featherstone (ed.) *Global Culture: Nationalism, Globalisation and Modernity*. London: Sage.

Atton, Chris (2002) *Alternative Media*. London: Sage.

Back, Les (1993) 'Race, Identity and Nation within an Adolescent Community in South London', *New Community*, 19(2): 217–33.

Back, Les (1996) *New Ethnicities and Urban Culture: Racisms and Multiculture in Young Lives*. London: UCL Press.

Bibliography

Bakhtin, Mikhai M. (1984) *Rabelais and his World*, trans. H. Isowolsky. Cambridge, MA: MIT Press.

Ballaster, Ros, Beetham, Margaret, Frazer, Elizabeth and Hebron, Sandra (1991) *Women's Worlds: Ideology, Femininity and the Woman's Magazine*. Basingstoke: Macmillan.

Banerji, Sabita and Baumann, Gerd (1990) 'Bhangra 1984–88: Fusion and Professionalization in a Genre of South Asian Dance Music', in P. Oliver (ed.) *Black Music in Britain: Essays on the Afro-Asian Contribution to Popular Music*. Milton Keynes: Open University Press.

Barker, Chris and Andre, Julie (1996) 'Did You See? Soaps, Teenage Talks and Gendered Identity', *Young: Nordic Journal of Youth Research*, 4(4): 21–38.

Barnard, Malcolm (1996) *Fashion as Communication*. London: Routledge.

Barthes, Roland (1972) *Mythologies*. London: Paladin.

Bassett, Caroline (1991) 'Virtually Gendered: Life in an on-line world', in K. Gelder and S. Thornton (eds) (1997) *The Subcultures Reader*. London: Routledge.

Baudrillard, Jean (1983) *Simulations*. New York: Semiotext(e).

Baudrillard, Jean (1988) *America*, trans. C. Turner. London: Verso.

Baudrillard, Jean (1991) 'The Reality Gulf', The *Guardian*, 11 January: 25.

Baudrillard, Jean (1992) 'Simulacra and Simulations', in P. Brooker (ed.) *Modernism/Postmodernism*. London: Longman.

Bauman, Zygmunt (1992) *Intimations of Postmodernity*. London: Routledge.

Bauman, Zygmunt (1997) *Postmodernity and its Discontents*. Cambridge: Polity.

Baumann, Gerd (1990) 'The Re-Invention of Bhangra: Social Change and Aesthetic Shifts in a Punjabi Music in Britain', *Journal of the International Institute for Comparative Music Studies and Documentation*, 32(2): 81–95.

Baumann, Gerd (1997) 'Dominant and Demotic Discourses of Culture: Their Relevance to Multi-Ethnic Alliances', in P. Werbner and T. Modood (eds) *Debating Cultural Hybridity: Multi-Cultural Identities and the Politics of Anti-Racism*. London: Zed Books.

Bausinger, Hermann (1984) 'Media, Technology and Daily Life', *Media, Culture and Society*, 6: 343–51.

Beardsworth, Alan and Keil, Teresa (1992) 'The Vegetarian Option: Varieties, Conversions, Motives and Careers', *The Sociological Review*, 40(2): 253–93.

Beattie, Geoffrey (1990) *England After Dark*. London: Weidenfeld and Nicolson.

Beck, Ulrich (1992) *The Risk Society: Towards a New Modernity*, trans. M. Ritter. London: Sage.

Beck, Ulrich (1998) 'Politics of Risk Society', in J. Franklin (ed.) *The Politics of Risk Society*. Cambridge: Polity.

Becker, Howard S. (1951) 'The Professional Jazz Musician and his Audience', in R.S. Denisoff and R.A. Peterson (eds) (1972) *The Sounds of Social Change*. Chicago: Rand McNally and Company.

Bell, Claudia (2002) 'The Big "OE": Young New Zealand Travellers as Secular Pilgrims', *Tourist Studies*, 2(2): 143–58.

Bell, Daniel (1976) *The Cultural Contradictions of Capitalism*. London: Heinemann.

Bennett, Andy (1997) '"Going Down the Pub": The Pub Rock Scene as Resource for the Consumption of Popular Music', *Popular Music*, 16(1): 97–108.

Bennett, Andy (1999) 'Hip Hop am Main: The Localisation of Rap Music and Hip Hop Culture', *Media, Culture and Society*, 21(1): 77–91.

Bennett, Andy (2000) *Popular Music and Youth Culture: Music, Identity and Place*. Basingstoke: Macmillan.

Bennett, Andy (2001a) 'Plug in and Play! UK Indie Guitar Culture', in A. Bennett and K. Dawe (eds) *Guitar Cultures*. Oxford: Berg.

Bennett, Andy (2001b) *Cultures of Popular Music*. Buckingham: Open University Press.

Bennett, Andy (2002) 'Music, Media and Urban Mythscapes: A Study of the Canterbury Sound', *Media, Culture and Society*, 24(1): 107–20.

Bennett, Andy (2004) 'New Tales from Canterbury: The Making of a Virtual Music Scene', in A. Bennett and R.A. Peterson (eds) *Music Scenes: Local, Trans-Local and Virtual*, Nashville, TN: Vanderbilt University Press.

Bennett, Andy and Peterson, Richard A. (eds) (2004) *Music Scenes: Local, Trans-local and Virtual*. Nashville, TN: Vanderbilt University Press.

Bennett, Tony (1986a) 'Introduction: Popular Culture and the Turn to Gramsci', in T. Bennett, C. Mercer and J. Woolacott (eds) *Popular Culture and Social Relations*. Milton Keynes: Open University Press.

Bennett, Tony (1986b) 'The Politics of the "Popular" and Popular Culture', in T. Bennett, C. Mercer and J. Woolacott (eds) *Popular Culture and Social Relations*. Milton Keynes: Open University Press.

Bennett, Tony, Martin, Graham, Mercer, Colin and Woollacott, Janet (eds) (1981) *Culture, Ideology and Social Process*. London: Open University Press.

Berger, Harris M. (1999) *Metal, Rock and Jazz: Perception and the Phenomenology of Musical Experience*. Hanover, NH: Wesleyen University Press.

Berman, Marshall (1992) 'Why Modernism Still Matters', in S. Lash and J. Friedman (eds) *Modernity and Identity*. Oxford: Blackwell.

Best, Steven and Kellner, Douglas (1997) *The Postmodern Turn*. London: The Guildford Press.

Bhachu, Parminder (1991) 'Culture, Ethnicity and Class Among Punjabi Sikh Women in 1990s Britain', *New Community*, 17(3): 401–12.

Bhatt, Chetan (1997) *Liberation and Purity: Race, New Religious Movements and the Ethics of Postmodernity*. London: UCL Press.

Björnberg, Alf and Stockfelt, Ola (1996) 'Kristen Klatvask fra Vejle: Danish Pub Music, Mythscapes and "Local Camp"', *Popular Music*, 15(2): 131–47.

Bjurström, Erling (1997) 'The Struggle for Ethnicity: Swedish Youth Styles and the Construction of Ethnic Identities', *Young: Nordic Journal of Youth Research*, 5(3): 44–58.

Bocock, Robert (1993) *Consumption*. London: Routledge.

Borden, Iain (2001) *Skateboarding, Space and the City: Architecture and the Body*. Oxford: Berg.

Bottomore, Tom (1984) *The Frankfurt School*. London: Tavistock Publications Ltd.

Bourdieu, Pierre (1984) *Distinction: A Social Critique of the Judgement of Taste*, trans. R. Nice. London: Routledge and Kegan Paul.

Bradley, Dick (1992) *Understanding Rock 'n' Roll: Popular Music in Britain 1955–1964*. Buckingham: Open University Press.

Breward, Christopher (1995) *The Culture of Fashion: A New History of Fashionable Dress*. Manchester: Manchester University Press.

Brown, Adam (ed.) (1998) *Fanatics! Power, Identity and Fandom in Football*. London: Routledge.

Brydon, Anne and Niessen, Sandra (eds) (1998) *Consuming Fashion: Adorning the Transnational Body*. Oxford: Berg.

Bryman, Alan (1999a) 'Theme Parks and McDonaldization', in B. Smart (ed.) *Resisting McDonaldization*. London: Sage.

Bryman, Alan (1999b) 'The Disneyization of Society', *The Sociological Review*, 47(1): 25–47.

Buck-Morss, Susan (1989) *The Dialectics of Seeing: Walter Benjamin and the Arcades Project*. Cambridge, MA: MIT Press.

Bull, Michael (2000) *Sounding Out the City: Personal Stereos and the Management of Everyday Life*. Oxford: Berg.

Calabrese, Andrew (2001) 'Why Localism? Communication Technology and the Shifting Scales of Political Community', in J. Gregory and E.W. Rothenbuhler (eds) *Communication and Community*. London: Lawrence Erlbaum.

Callinicos, Alex (1989) *Against Postmodernism: A Marxist Critique*. London: Polity.

Campbell, Colin and McIver, Shirley (1987) 'Cultural Sources of Support for Contemporary Occultism', *Social Compass*, 34(1): 41–60.

Cannon, Aubrey (1998) 'The Cultural and Historical Contexts of Fashion', in A. Brydon and S. Niessen (eds) (1998) *Consuming Fashion: Adorning the Transnational Body*. Oxford: Berg.

Carrington, Ben and Wilson, Brian (2002) 'Global Clubcultures: Cultural Flows and Late Modern Dance Music Culture', in M. Cieslik and G. Pollock (eds) *Young People in Risk Society: The Restructuring of Youth Identities and Transitions in Late Modernity*. Aldershot: Ashgate.

Carter, Erica (1984) 'Alice in the Consumer Wonderland: West German Case Studies in Gender and Consumer Culture', in A. McRobbie and M. Nava (eds) *Gender and Generation*. Basingstoke: Macmillan.

Carter, Erica, James, Donald and Squires, Judith (eds) (1993) *Space and Place: Theories of Identity and Location*. London: Lawrence and Wishart.

Cashmore, Ellis (1983) *Rastaman: The Rastafarian Movement in England*. London: George Allen and Unwin Ltd.

Cashmore, Ellis (1984) *No Future: Youth and Society*. London: Heinemann.

Chambers, Iain (1985) *Urban Rhythms: Pop Music and Popular Culture*. Basingstoke: Macmillan.

Chambers, Iain (1990) *Border Dialogues: Journeys in Postmodernity*. London: Routledge.

Chaney, David (1994) *The Cultural Turn: Scene Setting Essays on Contemporary Cultural History*. London: Routledge.

Chaney, David (1996) *Lifestyles*. London: Routledge.

Chaney, David (2002a) *Cultural Change and Everyday Life*. Basingstoke: Palgrave.

Chaney, David (2002b) 'The Power of Metaphors in Tourism Theory', in S. Coleman and M. Crang (eds) *Tourism: Between Place and Performance*. Oxford: Berghahn Books.

Charles, Nicki and Kerr, Masion (1988) *Women, Food and Families*. Manchester: Manchester University Press.

Clarke, John (1976) 'The Skinheads and the Magical Recovery of Community', in S. Hall and T. Jefferson (eds) *Resistance Through Rituals: Youth Subcultures in Post-War Britain*. London: Hutchinson.

Clarke, John, Hall, Stuart, Jefferson, Tony and Roberts, Brian (1976) 'Subcultures, Cultures and Class: A Theoretical Overview', in S. Hall and T. Jefferson (eds) *Resistance Through Rituals: Youth Subcultures in Post-War Britain*. London: Hutchinson.

Cohen, Phil (1972) *Subcultural Conflict and Working Class Community*, Working Papers in Cultural Studies 2. Birmingham: University of Birmingham.

Cohen, Sara (1991) *Rock Culture in Liverpool: Popular Music in the Making*. Oxford: Clarendon Press.

Cohen, Sara (1997) 'More than the Beatles: Popular Music, Tourism and Urban Regeneration', in S. Abram, J. Waldren and D.V.L. Macleod (eds) *Tourism and Tourists: Identifying with People and Places*. Oxford: Berg.

Cohen, Stanley (1987) *Folk Devils and Moral Panics: The Creation of the Mods and Rockers*, 3rd edn. Oxford: Basil Blackwell.

Cohen, Stanley and Taylor, Laurie (1976) *Escape Attempts: The Theory and Practice of Resistance to Everyday Life*. London: Penguin.

Connor, Steven (1989) *Postmodern Culture: An Introduction to Theories of the Contemporary*. Oxford: Blackwell.

Craik, Jennifer (1994) *The Face of Fashion: Cultural Studies in Fashion*. London: Routledge.

Craik, Jennifer (1997) 'The Culture of Tourism', in C. Rojek and J. Urry (eds) *Touring Cultures: Transformations of Travel and Theory*. London: Routledge.

Crawshaw, Carol and Urry, John (1997) 'Tourism and the Photographic Eye', in C. Rojek and J. Urry (eds) *Touring Cultures: Transformations of Travel and Theory*. London: Routledge.

Creeber, Glen (2001) '"Taking Our Personal Lives Seriously": Intimacy, Continuity and Memory in the Television Drama Serial', *Media, Culture and Society*, 23(4): 439–55.

Crook, Stephen (1998) 'Minotaurs and Other Monsters: "Everyday Life" in Recent Social Theory', *Sociology*, 32(2): 523–40.

Crouch, David, Aronsson, Lars and Wahlström, Lage (2001) 'Tourist Encounters', *Tourist Studies*, 1(3): 253–70.

Dawe, Kevin and Bennett, Andy (2001) 'Introduction: Guitars, People and Places', in A. Bennett and K. Dawe (eds) *Guitar Cultures*. Oxford: Berg.

Denisoff, R.S. and Romanowski, William D. (1991) *Risky Business: Rock in Film*. New Jersey: Transaction.

de Certeau, Michel (1984) *The Practice of Everyday Life*. London: University of California Press.

Denisoff, R.S. and Peterson, R.A. (eds) (1972) *The Sounds of Social Change*. Chicago: Rand McNally and Company.

DeNora, Tia (2000) *Music in Everyday Life*. Cambridge. Cambridge University Press.

Denzin, Norman K. (1991) '*Paris, Texas* and Baudrillard on America', *Theory, Culture and Society*, 8(2): 121–33.

Desforges, Luke (1998) '"Checking Out the Planet": Global Representations/Local Identities and Youth Travel', in T. Skelton and G. Valentine (eds) *Cool Places: Geographies of Youth Culture*. London: Routledge.

Douglas, Mary (1992) *Risk and Blame: Essays in Cultural Theory*. London: Routledge.

Drew, Robert S. (1997) 'Embracing the Role of the Amatuer: How Karaoke Bar Patrons Become Regular Performers', *Journal of Contemporary Ethnography*, 25(4): 449–68.

Drew, Rob (2001) *Karaoke Nights: An Ethnographic Rhapsody*. Walnut Creek, CA: Alta Mira Press.

Drew, Rob (2004) '"Scenes" Dimensions of Karaoke in the US', in A. Bennett and R.A. Peterson (eds) (2004) *Music Scenes: Local, Trans-local and Virtual*. Nashville, TN: Vanderbilt University Press.

Drotner, Kirstin (2000) 'Difference and Diversity: Trends in Young Danes' Media Uses', *Media, Culture and Society*, 22(2): 149–66.

Duncombe, Stephen (1997) *Notes from the Underground: Zines and the Politics of Alternative Culture*. London: Verso.

Dürrschmidt, Jörg (2000) *Everyday Lives in the Global City: The Delinking of Locale and Milieau*. London: Routledge.

Dwyer, Claire (1998) 'Contested Identities: Challenging Dominant Representations of Young British Muslim Women', in T. Skelton and G. Valentine (eds) *Cool Places: Geographies of Youth Culture*. London: Routledge.

Eade, John (2002) 'Adventure Tourists and Locals in a Global City: Resisting Tourist Performances in London's "East End"', in S. Coleman and M. Crang (eds) *Tourism: Between Place and Performance*. Oxford: Berghahn Books.

Eco, Umberto (1987) *Travels in Hyperreality*. London: Picador.

Eicher, Joanne B. and Sumberg, Barbara (1995) 'World Fashion, Ethnic and National Dress', in J.B. Eicher (ed.) *Dress and Ethnicity: Change Across Space and Time*. Oxford: Berg.

Eldridge, John (ed.) (1995) *The Glasgow University Media Group Reader: News Content, Language and Visuals*. London: Routledge.

Ellis, Bill (2000) *Raising the Devil: Satanism, New Religions and the Media*. Lexington: The University Press of Kentucky.

Ellis, Bill (2001) *Aliens, Ghosts, and Cults: Legends We Live*. Jackson: University Press of Mississippi.

Elsrud, Torun (2001) 'Risk Creation in Traveling: Backpacker Adventure Narration', in *Annals of Tourism Research*, 28(3): 597–617.

Emmons, Charles F. and Sobal, Jeff (1981) 'Paranormal Beliefs: Testing the Marginality Hypothesis', *Sociological Focus*, 14(1): 49–56.

Entwistle, Joanne (2000) *The Fashioned Body: Fashion, Dress and Modern Social Theory*. Cambridge: Polity.

Eyerman, Ron and Jamison, Andrew (1998) *Music and Social Movements: Mobilizing Traditions in the Twentieth Century*. Cambridge: Cambridge University Press.

Facer, Keri and Furlong, Ruth (2001) 'Beyond the Myth of the "Cyberkid": Young People at the Margins of the Information Revolution', *Journal of Youth Studies*, 4(4): 451–69.

Featherstone, Mike (1988) 'In Pursuit of the Postmodern: An Introduction', *Theory, Culture and Society*, 5(2): 195–215.

Featherstone, Mike (1991) *Consumer Culture and Postmodernism*. London: Sage.

Featherstone, Mike (1995) *Undoing Culture: Globalization, Postmodernism and Identity*. London: Sage.

Filipucci, Paolo (2002) 'Acting Local: Two Performances in Northern Italy', in S. Coleman and M. Crang (eds) *Tourism: Between Place and Performance*. Oxford: Berghahn Books.

Finkelstein, Joanne (1996) *After a Fashion*. Melbourne: Melbourne University Press.

Finkelstein, Joanne (1999) 'Chic – A Look That's Hard to See', *Fashion Theory*, 3(3): 363–86.

Finnegan, Ruth (1989) *The Hidden Musicians: Music-Making in an English Town*, Cambridge University Press, Cambridge.

Fiske, John (1989a) *Understanding Popular Culture*. London: Routledge.

Fiske, John (1989b) *Reading the Popular*. London: Routledge.

Fonarow, Wendy (1997) 'The Spatial Organisation of the Indie Music Gig', in K. Gelder and S. Thornton (eds) *The Subcultures Reader*. London: Routledge.

Fornäs, Johan (1994) 'Karaoke: Subjectivity, Play and Interactive Media', *Nordicom Review*, 1: 87–103.

Forrest, Emma (1994) 'Generation X', The *Sunday Times*, 10 July: 17.

Fountain, Nigel (1988) *Underground: The London Alternative Press 1966–74*. London: Comedia/Routledge.

Fowler, David (1992) 'Teenage Consumers? Young Wage-Earners and Leisure in Manchester, 1919–1939', in A. Davies and S. Fielding (eds) *Workers' Worlds: Cultures and Communities in Manchester and Salford, 1880–1939*. Manchester: Manchester University Press.

Fox, Phillis (1979) 'Social and Cultural Factors Influencing Beliefs About UFOs', in R.F. Haines (ed.) *UFO Phenomena and the Behavioral Scientist*. Metuchen, NJ: The Scarecrow Press.

Frisby, David and Featherstone, Mike (1997) *Simmel on Culture: Selected Writings*. London: Sage.

Frith, Simon (1981) 'The Magic That Can Set You Free: The Ideology of Folk and the Myth of Rock', *Popular Music*, 1: 159–68.

Frith, Simon (1983) *Sound Effects: Youth, Leisure and the Politics of Rock*. London: Constable.

Frith, Simon (1987) 'Towards an Aesthetic of Popular Music', in R. Leppert and S. McClary (eds) *Music and Society: The Politics of Composition, Performance and Reception*. Cambridge: Cambridge University Press.

Frith, Simon (1990) 'Video Pop: Picking Up the Pieces', in S. Frith (ed.) *Facing the Music: Essays on Pop, Rock and Culture*. London: Mandarin.

Froehling, Oliver (1999) 'Internauts and Guerrilleros: The Zapatista Rebellion in Chipas, Mexico and its Extension into Cyberspace', in M. Crang, P. Crang and J. May (eds) *Virtual Geographies: Bodies, Space and Relations*. London: Routledge.

Fruehling Springwood, Charles (2002) 'Farming, Dreaming, and Playing in Iowa: Japanese Mythopoetics and Agrarian Utopia', in S. Coleman and M. Crang (eds) *Tourism: Between Place and Performance*. Oxford: Berghahn Books.

Furedi, Frank (1997) *The Culture of Fear: Risk-Taking and the Morality of Low Expectation*. London: Cassell.

Ganetz, Hillevi (1995) 'The Shop, the Home and Feminity as a Masquerade', in J. Fornäs and G. Bolin (eds) *Youth Culture in Late Modernity*. London: Sage.

Gardiner, Michael E. (2000) *Critiques of Everyday Life*. London: Routledge.

Gauntlett, David and Hill, Annette (1999) *TV Living: Television Culture and Everyday Life*. London: Routledge/British Film Institute.

Geraghty, Christine (1981) 'The Continuous Serial – A Definition', in R. Dyer, C. Geraghty, M. Jordan, T. Lovell, R. Paterson and J. Stewart (eds) *Television Monograph: Coronation Street*. London: BFI.

Geraghty, Christine (1991) *Women and Soap Opera: A Study of Prime Time Soaps*. Cambridge: Polity.

Geraghty, Christine (1992) 'British Soaps in the 1980s', in D. Strinati and S. Wagg (eds) *Come on Down?: Popular Media Culture in Post-War Britain*. London: Routledge.

Gergen, Kenneth J. (1996) 'Postmodern Culture and the Revision of Alienation', in F. Geyer (ed.) *Alienation, Ethnicity, and Postmodernity*. London: Greenwood Press.

Giddens, Anthony (1991) *Modernity and Self Identity: Self and Society in the Late Modern Age*. Cambridge: Polity.

Giddens, Anthony (1998) 'Risk Society: The Context of British Politics', in J. Franklin (ed.) *The Politics of Risk Society*. Cambridge: Polity.

Gill, Alison (1998) 'Deconstruction Fashion: The Making of Unfinished, Decomposing and Re-assembled Clothes', *Fashion Theory*, 2(1): 25–50.

Gillespie, Marie (1995) *Television, Ethnicity and Cultural Change*. London: Routledge.

Gilroy, Paul (1993) *The Black Atlantic: Modernity and Double Consciousness*. London: Verso.

Gledhill, Christine (ed.) (1991) *Stardom: Industry of Desire*. London: Routledge.

Gold, John and Gold, Margaret (2000) *Cities of Culture: Tourism, Promotion and Consumption of Spectacle in Western Cities Since 1851*. Aldershot: Ashgate.

Goldman, Jane (1995) *The X Files: Book of the Unexplained, Volume 1*. London: Simon and Schuster.

Goffman, Erving (1959) *The Presentation of the Self in Everyday Life*. Harmondsworth: Penguin.

Gramsci, Antonio (1971) *Selections From the Prison Notebooks*. London: Lawrence and Wishart.

Grazian, David (2003) *Blue Chicago: The Search for Authenticity in Urban Blues Clubs*. Chicago: University of Chicago Press.

Greeley, Andrew M. (1975) *The Sociology of the Paranormal: A Reconnaissance.* Sage: London.

Green (ed.) *Young People, Creativity and New Technologies: The Challenge of Digital Arts.* London: Routledge.

Greenwood, Susan (2000) *Magic, Witchcraft and the Otherworld: An Anthropology.* Oxford: Berg.

Gregson, Nicky, Brooks, Kate and Crewe, Louise (2001) 'Bjorn Again? Rethinking 70s Revivalism through the Reappropriation of 70s Clothing', *Fashion Theory*, 5(1): 3–28.

Grossberg, Lawrence (1986) 'Is There Rock After Punk?', *Critical Studies in Mass Communication*, 3(1): 50–74.

Grossberg, Lawrence (1992) *We Gotta Get Out Of This Place: Popular Conservatism and Postmodern Culture.* London: Routledge.

Grossberg, Lawrence (1994) 'Is Anybody Listening? Does Anybody Care?: On Talking About "The State of Rock"', in A. Ross and T. Rose (eds) *Microphone Fiends: Youth Music and Youth Culture.* London: Routledge.

Habermas, Jürgen (1987) *The Theory of Communicative Action (Vol. 2).* Cambridge: Polity.

Hall, Roz and Newbury, Darren (1999) '"What Makes You Switch On?" Young People, the Internet and Cultural Participation', in J. Sefton-Green (ed.) *Young People, Creativity and New Technologies: The Challenge of Digital Arts.* London: Routledge.

Hall, Stuart (1968) 'The Hippies: An American "Moment"', Birmingham Centre for Contemporary Cultural Studies: University of Birmingham.

Hall, Stuart (1971) 'Technics of the Medium', in J. Corner and S. Harvey (eds) (1996) *Television Times: A Reader.* London: Arnold.

Hall, Stuart (1973) 'Encoding and Decoding in the Television Discourse', CCCS Stencilled Paper 7, University of Birmingham.

Hall, Stuart (1980) 'Cultural Studies: Two Paradigms', in T. Bennett, G. Martin, C. Mercer and J. Woollacott (eds) (1981) *Culture, Ideology and Social Process.* London: Open University Press/Batsford.

Hall, Stuart and Jefferson, Tony (eds) (1976) *Resistance Through Rituals: Youth Subcultures in Post-War Britain.* London: Hutchinson.

Hamilton, Peter (2002) 'The Street and Everyday Life', in T. Bennett and D. Watson (ed.) *Understanding Everyday Life.* Oxford: Open University and Blackwell.

Hanke, Robert (1989) 'Mass Media and Lifestyle Differentiation: An Analysis of the Public Discourse About Food', *Communication*, 11: 221–38.

Hanna, Judith Lynne (1992) 'Moving Messages: Identity and Desire in Popular Music and Social Dance', in J. Lull (ed.) *Popular Music and Communication*, 2nd edn. London: Sage.

Hannerz, Ulf (1990) 'Cosmopolitans and Locals in World Culture', in M. Featherstone (ed.) *Global Culture: Nationalism, Globalisation and Modernity.* London: Sage.

Hardin, Michael (1999) 'Mar(k)ing the Objected Body: A Reading of Contemporary Female Tattooing', *Fashion Theory*, 3(1): 81–108.

Harrell, Jack (1994) 'The Poetics of Destruction: Death Metal Rock', *Popular Music and Society*, 18(1): 91–107.

Bibliography

Harris, David (1992) *From Class Struggle to the Politics of Pleasure: The Effects of Gramscianism on Cultural Studies*. London: Routledge.

Harris, Keith (2000) 'Roots?: The Relationship Between the Global and the Local Within the Extreme Metal Scene', *Popular Music*, 19(1): 13–30.

Havens, Timothy (2000) '"The Biggest Show in the World": Race and the Global Popularity of *The Cosby Show*', *Media, Culture and Society*, 22(4): 371–91.

Healy, Dave (1997) 'Cyberspace and Place: The Internet as Middle Landscape on the Electronic Frontier', in D. Porter (ed.) *Internet Culture*. London: Routledge.

Hebdige, Dick (1976) 'The Meaning of Mod', in S. Hall and T. Jefferson (eds) *Resistance Through Rituals: Youth Subcultures in Post-War Britain*. London: Hutchinson.

Hebdige, Dick (1979) *Subculture: The Meaning of Style*. London: Routledge.

Hebdige, Dick (1987) *Cut 'n' Mix: Culture, Identity and Caribbean Music*. London: Routledge.

Hebdige, Dick (1988) *Hiding in the Light: On Images and Things*. London: Routledge.

Heller, Agnes (1984) *Everyday Life*, trans. G.L. Campbell. London: Routledge and Kegan Paul.

Hermes, Joke (1995) *Reading Women's Magazines: An Analysis of Everyday Media Use*. Cambridge: Polity.

Hetherington, Kevin (1992) 'Stonehenge and its Festival: Spaces of Consumption', in R. Shields (ed.) *Lifestyle Shopping: The Subject of Consumption*. London: Routledge.

Hetherington, Kevin (1998) 'Vanloads of Uproarious Humanity: New Age Travellers and the Utopics of the Countryside', in T. Skelton and G. Valentine (eds) *Cool Places: Geographies of Youth Culture*. London: Routledge.

Highmore, Ben (2002) *Everyday Life and Cultural Theory: An Introduction*. London: Routledge.

Hobson, D. (1989) 'Soap Operas at Work', in E. Sieter, H. Borchers, G. Kreutzner and E.M. Warth (eds) *Remote Control: Television, Audiences, and Cultural Power*. London: Routledge.

Hodkinson, Paul (2002) *Goth: Identity, Style and Subculture*. Oxford: Berg.

Hodkinson, Paul (2004) 'Trans-Local Connections in the Goth Scene', in A. Bennett, and R.A. Peterson (eds) *Music Scenes: Local, Trans-local and Virtual*. Nashville, TN: Vanderbilt University Press.

Hoggart, Richard (1957) *The Uses of Literacy*. Harmondsworth: Penguin.

Holton, Robert J. and Turner, Bryan S. (1989) *Max Weber on Economy and Society*. London: Routledge.

Hosokawa, Shuhei (1984) 'The Walkman Effect', *Popular Music*, 4(4): 165–80.

Huq, Rupa (1996) 'Asian Kool? Bhangra and Beyond', in S. Sharma, J. Hutnyk and A. Sharma (eds) *Dis-Orienting Rhythms: The Politics of the New Asian Dance Music*. London: Zed Books.

Huq, Rupa (1999) 'Living in France: The Parallel Universe of Hexagonal Pop', in A. Blake (ed.) *Living Through Pop*. London: Routledge.

Inglis, David and Hughson, John (2003) *Confronting Culture: Sociological Vistas*. Cambridge: Polity.

Jackson, Peter, Stevenson, Nick and Brooks, Kate (2001) *Making Sense of Men's Magazines*. Cambridge: Polity.

Jameson, Fredric (1984) 'Postmodernism or the Cultural Logic of Late Capitalism', *New Left Review*, No. 146.

Jameson, Fredric (1992) 'Postmodernism and Consumer Society', in P. Brooker (ed.) *Modernism/Postmodernism*. London: Longman.

Jay, Martin (1973) *The Dialectical Imagination: A History of the Frankfurt School and the Institute of Social Research 1923–1950*. London: Heinemann Educational Books.

Jenks, Chris (1993) *Culture*. London: Routledge.

Jones, Steve (ed.) (1997) *Virtual Culture: Identity and Communication in Cybersociety*. London: Sage.

Jorgensen, Danny L. and Jorgensen, Lin (1982) 'Social Meanings of the Occult', *The Sociological Quarterly*, 23: 373–89.

Kaplan, E. Ann (1987) *Rocking Around the Clock: Music Television, Postmodernism and Consumer Culture*. London: Methuen.

Kahn, Naseem (1993) 'Asian Women's Dress: From Burqah to Bloggs: Changing Clothes for Changing Times', in J. Ash and E. Wilson (eds) *Cheap Thrills: A Fashion Reader*. Berkeley and Los Angeles: University of California Press.

Kaur, Raminder and Kalra, Virinder S. (1996) 'New Paths For South Asian Identity and Creativity', in S. Sharma, J. Hutnyk and A. Sharma (eds) *Dis-Orienting Rhythms: The Politics of the New Asian Dance Music*. London: Zed Books.

Kaya, Ayhan (2001) *'Sicher in Kreuzberg' – Constructing Diasporas: Turkish Hip-Hop Youth in Berlin*. Piscataway: Transaction Publishers.

Kellner, Douglas (1992) 'Popular Culture and the Construction of Postmodern Identities', in S. Lash and J. Friedman (eds) *Modernity and Identity*. Oxford: Blackwell.

Kellner, Douglas (1995) *Media Culture*. London: Routledge.

Kibby, Marjorie D. (2000) 'Home on the Page: A Virtual Place of Music Community', *Popular Music*, 19(1): 91–100.

Knight, Peter (2000) *Conspiracy Culture: From Kennedy to the X Files*. London: Routledge.

Kotarba, Joseph A. (1994) 'The Postmodernization of Rock 'n' Roll Music: The Case of Metallica', in J. Epstein (ed.) *Adolescents and their Music: If it's too Loud you're too Old*. New York: Garland.

Kraidy, Marwan M. (1999) 'The Local, the Global and the Hybrid: A Native Ethnography of Glocalization', *Critical Studies in Media Communication*, 16(4): 456–477.

Kumar, Krishan (1995) *From Post-Industrial to Post-Modern Society: New Theories of the Contemporary World*. Oxford: Blackwell.

Laba, Martin (1986) 'Popular Culture and Folklore: The Social Dimension', in P. Narváez and M. Laba (eds) *Media Sense: The Folklore-Popular Culture Continuum*. Bowling Green, OH: Bowling Green State University Popular Press.

Laing, Dave (1994) 'Scrutiny to Subcultures: Notes on Literary Criticism and Popular Music', *Popular Music*, 13(2): 179–190.

Langman, Lauren (1992) 'Neon Cages: Shopping for Subjectivity', in R. Shields (ed.) *Lifestyle Shopping: The Subject of Consumption*. London: Routledge.

Langman, Lauren and Scatamburlo, Valerie (1996) 'The Self Strikes Back: Identity Politics in the Postmodern Age', in F. Geyer (ed.) *Alienation, Ethnicity and Postmodernity*. London: Greenwood Press.

Lanza, Joseph (1994) *Elevator Music: a Surreal History of Muzak, Easy-Listening and other Moodsong*. London: Quartet.

Lash, Scott (1990) *Sociology of Postmodernism*. London: Routledge.

Lefebvre, Henri (1971) *Everyday Life in the Modern World*, trans. S. Rabinovitch. London: Penguin.

Lefebvre, Henri (1991) *Critique of Everyday Life, Volume 1*, trans. J. Moore. London: Verso.

Lewis, George H. (1992) 'Who Do You Love?: The Dimensions of Musical Taste', in J. Lull (ed.) *Popular Music and Communication*, 2nd edn. London: Sage.

Lewis, Lisa A. (ed.) (1992) *The Adoring Audience: Fan Culture and Popular Media*. London: Routledge.

Liebes, Tamar and Katz, Elihu (1989) 'On the Critical Abilities of Television Viewers', in E. Sieter, H. Borchers, G. Kreutzner and E.M. Warth (eds) *Remote Control: Telvision, Audiences, and Cultural Power*. London: Routledge.

Lipsitz, George (1994) *Dangerous Crossroads: Popular Music, Postmodernism and the Poetics of Place*. London: Verso.

Lockard, Joseph (1997) 'Progressive Politics, Electronic Individualism and the Myth of Virtual Community', in D. Porter (ed.) *Internet Culture*. London: Routledge.

Lopes, Paul (2002) *The Rise of a Jazz Art World*. Cambridge: Cambridge University Press.

Löwith, Karl (1993) *Max Weber and Karl Marx*. London: Routledge.

Lull, James (ed.) (1988) *World Families Watch Television*. London: Sage.

Lull, James (1995) *Media, Communication, Culture: A Global Approach*. Cambridge: Polity Press.

Lury, Celia (2002) 'Everyday Life and the Economy', in T. Bennett and D. Watson (eds) *Understanding Everyday Life*. Oxford: Open University and Blackwell.

Lyotard, Jean-François (1984) *The Postmodern Condition: A Report on Knowledge*, trans. G. Bennington and B. Massumi. Manchester: Manchester University Press.

Lyotard, Jean-François (1986–7) 'Rules and Paradoxes or Svelt Appendix', *Cultural Critique*, 5: 209–19.

MacCannell, Dean (1976) *The Tourist: A New Theory of the Leisure Class*. London: The Macmillan Press Ltd.

MacCannell, Dean and Flower MacCannell, Juliet (1993) 'Social Class in Postmodernity: *Simulacrum* or Return of the Real?', in C. Rojek and B.S. Turner (eds) *Forget Baudrillard?* London: Routledge.

Macdonald, Dwight (1953) 'A Theory of Mass Culture', in B. Rosenberg and D. White (eds) (1957) *Mass Culture: The Popular Arts in America*. Glencoe, IL: The Free Press.

MacKinnon, Niall (1993) *The British Folk Scene: Musical Performance and Social Identity*. Buckingham: Open University Press.

MacLeod, Donald V.L. (1997) 'Alternative Tourists on a Canary Island', in S. Abram, J. Waldren and D.V.L. Macleod (eds) *Tourism and Tourists: Identifying with People and Places.* Oxford: Berg.

McGuigan, Jim (1999) *Modernity and Postmodern Culture.* Buckingham: Open University Press.

McKay, George (1996) *Senseless Acts of Beauty: Cultures of Resistance Since the Sixties.* London: Verso.

McKay, George (ed.) (1998) *DIY Culture: Party and Protest in Nineties Britain.* London: Verso.

McRobbie, Angela (1980) 'Settling Accounts with Subcultures: A Feminist Critique' in S. Frith and A. Goodwin (eds) (1990) *On Record: Rock Pop and the Written Word.* London: Routledge.

McRobbie, Angela (1984) 'Dance and Social Fantasy', in A. McRobbie and M. Nava (eds) *Gender and Generation.* London: Macmillan.

McRobbie, Angela (1991) *Feminism and Youth Culture: From Jackie to Just Seventeen.* Basingstoke: Macmillan.

McRobbie, Angela (1994) *Postmodernism and Popular Culture.* London: Routledge.

McRobbie, Angela (1997) 'New Sexualities in Girls' and Women's Magazines', in A. McRobbie (ed.) *Back to Reality? Social Experience and Cultural Studies.* Manchester: Manchester University Press.

McRobbie, Angela and Garber, Jenny (1976) 'Girls and Subcultures: An Exploration' in S. Hall and T. Jefferson (eds) *Resistance Through Rituals: Youth Subcultures in Post-War Britain.* London: Hutchinson.

Mack, John E. (1994) *Abduction: Human Encounters With Aliens.* London: Simon and Schuster.

Maffesoli, Michel (1996) *The Time of the Tribes: The Decline of Individualism in Mass Society,* trans. D. Smith. London: Sage.

Magliocco, Sabina (2001) *Neo-Pagan Sacred Art and Altars: Making Things Whole.* Jackson: University Press of Mississippi.

Malbon, Ben (1999) *Clubbing: Dancing, Ecstasy and Vitality.* London: Routledge.

Malmstrom, Frederick V. and Coffman, Richard M. (1979) 'Humanoids Reported in UFOs, Religion and Folktales: Human Bias Towards Human Life Forms?', in R.F. Haines (ed.) *UFO Phenomena and the Behavioral Scientist.* Metuchen, NJ: The Scarecrow Press.

Malyon, Tim (1998) 'Tossed in the Fire and They Never Got Burned: The Exodus Collective', in G. McKay (ed.) *DIY Culture: Party and Protest in Nineties Britain.* London: Verso.

Marcuse, Herbert (1964) *One-Dimensional Man.* Boston: Beacon Press.

Martin, Greg (2002) 'Conceptualizing Cultural Politics in Subcultural and Social Movement Studies', *Social Movement Studies,* 1(1): 73–88.

Massey, Doreen (1993) 'Power-Geometry and a Progressive Sense of Place', in J. Bird, B. Curtis, T. Putnam, G. Robertson and L. Tickner (eds) *Mapping the Futures: Local Cultures, Global Change.* London: Routledge.

May, Tim (1996) *Situating Social Theory.* Buckingham: Open University Press.

Bibliography

Melechi, Antonio (1993) 'The Ecstasy of Disappearance', in S. Redhead (ed.) *Rave Off: Politics and Deviance in Contemporary Youth Culture*. Aldershot: Avebury.

Melley, George (1970) *Revolt into Style: The Pop Arts in Britain*. London: Allen Lane.

Mercer, Kobena (1987) 'Black Hair/Style Politics', in K. Gelder and S. Thornton (eds) (1997) *The Subcultures Reader*. London: Routledge.

Miles, Steven (1998) *Consumerism as a Way of Life*. London: Sage.

Miles, Steven (2000) *Youth Lifestyles in a Changing World*. Buckingham: Open University Press.

Miller, Toby and McHoul, Alec (1998) *Popular Culture and Everyday Life*. London: Sage.

Miller, Daniel and Slater, Don (2000) *The Internet: An Ethnographic Approach*. Oxford: Berg.

Mitchell, Tony (1996) *Popular Music and Local Identity: Rock, Pop and Rap in Europe and Oceania*. London: Leicester University Press.

Monbiot, George (1998) 'Reclaim the Fields and the Country Lanes! The Land is Ours Campaign', in G. McKay (ed.) *DIY Culture: Party and Protest in Nineties Britain*. London: Verso.

Moody, Edward J. (1974) 'Urban Witches', in E.A. Tiryakian (ed.) *On the Margin of the Visible: Sociology, the Esoteric, the Occult*. New York: John Wiley and Sons.

Moores, Shaun (1993) *Interpreting Audiences: The Ethnography of Media Consumption*. London: Sage.

Morley, David (1980) *The 'Nationwide' Audience: Structure and Decoding*. London: British Film Institute.

Morley, David (1986) *Family Television: Cultural Power and Domestic Leisure*. London: Comedia.

Morley, David (1992) *Television, Audiences and Cultural Studies*. London: Routledge.

Morley, David (1995) 'Theories of Consumption in Media Studies', in D. Miller (ed.) *Acknowledging Consumption: A Review of New Studies*. London: Routledge.

Morley, David (1996) 'The Geography of Television: Ethnography, Communications and Community', in J. Hay, L. Grossberg and E. Wartella (eds) *The Audience and its Landscape*. Boulder, CO: Westview Press.

Morley, David and Robins, Kevin (1989) 'Spaces of Identity', *Screen*, 30(4): 10–34.

Morrison, Ken (1995) *Marx, Durkheim, Weber*. London: Sage.

Mort, Frank (1996) *Cultures of Consumption: Masculinities and Social Space in Late Twentieth-Century Britain*. London: Routledge.

Muggleton, David (2000) *Inside Subculture: The Postmodern Meaning of Style*. Oxford: Berg.

Mutsaers, Lutgard (1990) 'Indorock: An Early Eurorock Style', *Popular Music*, 9(3): 307–20.

Nederman, Cary J. and Goulding, James W. (1981) 'Popular Occultism and Critical Theory: Exploring Some Themes of Astrology and the Occult', *Sociological Analysis*, 42(4): 325–32.

Negus, Keith (1992) *Producing Pop: Culture and Conflict in the Popular Music Industry*. London: Edward Arnold.

Nelson, G.K. (1975) 'Towards a Sociology of the Psychic', *Review of Religious Research*, 16(3): 166–73.

Nippert-Eng, Christine (1996) *Home and Work: Negotiating Boundaries Through Everyday Life*. Chicago: University of Chicago Press.

Nixon, Sean (1992) 'Have You Got The Look? Masculinities and Shopping Spectacle', in R. Shields (ed.) *Lifestyle Shopping: The Subject of Consumption*. London: Routledge.

Nixon, Sean (1997) 'Designs on Masculinity: Menswear Retailing and the Role of Retail Design', in A. McRobbie (ed.) *Back to Reality: Social Experience and Cultural Studies*. Manchester: Manchester University Press.

Novack, Cynthia J. (1990) *Sharing the Dance: Contact Improvisation and American Culture*. Madison, Winsconsin: The University of Wisconsin Press, Wisconsin.

Nuttall, Mark (1997) 'Packaging the Wild: Tourism Development in Alaska', in S. Abram, J. Waldren and D.V.L. MacLeod (eds) *Tourism and Tourists: Identifying with People and Places*. Oxford: Berg.

O'Shea Borrelli, Laird (1997) 'Dressing Up and Talking About It: Fashion Writing in Vogue from 1968 to 1963', *Fashion Theory*, 1(3): 247–60.

Paddison, Max (1996) *Adorno, Modernism and Mass Culture: Essays on Critical Theory and Music*. London: Kahn and Averill.

Partington, Angela (1993) 'Popular Fashion and Working-Class Affluence', in J. Ash and E. Wilson (eds) *Cheap Thrills: A Fashion Reader*. Berkeley and Los Angeles: University of California Press.

Peel, Frank (1968) *The Risings of the Luddites, Chartists and Plug-Drawers*, 4th edn. London: Cass.

Pendragon, Arthur and Stone, Christopher, James (2003) *The Trails of Arthur: The Life and Times of a Modern-Day King*. Element: London.

Peterson, Richard A. and Bennett, Andy (eds) (2004) 'Introducing Music Scenes', in A. Bennett and R.A. Peterson (eds) *Music Scenes: Local, Trans-local and Virtual*. Nashville, TN: Vanderbilt University Press.

Perry, Nick (1998) *Hyperreality and Global Culture*. London: Routledge.

Pickering, Michael (1984) 'Popular Song at Juniper Hill', *Folk Music Journal*, 4(5): 481–503.

Pickering, Michael and Green, Anthony (1987) 'Towards a Cartography of the Vernacular Milieu', in M. Pickering and A. Green (eds) *Everyday Culture: Popular Song and the Vernacular Milieu*. Milton Keynes: Open University Press.

Pieterse, Jan Nederveen (1995) 'Globalization as Hybridization', in M. Featherstone, S. Lash and R. Robertson (eds) *Global Modernities*. London: Sage.

Pimple, Kenneth, D. (1995) 'Ghosts, Spirits, and Scholars: The Origins of Modern Spiritualism', in B. Walker (ed.) *Out of the Ordinary: Folklore and the Supernatural*. Logan, UT: Utah State University Press.

Pini, Maria (1997) 'Women and the Early British Rave Scene', in A. McRobbie (ed.) *Back to Reality: Social Experience and Cultural Studies*. Manchester: Manchester University Press.

Plows, Alex (1998) 'Earth First! Defending Mother Earth, Direct-Style', in G. McKay (ed.) *DIY Culture: Party and Protest in Nineties Britain*. London: Verso.

Polhemus, Ted (1997) 'In the Supermarket of Style', in S. Redhead, D. Wynne and J. O'Connor (eds) *The Clubcultures Reader: Readings in Popular Cultural Studies*. Oxford: Blackwell.

Porter, Roy (1993) 'Baudrillard: History, Hysteria and Consumption', in C. Rojek and B.S. Turner (eds) *Forget Baudrillard?* London: Routledge.

Potter, Russell, A. (1995) *Spectacular Vernaculars: Hip Hop and the Politics of Postmodernism*. New York: State University of New York Press.

Price, Ken (1981) 'Black Identity and the Role of Reggae', in D. Potter (ed.) *Society and the Social Sciences: An Introduction*. London: Routledge/Open University Press.

Pritchard, Annette (2001) 'Tourism and Representation: A Scale for Measuring Gender Portrayals', *Leisure Studies*, 20(2): 79–94.

Redhead, Steve (1990) *The End-of-the-Century Party: Youth and Pop Towards 2000*. Manchester: Manchester University Press.

Redhead, Steve (1997) *Post-Fandom and the Millenial Blues: The Transformation of Soccer Culture*. London: Routledge.

Regan Shade, Leslie (1996) 'Is there Free Speech on the Net? Censorship in the Global Information Infrastructure', in R. Shields (ed.) *Cultures of Internet: Virtual Spaces, Real Histories, Living Bodies*. London: Sage.

Reich, Charles A. (1971) *The Greening of America*. Middlesex, England: Allen Lane.

Reimer, Bo (1995a) 'Youth and Modern Lifestyles', in J. Fornäs and G. Bolin (eds) *Youth Culture in Late Modernity*. London: Sage.

Reimer, Bo (1995b) 'The Media in Public and Private Spheres', in J. Fornäs and G. Bolin (eds) *Youth Culture in Late Modernity*. London: Sage.

Rheingold, Howard (1994) *The Virtual Community: Finding Connection in a Computerized World*. London: Secker and Warburg.

Richardson, James T. (1991) 'Satanism in the Courts: From Murder to Heavy Metal', in J.T. Richardson, J. Best and D.G. Bromley (eds) *The Satanism Scare*. New York: Aldine de Gruyter.

Ritzer, George (1993) *The McDonaldization of Society: An Investigation Into the Changing Character of Contemporary Social Life*. London: Pine Forge Press.

Ritzer, George and Liska, Allan (1997) '"McDisneyization" and "Post-Tourism"', in C. Rojek and J. Urry (eds) *Touring Cultures: Transformations of Travel and Theory*. London: Routledge.

Roberts, Robert (1971) *The Classic Slum*. Manchester: Manchester University Press.

Robertson, Roland (1995) 'Glocalization: Time-Space and Homogeneity-Heterogeneity', in M. Featherstone, S. Lash and R. Robertson (eds) *Global Modernities*. London: Sage.

Rojek, Chris (1993) *Ways of Escape: Modern Transformations in Leisure and Travel*. Basingstoke: Macmillan.

Rojek, Chris (1995) *Decentring Leisure: Rethinking Leisure Theory*. London: Sage.

Rojcewicz, Peter M. (1991) 'Between One Eye Blink and the Next: Fairies, UFOs, and Problems', in P. Narváez (ed.) *The Good People*. Lexington, KY: The University Press of Kentucky.

Rose, Tricia (1994) *Black Noise: Rap Music and Black Culture in Contemporary America*. London: Wesleyan University Press.

Rosen, Ruth (1986) 'Soap Operas: Search for Yesterday', in T. Gitlin (ed.) *Watching Television*. New York: Pantheon.

Ross, Andrew (1994) 'Introduction', *Microphone Fiends: Youth Music and Youth Culture*. London: Routledge.

Roszak, Theodore (1969) *The Making of a Counter Culture: Reflections on the Technocratic Society and its Youthful Opposition*. London: Faber and Faber.

Rucker, Margaret, Anderson, Elizabeth and Kangas, April (1999) 'Clothing, Power and the Workplace', in K.K.P. Johnson and S.J. Lennon (eds) *Appearance and Power*. Oxford: Berg.

Saldanha, Arun (2002) 'Music Tourism and Factions of Bodies in Goa', *Tourist Studies*, 2(1): 43–62.

Sampson, Wallace (1996) 'Antiscience Trends in the Rise of the "Alternative Medicine" Movement', in P.R. Gross, N. Levitt and M.W. Lewis (eds) *The Flight From Science and Reason*. New York: The New York Academy of Sciences.

Sánchez Taylor, Jaqueline (2001) 'Dollars are a Girl's Best Friend? Female Tourists' Sexual Behaviour in the Carribean', *Sociology*, 35(3): 749–64.

Sardiello, Robert (1998) 'Identity and Status Stratification in Deadhead Subculture', in J.S. Epstein (ed.) *Youth Culture: Identity in a Postmodern World*. Oxford: Blackwell.

Saussure, Ferdinand de (1974) *Course in General Linguistics*. London: Fontana.

Savage, Jon (1990) 'The Enemy Within: Sex, Rock and Identity', in S. Frith (ed.) (1990) *Facing the Music: Essays on Pop, Rock and Culture*, 2nd edn. London: Mandarin.

Savan, Leslie (1993) 'Commercials Go Rock', in S. Frith, A. Goodwin and L. Grossberg (eds) *Sound the Vision: The Music Video Reader*. London: Routledge.

Schacht, Richard (1996) 'Alienation Redux: From Here to Postmodernity', in F. Geyer (ed.) *Alienation, Ethnicity, and Postmodernity*. London: Greenwood Press.

Schechner, Richard (1981) 'Restoration of Behavior', *Studies in Visual Communication*, 7: 2–45.

Schmalenbach, Herman (1977) *On Society and Experience*. edited by G. Lüschen and G.P. Stone. Chicago: The University of Chicago Press.

Shank, Barry (1994) *Dissonant Identities: The Rock 'n' Roll Scene in Austin, Texas*. London: Wesleyan University Press.

Sharma, Sanjay, Hutnyk, John and Sharma, Ashanwi (eds) (1996) *Dis-Orienting Rhythms: The Politics of the New Asian Dance Music*. London: Zed Books.

Shields, Rob (1991) *Places on the Margin: Alternative Geographies of Modernity*. London: Routledge.

Shields, Rob (1992a) 'Spaces for the Subject of Consumption', in R. Shields (ed.) *Lifestyle Shopping: The Subject of Consumption*. London: Routledge.

Shields, Rob (1992b) 'The Individual, Consumption Cultures and the Fate of Community', in R. Shields (ed.) *Lifestyle Shopping: The Subject of Consumption*. London: Routledge.

Shumway, David (1992) 'Rock and Roll as a Cultural Practice', in A. DeCurtis (ed.) *Present Tense: Rock and Roll and Culture*. Durham, NC: Duke University Press.

Singer, Pete (1998) 'A Vegetarian Philosophy', in S. Griffiths and J. Wallace (ed.) *Consuming Passions: Food in the Age of Anxiety*. Manchester: Mandolin.

Smart, Barry (1993a) *Postmodernity*. London: Routledge.

Bibliography

Smart, Barry (1993b) 'Europe/America: Baudrillard's Fatal Comparison', in C. Rojek and B.S. Turner (eds) *Forget Baudrillard?* London: Routledge.

Smith, Jackie (2001) 'Globalizing Resistance: The Battle of Seattle and the Future of Social Movements', *Mobilization: An International Journal*, 6(1): 1–19.

Spark, Ceridwen (2002) 'Brambuk Living Cultural Centre: Indigenous Culture and the Production of Place', *Tourist Studies*, 2(1): 23–42.

Stevenson, Nick (1995) *Understanding Media Cultures*. London: Sage.

Stokes, Martin (ed.) (1994) *Ethnicity, Identity and Music: The Musical Construction of Place*. Oxford: Berg.

Storry, John (1997) *An Introduction to Cultural Theory and Popular Culture*, 2nd edn. London: Prentice Hall.

Storrey, Mike and Childs, Peter (eds) (1997) *British Cultural Identities*. London: Routledge.

Straw, Will (1991) 'Systems of Articulation, Logics of Change: Communities and Scenes in Popular Music', *Cultural Studies*, 5(3): 368–88.

Street, John (1993) 'Local Differences?: Popular Music and the Local State', *Popular Music*, 12(1): 43–54.

Strinati, Dominic (1995) *An Introduction to Theories of Popular Culture*. London: Routledge.

Sweeting, Adam (1994) 'Wall of Sound', The *Guardian*, 10 October: 8–9.

Sweetman, Paul (2004) 'Tourists and Travellers? 'Subcultures', Reflexive Identities and Neo-Tribal Sociality', in A. Bennett and K. Kahn-Harris (eds) *After Subculture: Critical Studies in Contemporary Youth Culture*. London: Palgrave.

Swingewood, Alan (1977) *The Myth of Mass Culture*. London: Macmillan.

Syversten, Trine (2001) 'Ordinary People in Extraordinary Circumstances: A Study of Participants in Television Dating Games', *Media, Culture and Society*, 23(3): 319–37.

Szostak-Pierce, Suzanne (1999) 'Even Further: The Power of Subcultural Style in Techno Culture', in K.K.P. Johnson and S.J. Lennon (eds) *Appearance and Power*. Oxford: Berg.

Thomas, Helen (2003) *The Body, Dance and Cultural Theory*. Basingstoke: Palgrave.

Thompson, Dorothy (1984) *The Chartists: Popular Politics in the Industrial Revolution*. New York: Pantheon Books.

Thompson, John, B. (1995) *The Media and Modernity: A Social Theory of Modernity*. Cambridge: Polity Press.

Thornton, Sarah (1994) 'Moral Panic, the Media and British Rave Culture', in A. Ross and T. Rose (eds) *Microphone Fiends: Youth Music and Youth Culture*. London: Routledge.

Thornton, Sarah (1995) *Club Cultures: Music, Media and Subcultural Capital*. Cambridge: Polity Press.

Tomlinson, John (1991) *Cultural Imperialism: A Critical Introduction*. London: Pinter.

Truzzi, Marcello (1974) 'Witchcraft and Satanism', in E.A. Tiryakian (ed.) *On the Margin of the Visible: Sociology, the Esoteric, the Occult*. New York: John Wiley and Sons.

Truzzi, Marcello (1975) 'Astrology as Popular Culture', *Journal of Popular Culture*, 8: 906–11.

Tsitsos, William (1999) 'Rules of Rebellion: Slamdancing, Moshing and the American Alternative Scene', *Popular Music*, 18(3): 397–414.

Tulloch, Carol (1993) 'Rebel Without a Pause: Black Street Style and Black Designers', in J. Ash and E. Wilson (eds) *Cheap Thrills: A Fashion Reader*. Berkeley and Los Angeles: University of California Press.

Turner, Bryan S. (1993) 'Cruising America', in C. Rojek and B.S. Turner (eds) *Forget Baudrillard?* London: Routledge.

Urry, John (1990) *The Tourist Gaze: Leisure and Travel in Contemporary Societies*. London: Sage.

Urry, John (1995) *Consuming Places*. London: Routledge.

Van den Bulck, Hilde (2001) 'Public Service Television and National Identity as a Project of Modernity: The Example of Flemish Television', *Media Culture and Society*, 23(1): 53–69.

van Zoonen, Liesbet (2001) 'Desire and Resistance: *Big Brother* and the Recognition of Everyday Life', *Media, Culture and Society*, 23(5): 669–77.

Veblen, Thorstein (1994 [1924]) *The Theory of the Leisure Class: An Economic Study of Institutions*. New York: Mentor Books.

Vestel, Viggo (1999) 'Breakdance, Red Eyed Penguins, Vikings, Grunge and Straight Rock 'n' Roll: The Construction of Place in Musical Discourse in Rudenga, East Side Oslo', *Young: Nordic Journal of Youth Research*, 7(2): 4–24.

Wakeford, Nina (1999) 'Gender and the Landscapes of Computing in an Internet Café', in M. Crang, P. Crang and J. May (eds) *Virtual Geographies: Bodies, Space and Relations*. London: Routledge.

Walker, Barbara (ed.) (1995) *Out of the Ordinary: Folklore and the Supernatural*. Logan, UT: Utah State University Press.

Walter, Tony (2001) 'Reincarnation, Modernity and Identity', *Sociology*, 35(1): 21–38.

Warde, Alan (1997) *Consumption, Food and Taste: Culinary Antinomies and Commodity Culture*. Sage: London.

Watkins, Craig S. (1998) *Representing: Hip Hop Culture and the Production of Black Cinema*. Chicago: University of Chicago Press.

Wearing, Stephen and Wearing, Betsy (2001) 'Conceptualizing the Selves of Tourism', *Leisure Studies*, 20(2): 143–59.

Weber, Max (1968 [1921]) *Economy and Society* – 3 volumes. Totowa, New Jersey: Bedminster Press.

Weber, Max (1978 [1919]) 'The Distribution of Power Within the Political Community: Class, Status, Party', in *Economy and Society: An Outline of Interpretive Sociology*. Berkeley, CA: University of California Press.

Webster, Colin (1976) 'Communes: A Thematic Typology', in S. Hall and T. Jefferson (eds) *Resistance Through Rituals: Youth Subcultures in Post-War Britain*. London: Hutchinson.

Weinstein, Deena (2000) *Heavy Metal: The Music and its Culture*, 2nd edn. New York: Da Capo Press.

Weissmann, Gerald (1996) '"Sucking With Vampires": The Medicine of Unreason', in P.R. Gross, N. Levitt, M.W. Lewis (eds) *The Flight From Science and Reason*. New York: The New York Academy of Sciences.

Welsh, Ian (2000) 'New Social Movements', *Developments in Sociology*, 16: 43–60.

Wilbur, Shawn P. (1997) 'An Archaeology of Cyberspaces: Virtuality, Community, Identity', in D. Porter (ed.) *Internet Culture*. London: Routledge.

Williams, Raymond (1958) *Culture and Society 1780–1950*. London: Chatto & Windus.

Williams, Raymond (1961) *The Long Revolution*. Harmondsworth: Pengiun.

Willis, Paul (1978) *Profane Culture*. London: Routledge and Kegan Paul.

Willis, Paul (1990) *Common Culture: Symbolic Work at Play in the Everyday Cultures of the Young*. Milton Keynes: Open University Press.

Wilson, Elizabeth (1998) 'Bohemian Dress and the Heroism of Everyday Life', *Fashion Theory*, 2(3): 225–44.

Winship, Janice (1987) *Inside Women's Magazines*. London: Pandora.

Wooffitt, Robin (1988) 'On the Analysis of Accounts of Paranormal Phenomena', *Journal of the Society for Psychical Research*, 55: 139–49.

Woofitt, Robin (1992) *Telling Tales of the Unexpected: The Organisation of Factual Discourse*. Hemel Hempstead: Harvester Wheatsheaf.

Wooffitt, Robin (1994) 'Analysing Verbal Accounts of Spontaneous Paranormal Phenomena', *European Journal of Parapsychology*, 10: 45–63.

Wuthnow, Robert (1976) 'Astrology and Marginality', *Journal for the Scientific Study of Religion*, 15: 157–68.

Young, T. (1985) 'The Shock of the Old', *New Society*, 14 February: 246.

Zdatny, Steven (1997) 'The Boyish Look and the Liberated Woman: The Politics and Aesthetics of Women's Hairstyles', *Fashion Theory*, 1(4): 367–98.

Zweig, Ferdinand (1961) *The Worker in an Affluent Society: Family Life and Industry*. London: Heinemann.

Index

Index